BASEBALL IN ASHEVILLE

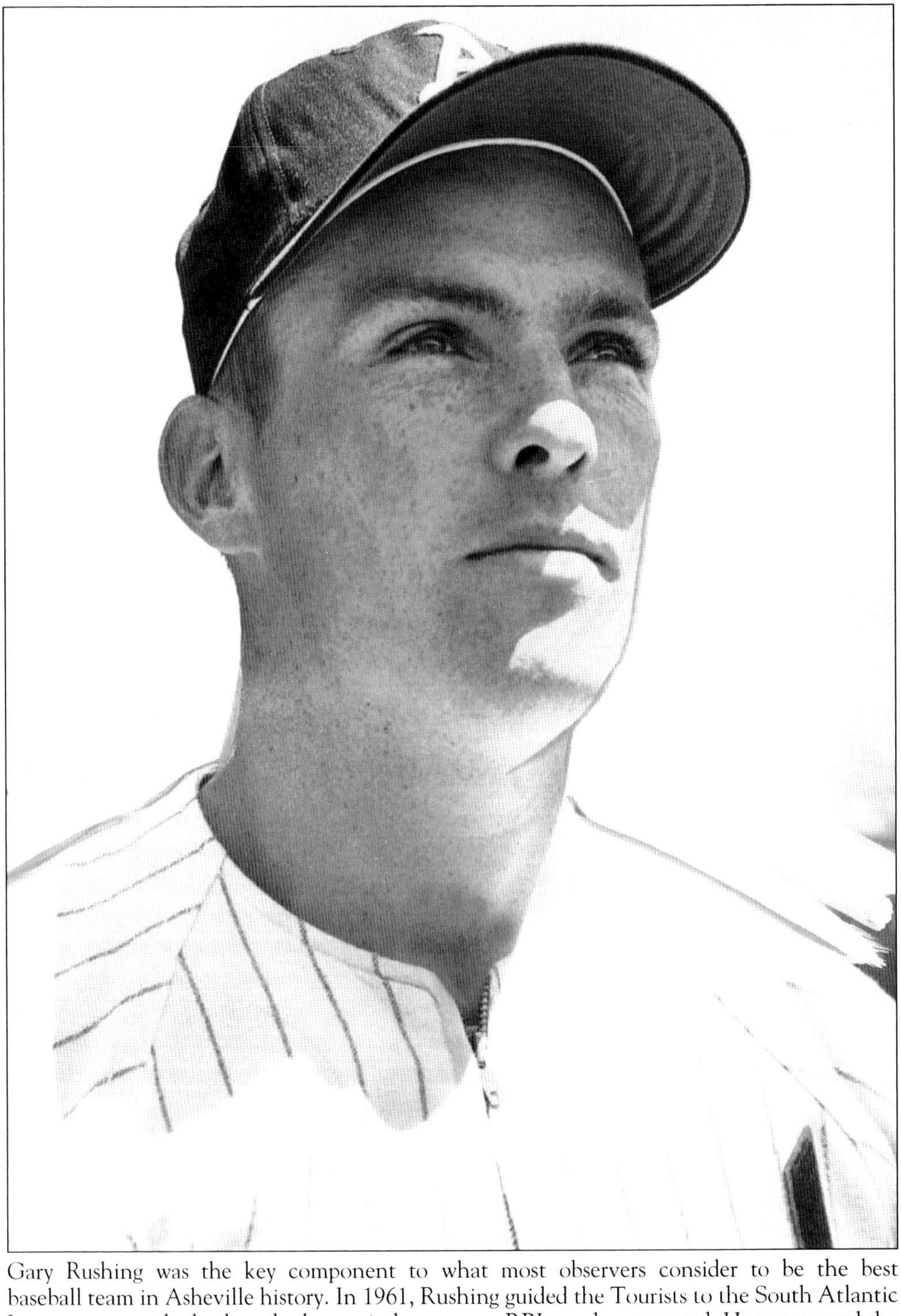

Gary Rushing was the key component to what most observers consider to be the best baseball team in Asheville history. In 1961, Rushing guided the Tourists to the South Atlantic League pennant by leading the league in home runs, RBIs, and runs scored. He was named the South Atlantic League Most Valuable Player at the end of the campaign. (*Asheville Citizen-Times* photograph.)

BASEBALL IN ASHEVILLE

Bill Ballew

ARCADIA
PUBLISHING

Copyright © by Bill Ballew
ISBN 978-0-7385-1610-3

Published by Arcadia Publishing
Charleston, South Carolina

Printed in the United States of America

Library of Congress Catalog Card Number: 2003114591

For all general information contact Arcadia Publishing at:
Telephone 843-853-2070
Fax 843-853-0044
E-mail sales@arcadiapublishing.com
For customer service and orders:
Toll-Free 1-888-313-2665

Visit us on the Internet at www.arcadiapublishing.com

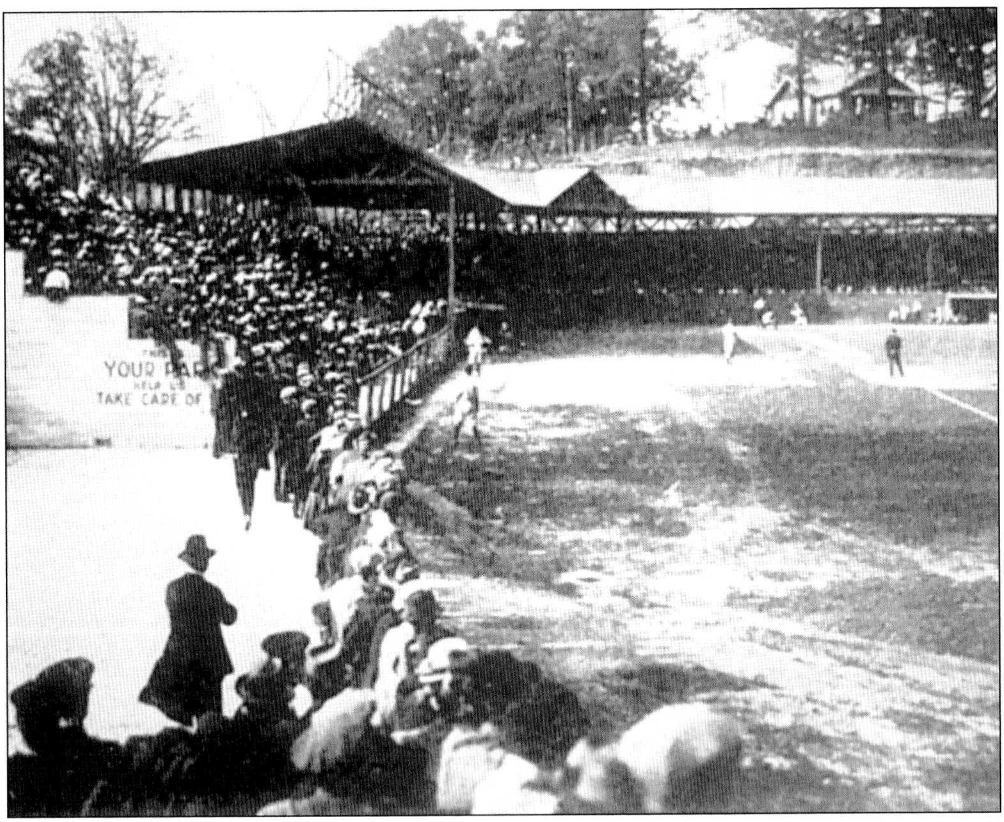

Fans pack McCormick Field in this 1926 photograph. A sign on the grandstand wall down the right field line reads, "This is your park. Help us take care of it." (Asheville Tourists photograph.)

CONTENTS

ACKNOWLEDGMENTS

Numerous people provided invaluable assistance to make this book a reality. What amazed me most is how many wanted to see this project come to completion and how many were willing to go beyond the call of duty to help make it happen.

Bob Gabordi, executive editor of the *Asheville Citizen-Times* and one of the most devoted baseball fans this country has known, provided access to the newspaper's archives. Without that, this book would have been impossible to publish in a timely manner. Holly McKenzie, the newspaper's archivist, and senior sports writer Keith Jarrett made my work much less stressful.

Bob Terrell, perhaps the foremost authority on the history of baseball in Western North Carolina, offered his treasure trove of photographs. Tony Farlow never batted an eye or muttered the slightest complaint when I requested prints of his excellent photographs more than once. Jim Baker provided his incredible insight into baseball's background in the city. Ann Wright and Zoe Rhine at Pack Memorial Public Library supplied their knowledge and pointed me in directions I would have never considered. Ewart Ball, who captured many of the enclosed images as a staff photographer with the *Asheville Citizen-Times*, deserves acknowledgement for his fine work over the years. Other key contributors include Mike Gore, Tom Smith, Bill Burdette, and David Cheadle. To all, scads of emotion and thanks.

The same feelings go to the front office staff of the Asheville Tourists. Ron and Carolyn McKee have made professional baseball in the Land of the Sky the rousing success it is today. Everyone who passes through the turnstiles at McCormick Field should feel a sense of gratitude to the McKees, who have given the last quarter-century of their lives to the game. No one has researched the history of baseball in Asheville more in-depth or with more passion than Chris Smith. Hopefully this book is a tribute to his hard work over the past decade. Larry Hawkins, Ben Ashby, Margarita Turner, David King, and Billie Jean Sheffron, who got this project rolling for me, deserve kudos as well.

Two special people at Arcadia were nothing less than vital for this project. Maggie Tiller showed the patience of Job while expressing constant support and enthusiasm to keep the work moving forward. Laura New, meanwhile, believed Asheville was worthy of a place in this incredible series. Her foresight will help the players who made the national pastime a hit in Asheville remain on our minds for years to come.

Finally, the people that put up with me need to know how much I appreciate them, especially my wife, Hope; sons, Brad and Bryce; and beagle, Brandy. My parents, Bill and Shirley Ballew; brother, Sam Ballew; and mother-in-law, Faith O'Kelley also deserve thanks for their constant support.

INTRODUCTION

Asheville joins much of the country in that the city's baseball roots can be traced to the Civil War. The newly created game and its immediate ancestors, including town ball and cricket, became commonplace during the first half of the 1800s in the northeastern portion of the United States. Despite all the death and destruction brought by nearly five years of battles and confrontations, the events and subsequent results of the Civil War introduced new cultures and interests, one of which was baseball.

Little physical damage was done to Western North Carolina during the conflict that will forever be known in the South as The War Between The States. The rugged mountain terrain of the region meant there were no key rail centers or gateways the Union deemed worthy of destroying. The lone event of the war in Asheville was the Battle of Asheville, featuring a few sporadic canon shots fired between the Confederate troops, positioned near downtown and Pritchard Park, and the Union army, located in Bent Creek, during the waning days of the war in April 1865. There were no casualties.

The major effect of the Civil War was the loss of life suffered by Asheville's male population. More than 580 soldiers, representing approximately 10 percent of the city's men, died in the Civil War. Most perished fighting for the Confederacy, although a fair number served in the Union forces. In fact, Asheville and Western North Carolina, comprised primarily of small farmers, hill folk, and some transplanted Northerners, supported the Union due to their overall disapproval of slavery. The result proved twofold: one, the loss of men hurt the economic landscape in Asheville for nearly a generation, thereby leaving little time for recreational activities; and, two, the area showed a more willing acceptance of some Northern lifestyles, which were acquired during peaceful interactions between the troops, many of which included baseball games.

Baseball was first played in Western North Carolina in prison camps during the war. According to noted author Bob Terrell, an old Currier and Ives print proves this. Newspaper accounts indicate that the first baseball game in Asheville was played in 1866 on Smith's 118-acre tract, an area known as the Barn Field, located between Grove Street and Aston Park. Baseball soon became known as a "club" sport, and "sandlot attractions" played among talented amateurs took place on a field near the end of Charlotte Street prior to the turn of the century. However, due to the lack of flat land and the time constraints of the work force, baseball did not blossom among Asheville boys until the first decade of the 20th century.

The first professional team in the area was the Asheville Moonshiners, who hosted games at Allandale Park, near the French Broad River, and played 21 games in the Southeastern League in 1897. Travel difficulties caused the circuit to eliminate Asheville and the Chattanooga Blues, leading the Moonshiners to form the Tri-State League, featuring competition from Concord, Swannanoa, Weaverville, Spartanburg, Columbia, and Knoxville. The fledgling league never materialized beyond exhibition games and professional baseball did not return to Asheville for a dozen years.

In 1909, the Asheville Red Birds joined the Western North Carolina League, which also fielded teams from Hendersonville, Canton, and Waynesville. Asheville played in a variety of circuits, including the Appalachian, Southeastern, and North Carolina State leagues, until 1917, when World War I brought professional baseball to a halt. Amateur and semi-pro clubs, including the Asheville Royal Giants, became more common during this period. Aiding the teams' cause was the construction of various facilities. Riverside Park, located along the French Broad River near Montford Avenue, was built in 1909, yet washed away during the Great Flood of July 16, 1916. Oates Park, a wooden ballpark at the corners of Southside, Choctaw, and McDowell Streets, was erected in 1914, and Pearson's Park was constructed in 1916. These facilities welcomed some of the most notable stars in the game. On April 8, 1913, Ty Cobb, who was holding out on his contract with the Detroit Tigers, brought a group of baseball "artists" to Asheville to play Tommy Stouch's Mountaineers at Oates Park. Jim Thorpe and a team of New York Giants rookies played in town shortly thereafter on April 9, 1914, with Thorpe hitting a three-run home run in a 9-5 win over Asheville.

Bigger things began to brew on the baseball front in 1916 when the Philadelphia A's scheduled an exhibition game for April 5 against a squad put together by S.A. Lynch Enterprises—the "Paramount" team. The *Asheville Citizen* reported that the contest was held with the hope of gauging interest in building a larger venue for the professional game in Asheville. The paper reported in its March 22, 1916, edition, "Bonds issued against the ball park will soon be placed on the market and will go far toward determining the future of baseball in the city. They will be placed on sale as an investment, paying six per cent interest and being redeemable in ten years. The club has provided for a special fund to take care of the interest and if they are all sold, as everything indicates they will be, the club will be placed on a sound financial basis for years to come." The newspaper added that Asheville baseball fans had been generous in the past without any hope of a return on their money.

Although World War I brought such hopes to a temporary halt, Asheville finally reserved its place on the baseball map when McCormick Field opened in 1924. The sport has been a constant in the city ever since. The rare absences on the professional front involved a pair of three-year absences due to World War II in the 1940s and in the second half of the 1950s, when McCormick Field became a temporary home for weekly stockcar races. Otherwise, Asheville has contributed its share of memories to the national pastime, providing fans and players with a winning trifecta of recreation, entertainment, and character that only baseball seems capable of offering.

One

The Early Years

Western North Carolina was receptive to baseball during the first two decades of the 20th century, although the professional game had difficulty gaining a stronghold in the area. After the Asheville Moonshiners made a couple of attempts at facing competition in 1897, the pro sport did not return to the city until 1909, when the Asheville Red Birds battled in the Western North Carolina League. The Asheville Moonshiners spent the 1910 slate in the Southeastern League and two years, 1911 and 1912, in the Appalachian League. The team was known as the Mountaineers for two seasons and the Tourists for the final three seasons during a five-year run, 1913 to 1917, in the North Carolina State League. That stint concluded when the Asheville and Raleigh teams disbanded on May 18, 1917, 12 days before the league ceased operations because of the country's participation in World War I.

Baseball grew immensely in popularity in Asheville during this same time. Youth leagues formed throughout the city. The game was played on schoolyards and became a frequent activity on vacant lots. The townspeople held great interest in the major leagues and crowded downtown streets to follow the World Series on game boards. Although such factors as economic hardships and a difficult terrain retarded the growth of baseball during the 1800s, the national pastime quickly became Asheville's passion in the early 1900s.

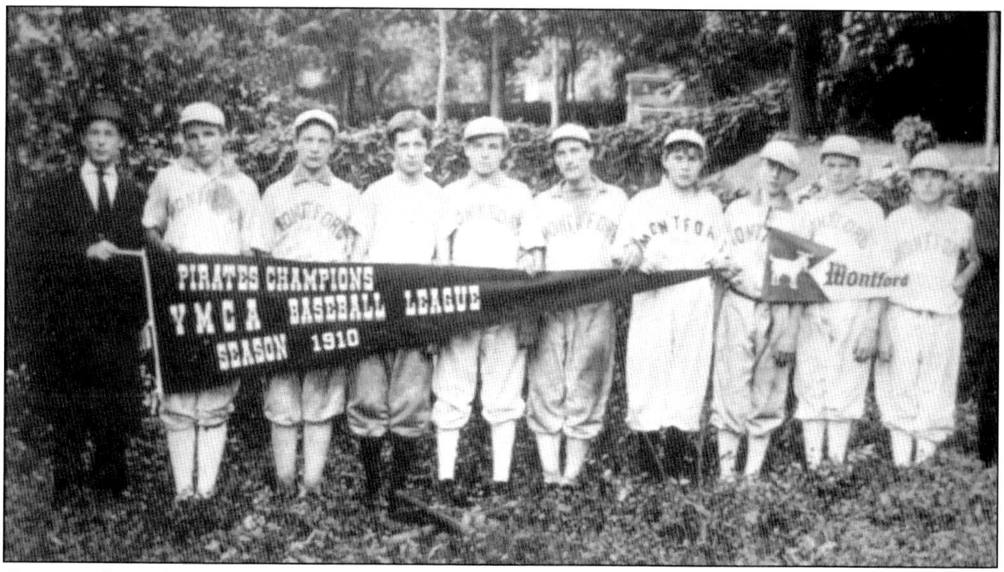

Organized youth leagues began to play in Asheville during the first decade of the 20th century. The Montford Goats won the YMCA baseball league championship in 1910. The following players are pictured from left to right: Henry Gudger, George Craig, Charles Tennent, John Tennent, "Nemo" Coleman, Walter Hunt, Phillip "Goat" Randolph, Stephen Adams, Allen Williamson, Dewey Hunt, and John Hunter. (Pack Memorial Public Library, Asheville, North Carolina, North Carolina Collection.)

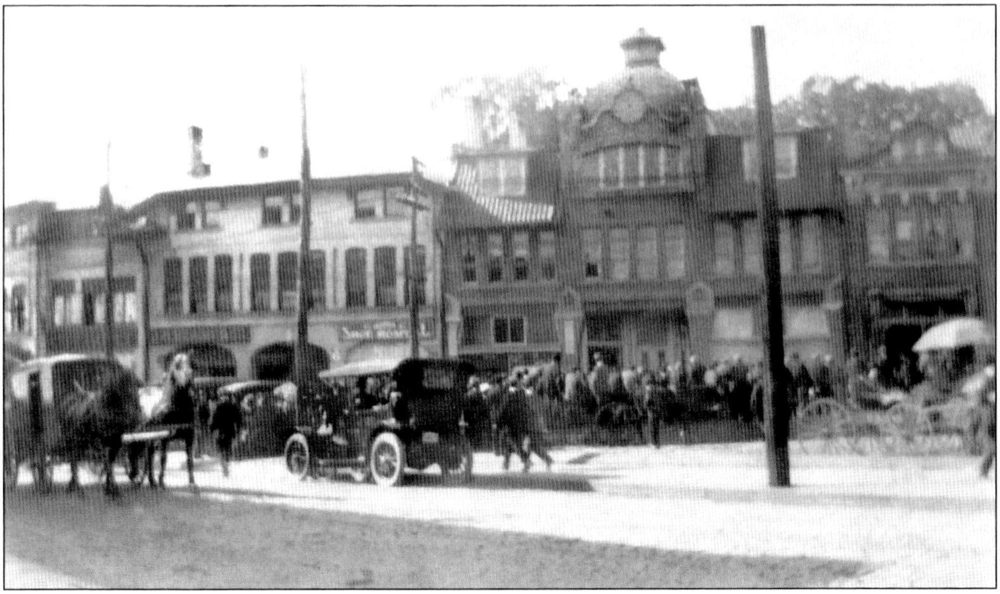

Though the World Series was in its infancy in 1911, fans throughout the country longed to follow the games' proceedings every October. Above, Ben Wolfe, brother of Thomas Wolfe, reads the Western Union dispatches of a game between the New York Giants and Philadelphia A's to a crowd gathered at Pack Square in downtown Asheville. (Pack Memorial Public Library, Asheville, North Carolina, Thomas Wolfe Collection.)

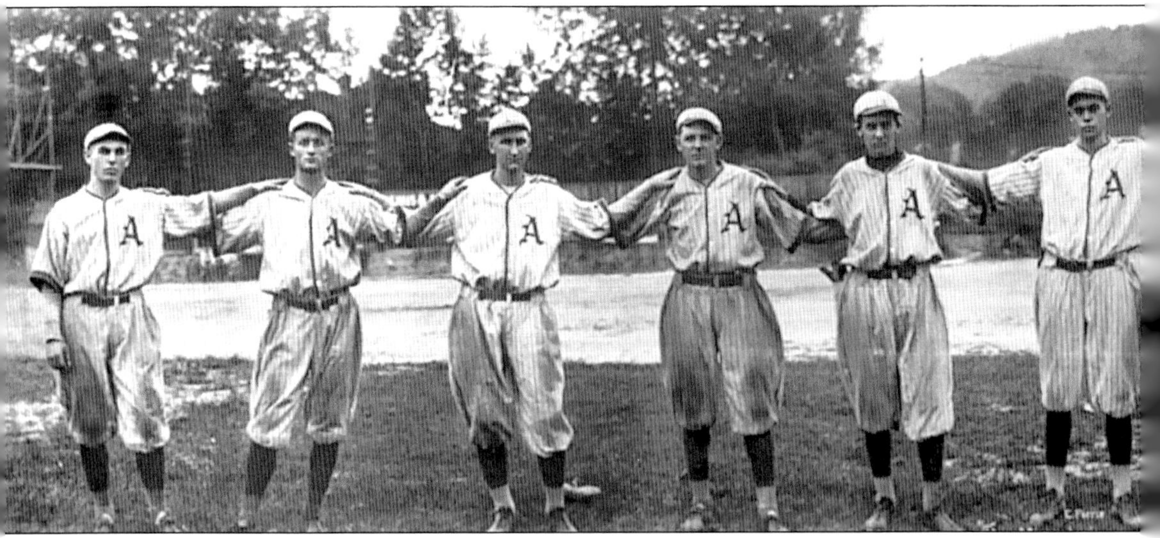

The 1915 Asheville Tourists won the first professional baseball championship in the city's history. One year after finishing in last place in the North Carolina State League, the team changed its name from the Mountaineers to the Tourists and posted a 74-46 record to capture

Thomas Wolfe's life-long love affair with baseball intensified in 1915 when he served as a part-time batboy for the Tourists in between warming up with players and handling other chores on game days at Oates Park. Pictured at age 15, Wolfe often recounted his days in Asheville. In a letter to Arthur Mann, Wolfe referred to Oates Park when he wrote, "And is there anything that can tell more about an American summer than, say, the smell of the wooden bleachers in a small-town baseball park, that resinous, sultry, and exciting smell of old dry wood." (Pack Memorial Public Library, Asheville, North Carolina, Thomas Wolfe Collection.)

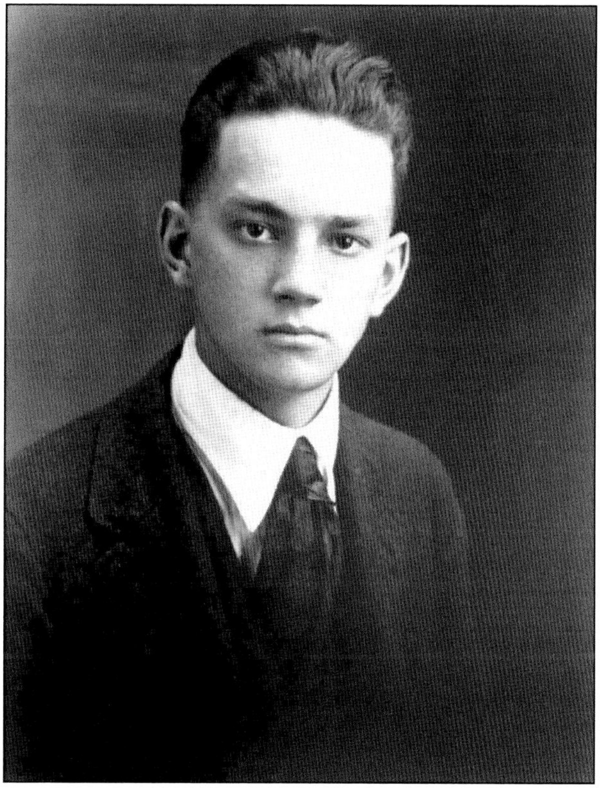

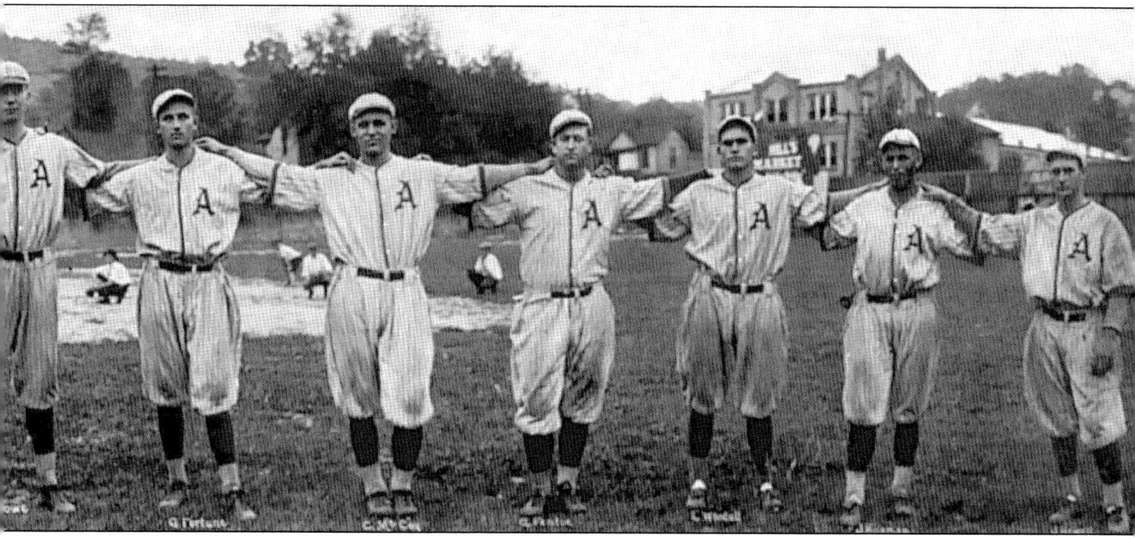

first place by five-and-a-half games over the Durham Bulls. Jimmy Hickman led the league with 14 home runs and 95 runs; he tied for the top spot with 127 hits. This picture was taken at Oates Park. (Bob Terrell collection.)

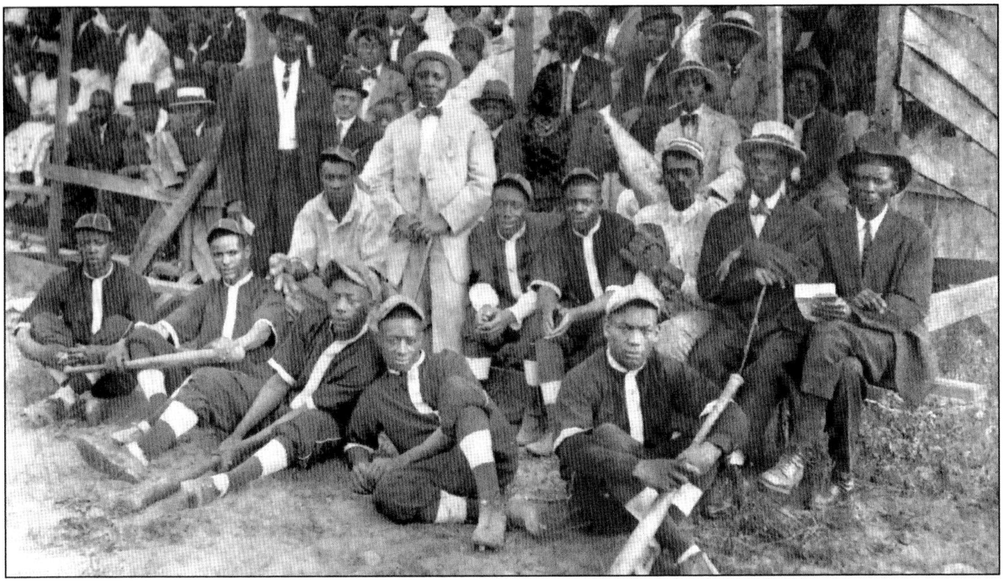

The Asheville Royal Giants were the city's first black baseball team. The team was formed by Edward W. Pearson Sr., a native of Burke County and a veteran of the Spanish-American War, who came to Asheville in August of 1906. Pearson founded the Buncombe County District Agricultural Fair and established Pearson's Park in West Asheville before organizing the Royal Giants. The club is pictured here at Pearson's Park in 1916. (Pack Memorial Public Library, Asheville, North Carolina, North Carolina Collection.)

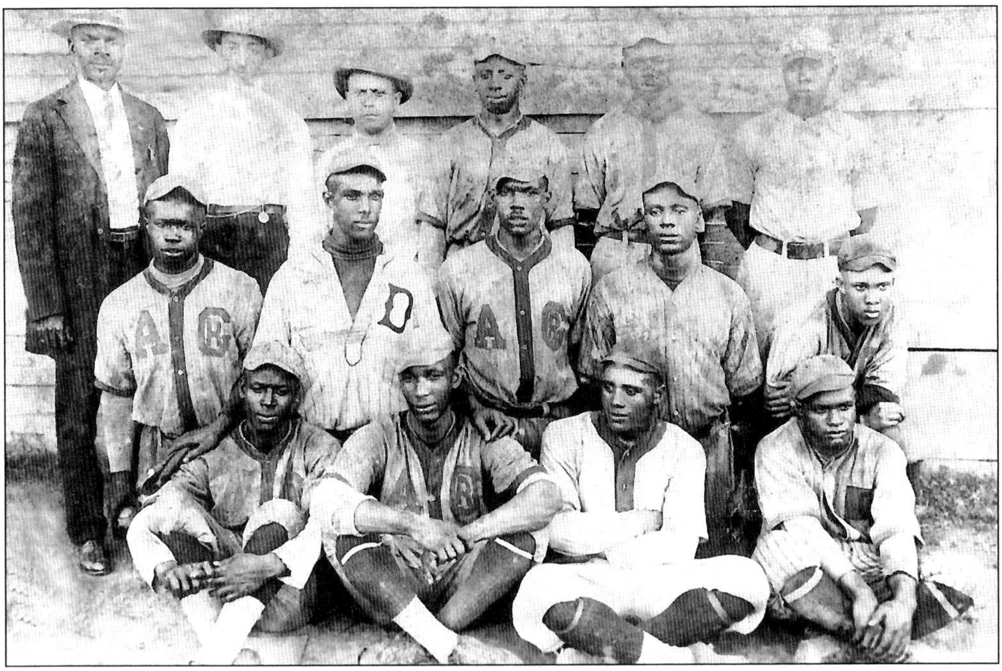

The Asheville Royal Giants thrilled fans throughout the black community during the late 1910s and early 1920s. There is some discrepancy regarding the actual date of this team picture. The original photograph records 1917 on the back and 1921 on the front. (Pack Memorial Public Library, Asheville, North Carolina, North Carolina Collection.)

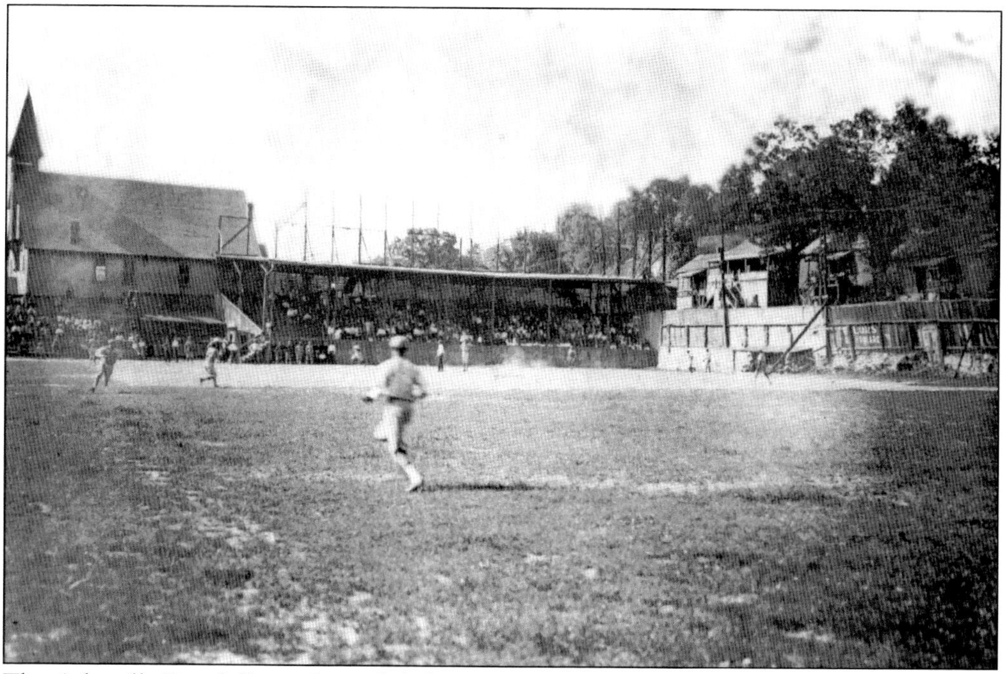

The Asheville Royal Giants hosted Atlanta at in 1918 at Oates Park, located on Southside Avenue near Choctaw Street. Southside AME Zion Church is on the left in the background. (Pack Memorial Public Library, Asheville, North Carolina, North Carolina Collection.)

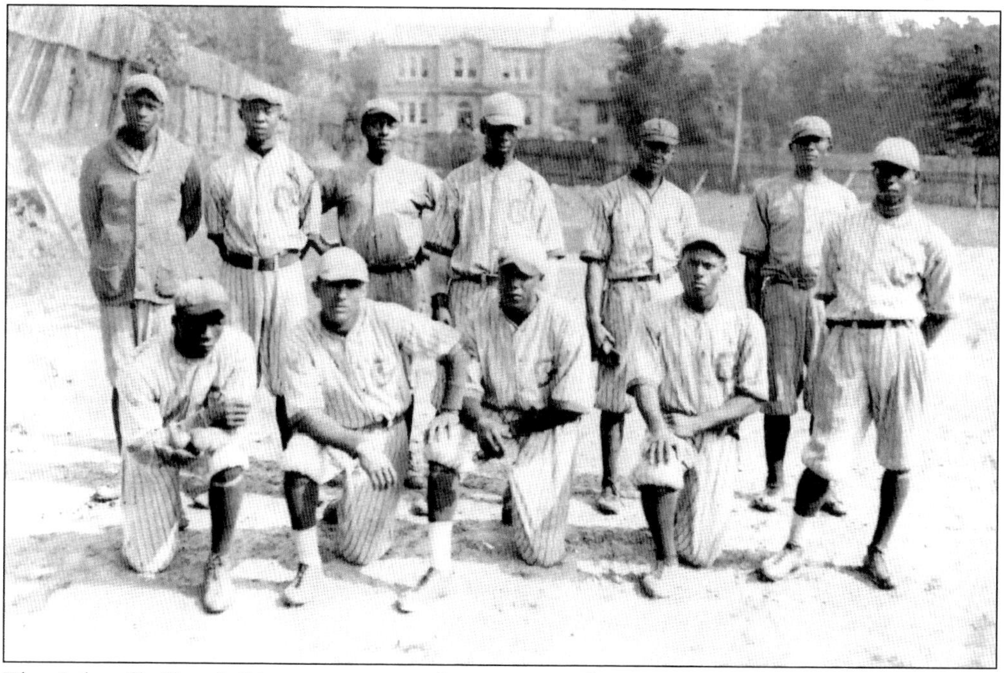

The Asheville Royal Giants were one of strongest and most stable teams among the loosely organized Negro League minors. The Royal Giants faced teams throughout the South and formed noted rivalries with Atlanta and Greenville. (Pack Memorial Public Library, Asheville, North Carolina, North Carolina Collection.)

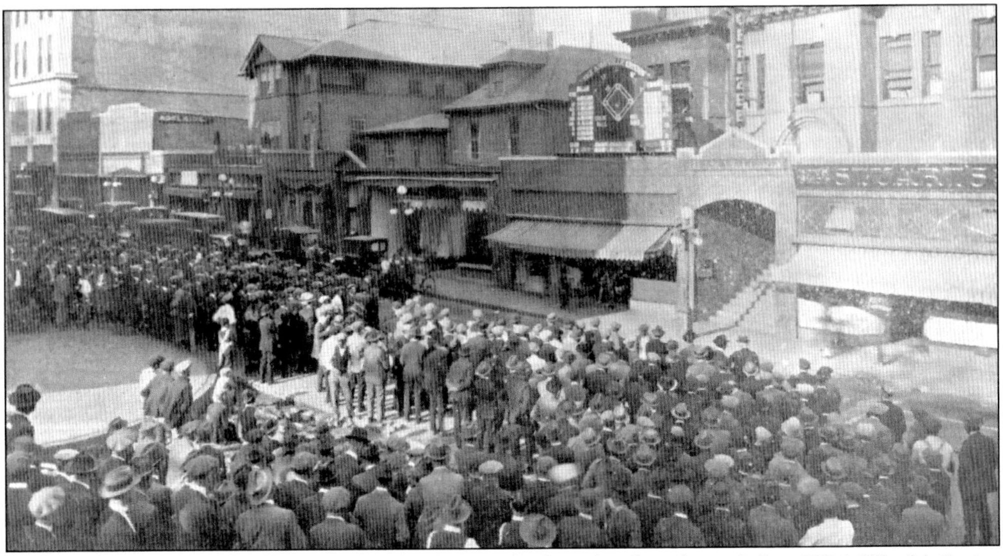

Fans gathered in downtown Asheville to watch the play-by-play of the 1924 World Series between the New York Giants and Washington Senators on a game board. Operators of the game board posted base runners on a diamond while recording runs, outs, and innings upon receiving the information via Western Union dispatches. (Pack Memorial Public Library, Asheville, North Carolina, North Carolina Collection.)

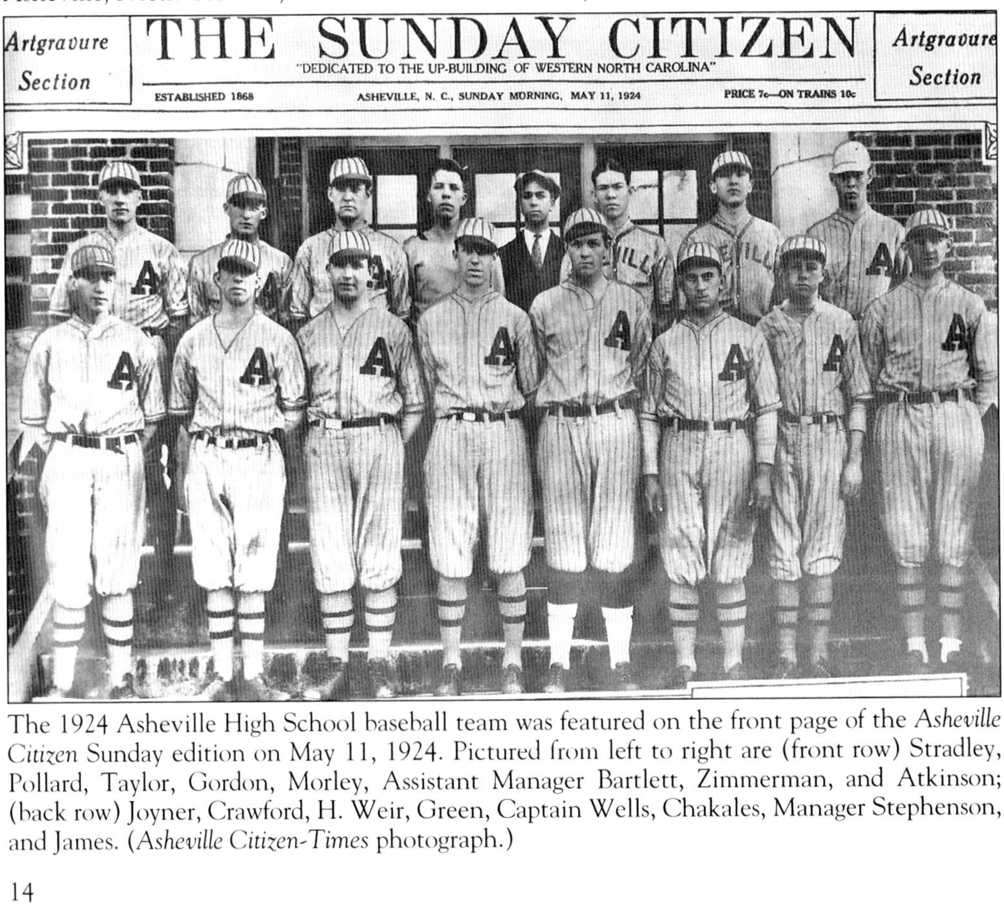

The 1924 Asheville High School baseball team was featured on the front page of the *Asheville Citizen* Sunday edition on May 11, 1924. Pictured from left to right are (front row) Stradley, Pollard, Taylor, Gordon, Morley, Assistant Manager Bartlett, Zimmerman, and Atkinson; (back row) Joyner, Crawford, H. Weir, Green, Captain Wells, Chakales, Manager Stephenson, and James. (*Asheville Citizen-Times* photograph.)

Two

Baseball Gets a New Home

Asheville garnered a place on the baseball map in 1924 with the opening of McCormick Field. Built for $200,000, the field was named for Dr. Lewis McCormick, the city's only bacteriologist, who started the "Swat That Fly" campaign in 1905 to reduce the area's burgeoning problem with the housefly. Although McCormick died unexpectedly in 1922, the facility that honors him was deemed a diamond in every sense of the word.

The Tourists played in the South Atlantic League/Association from 1924 to 1930 and in the Piedmont League from 1931 to 1942, except for 1933, when the city lost its franchise at the height of the Great Depression before receiving the Columbia Sandlappers franchise on June 7, 1934. During this time, Asheville fans were privy to exhibition games played by the New York Yankees, featuring Babe Ruth and Lou Gehrig, and other major league teams that worked their way north from spring training. One of the biggest events occurred in 1948 when the Brooklyn Dodgers and Jackie Robinson played at McCormick Field. The home nine also fielded competitive clubs, most notably manager Ray Kennedy's 1928 Tourists, which posted a 97-49 record and won the South Atlantic League by 18 games over the second-place Macon Peaches, and skipper Clay Bryant's 1948 Tourists, which won the Tri-State League in the team's third season on the Class B circuit.

Arc lights were employed in order to play the first night games in Asheville during the early 1930s. Night baseball disappeared when the Tourists folded in 1932 and did not return until permanent lights were installed at McCormick Field and christened on July 5, 1940, when 2,574 fans watched Norfolk defeat Asheville 4-0.

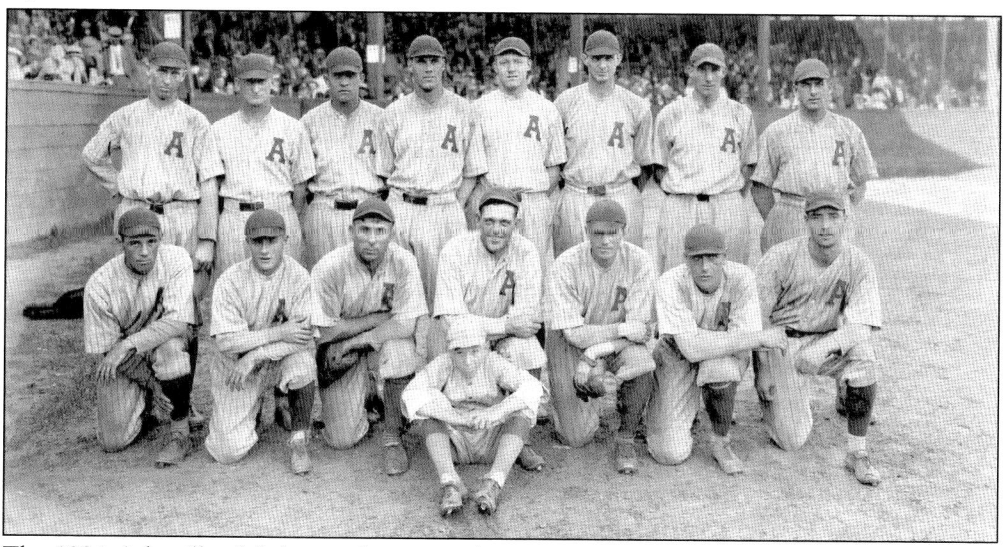

The 1924 Asheville club began the season known as the Skylanders before reverting to the more traditional Tourists during the campaign. Bob Higgins managed the club to a 58-63 record, placing the team fifth in the six-team Class B South Atlantic League. (Pack Memorial Public Library, Asheville, North Carolina, North Carolina Collection.)

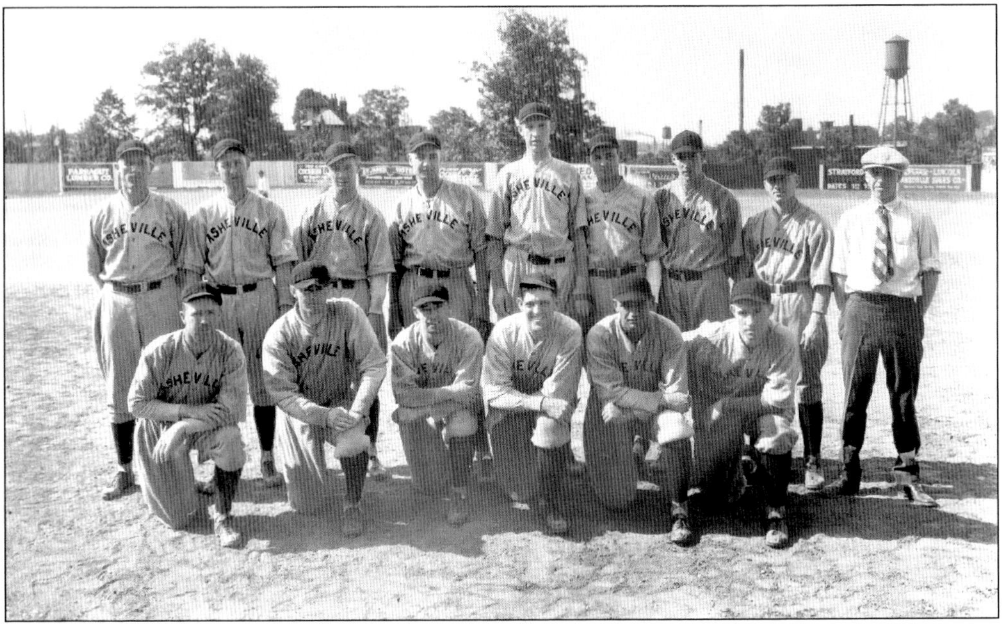

For the second time in as many seasons, the Asheville Tourists finished the 1925 campaign in the middle of the pack in the Class B South Atlantic League. The Tourists posted a 66-63 record and finished in fifth place on the eight-team circuit. (Pack Memorial Public Library, Asheville, North Carolina, North Carolina Collection.)

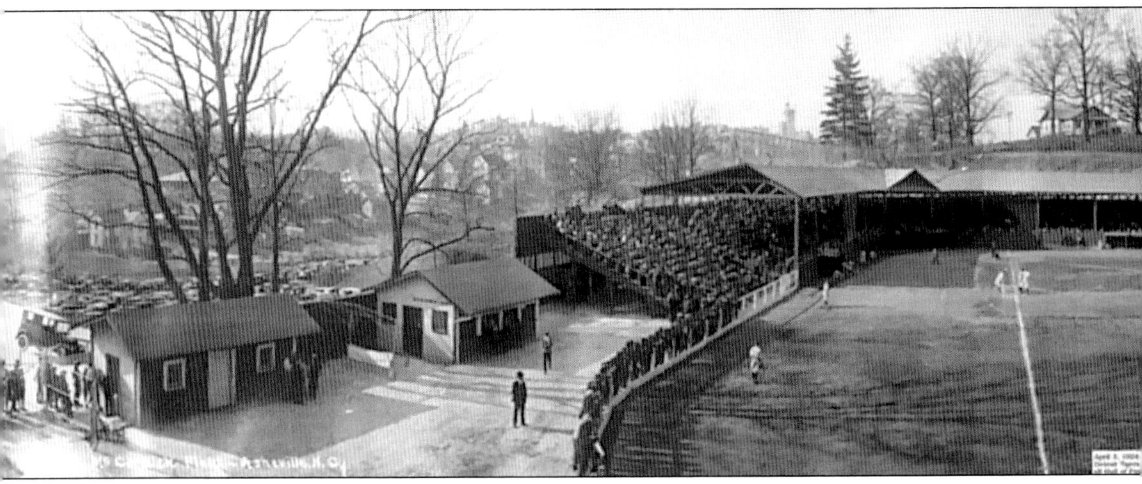

The first official game in McCormick Field history took place on April 3, 1924, when the Asheville Skylanders shocked the Detroit Tigers, 18-14. The Hall of Fame outfield of Heinie Manush, Ty Cobb, and Harry Heilmann manned the garden for the visitors, with the 37-year-old Cobb, who served as Detroit's player/manager, hitting the first home run in the new

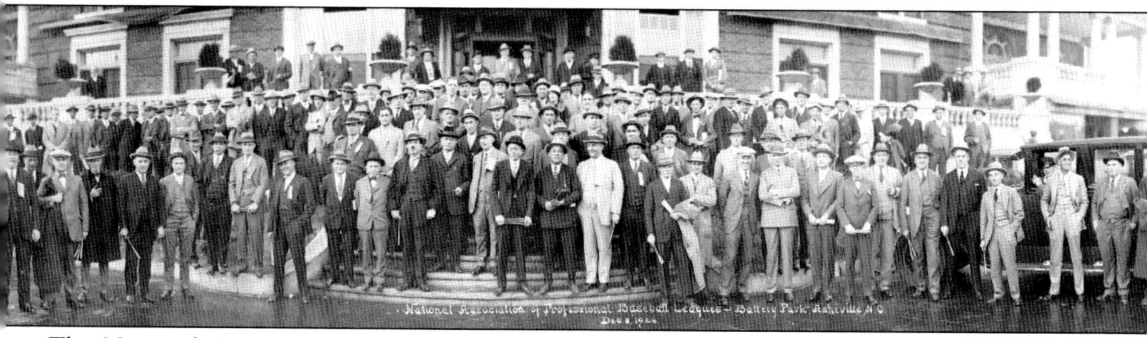

The National Association of Baseball Leagues, the governing body of the minor leagues, held its annual meeting in Asheville in 1926. This picture was taken on the front steps of the Battery Park Hotel. (Pack Memorial Public Library, Asheville, North Carolina, North Carolina Collection.)

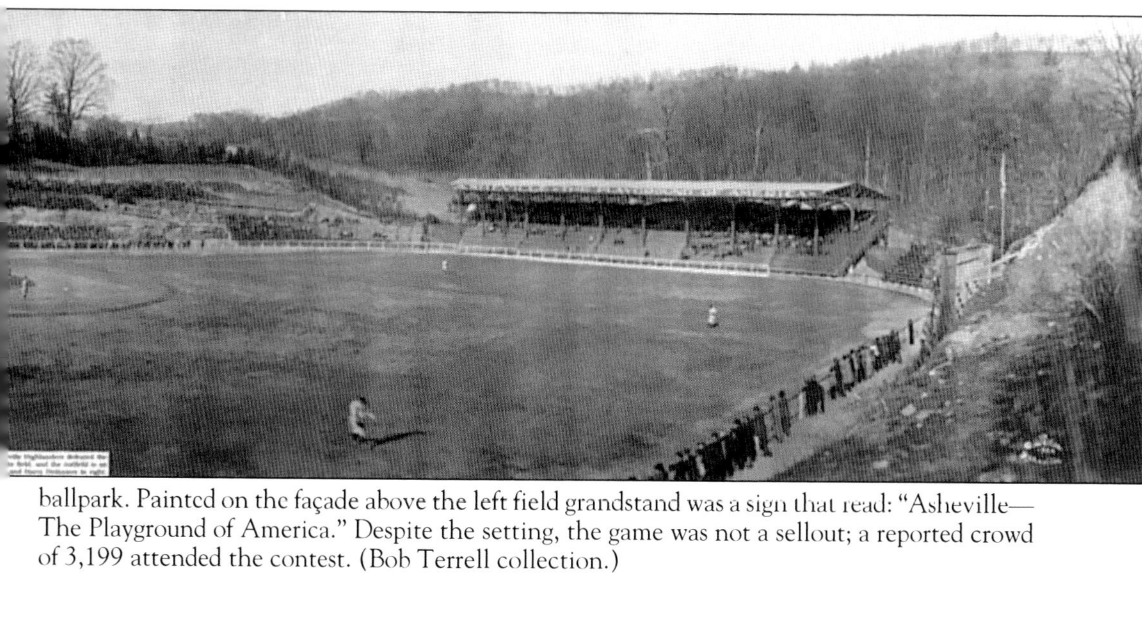

ballpark. Painted on the façade above the left field grandstand was a sign that read: "Asheville—The Playground of America." Despite the setting, the game was not a sellout; a reported crowd of 3,199 attended the contest. (Bob Terrell collection.)

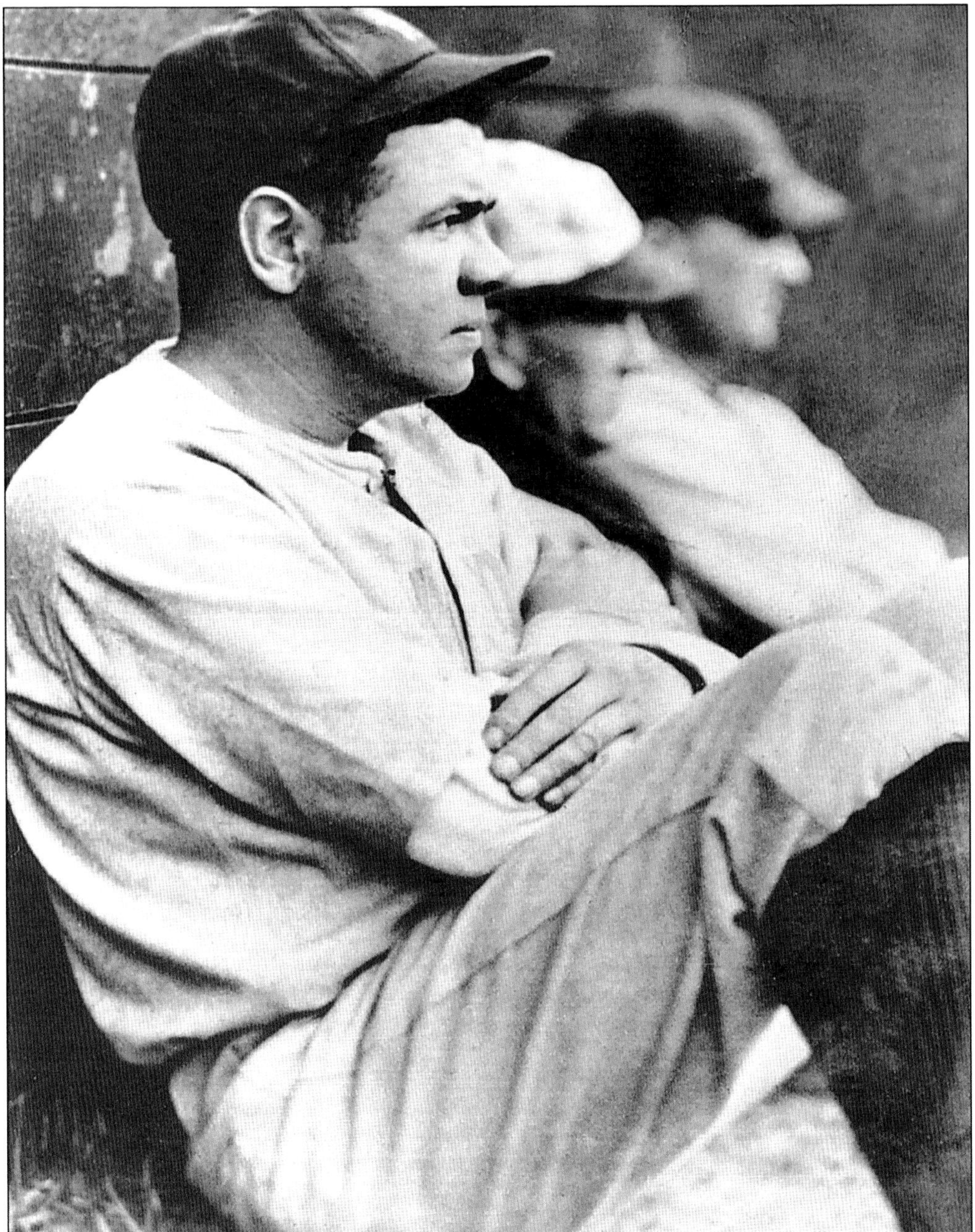

Babe Ruth, pictured here watching the action at McCormick Field, reportedly died in Asheville in 1925 from what became known as "The Bellyache Heard 'Round the World." The Yankees played several exhibition games annually while working their way north to New York from spring training. Ruth, who had been ill for most of the winter, collapsed upon departing the train in Asheville following the ride from Knoxville. Despite rumors to the contrary, Ruth survived and returned to Asheville on several other occasions. In 1926, he stood in the outfield, smelled the honeysuckle, and said, "My, my, what a beautiful place to play. Delightful. Damned delightful place!" Five years later, on April 8, 1931, Ruth and teammate Lou Gehrig both hit home runs in an 11-3 win in Asheville. (Asheville Tourists game program, 1995.)

In 1937, shortstop Lynn Myers scored seven runs in a game without an official at-bat. Myers accrued five walks and was hit by two pitches; he crossed the plate every time he reached base. The Tourists won the game 20-3 on their way to winning the Class B Piedmont League crown with an 89-50 record. Myers played two years in Asheville, hitting .269 in 1937 and .307 in 1938. (*Asheville Citizen-Times* photograph.)

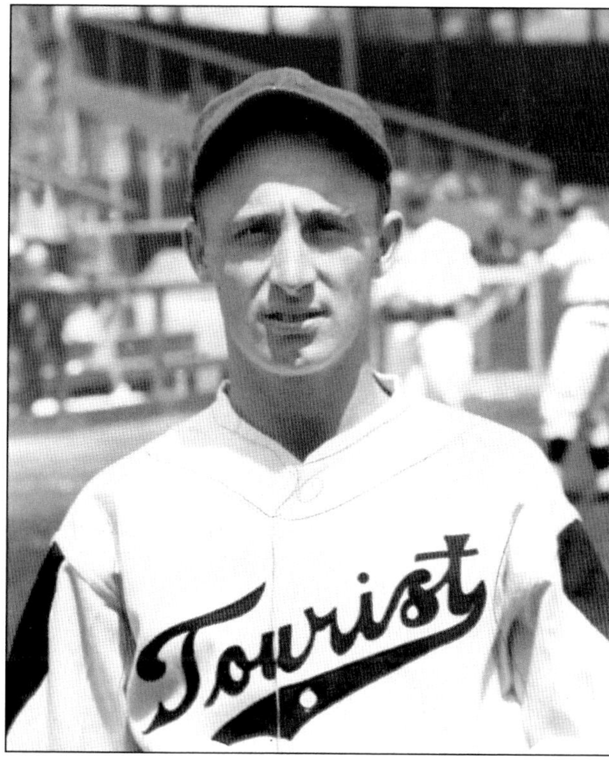

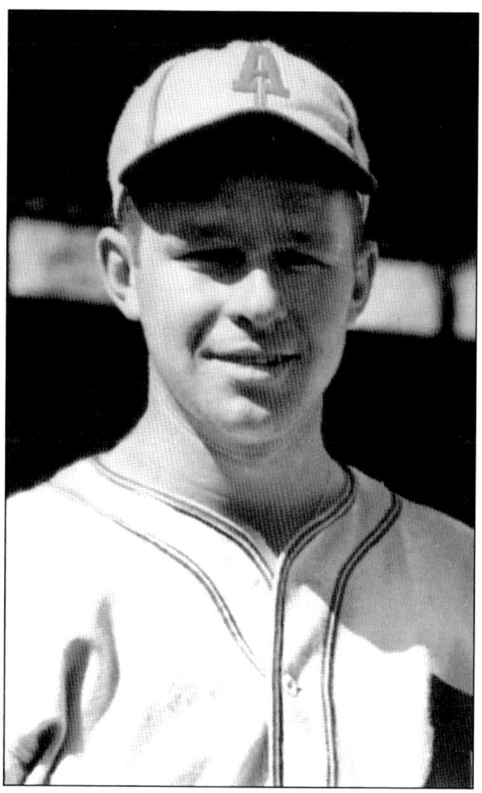

Joe Schultz produced the second-highest batting average on the Tourists in 1938, hitting at a .310 clip in 58 contests. Schultz became a premier pinch-hitter in nine major league seasons before managing the expansion Seattle Pilots in 1969. (*Asheville Citizen-Times* photograph.)

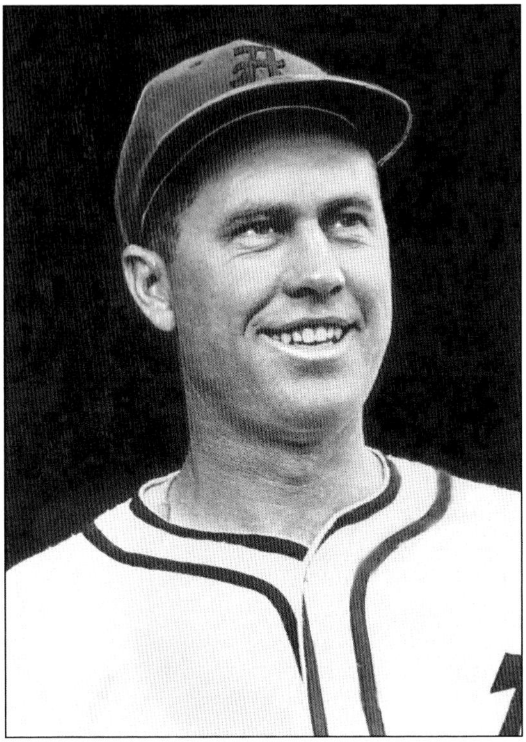

Tommy West managed the Tourists to a second-place finish and a playoff spot in the Class B Piedmont League in 1940. West also saw extensive action at catcher and led the team with a .303 batting average while contributing five home runs, 25 doubles, and 56 RBIs. West's Asheville squad went 75-60 during the regular season before falling to the Rocky Mount Red Sox, 3 games to 2, in the first round of postseason play. (*Asheville Citizen-Times* photograph.)

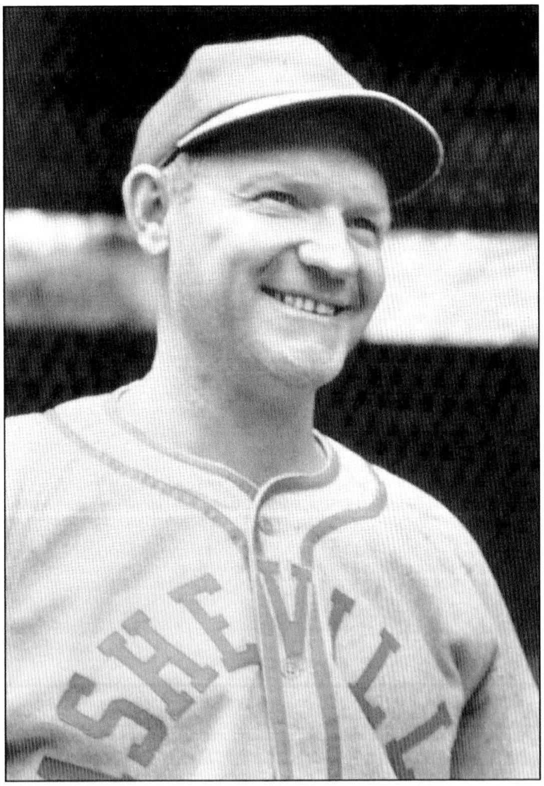

Nick Cullop, a former outfielder who played for five major league teams in five seasons, from 1926 to1931, managed the Tourists to a seventh-place finish in the Class B Piedmont League in 1941 with a 64-76 record. (*Asheville Citizen-Times* photograph.)

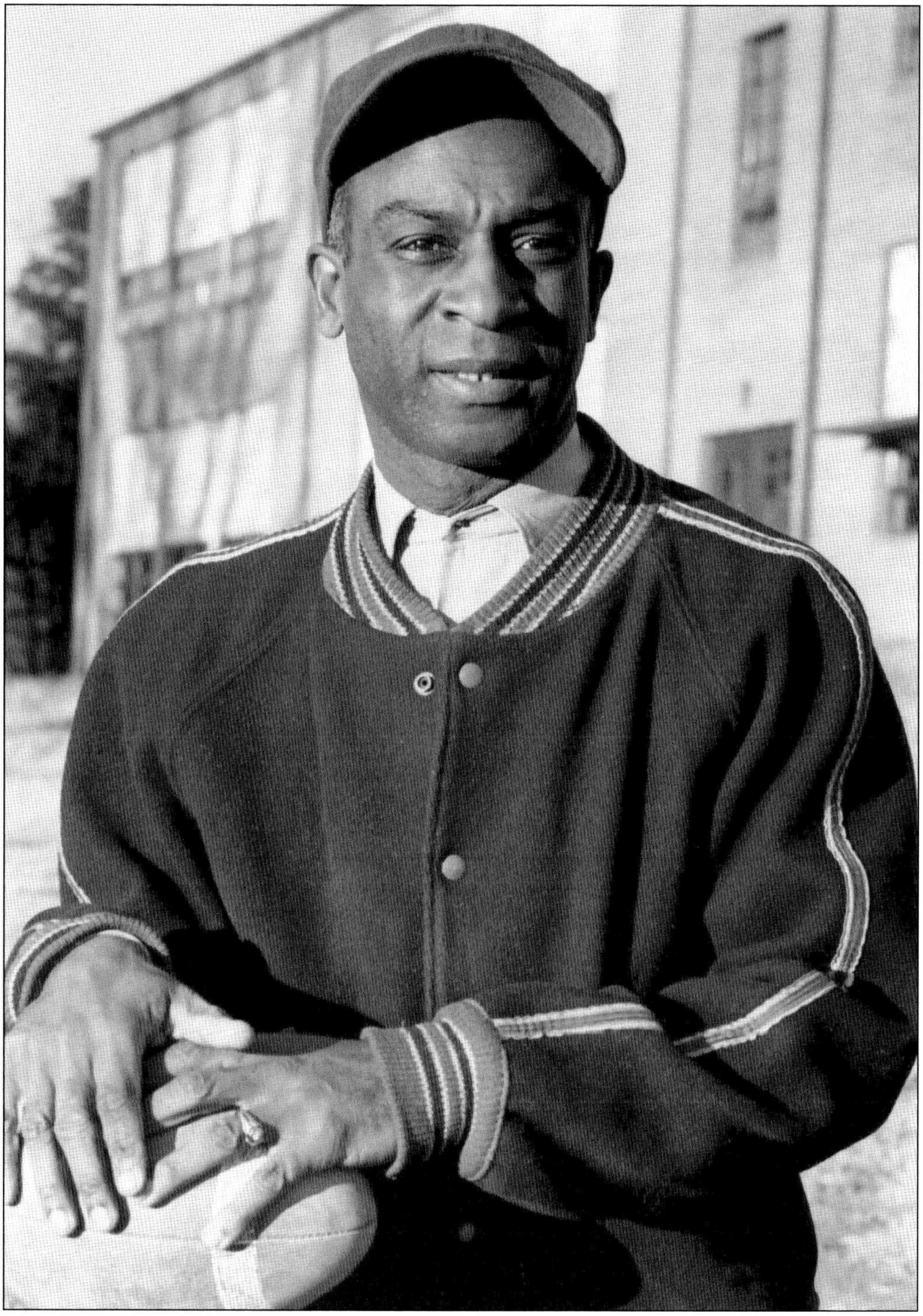

In 1944, C.L. Moore formed and served as player-manager of the Asheville Blues in the Negro Southern League. A semi-pro standout with the Chicago Union Giants and the Atlantic City Bacharach Giants, Moore guided the Blues to a pair of pennants as well as on a barnstorming tour with the renowned House of David in 1948. (*Asheville Citizen-Times* photograph.)

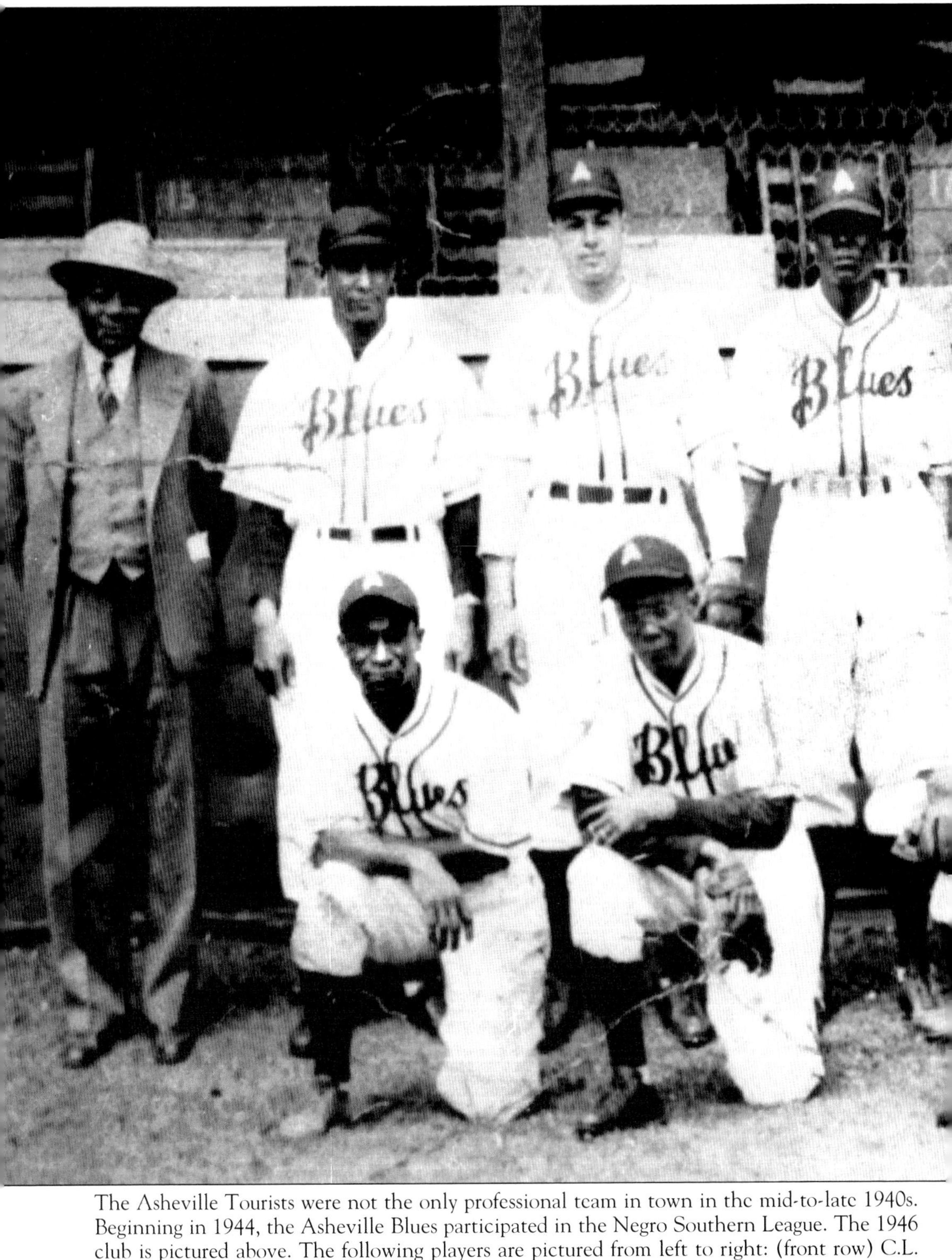

The Asheville Tourists were not the only professional team in town in the mid-to-late 1940s. Beginning in 1944, the Asheville Blues participated in the Negro Southern League. The 1946 club is pictured above. The following players are pictured from left to right: (front row) C.L. Moore, Waldo "Cane Creek" Donlap, A.C. Neeley, Rufus Hatten, mascot Robert Moore, Fred

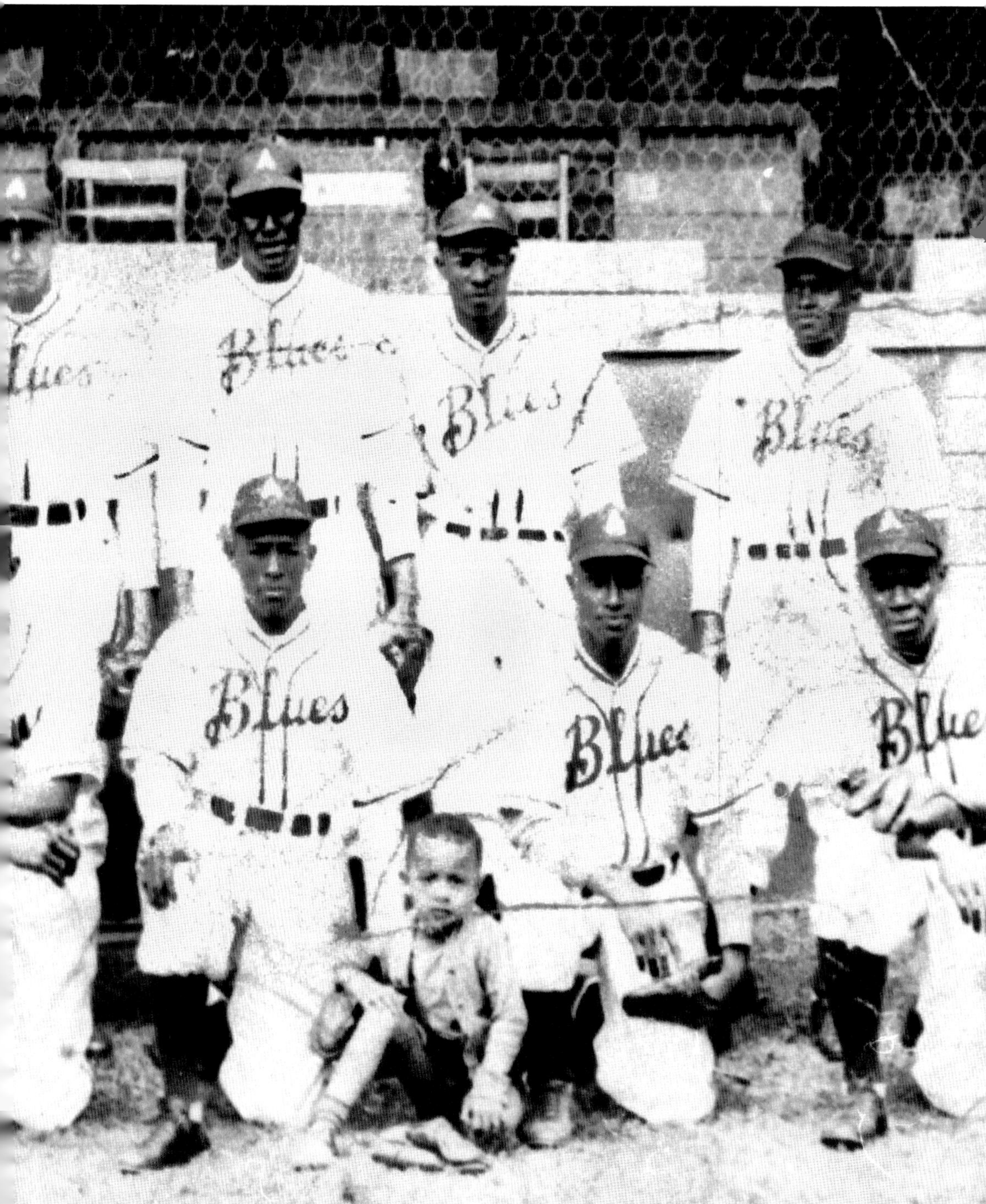

Worthy, and Spencer Alexander; (back row) Dr. White, Herman Taylor, Vernon Phillips, Frank Flemming, Robert Bowman, ? Brandon, Arthur Hefner, and unidentified. (National Baseball Hall of Fame Library, Cooperstown, New York.)

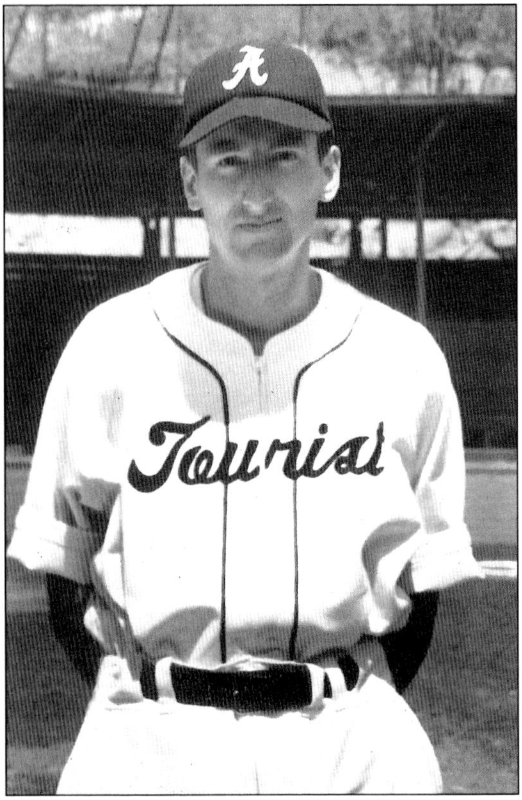

Sam Patton ranked third in the Class B Tri-State League in 1946 with 171 hits and placed seventh with a .333 batting average. Patton was a premier defensive outfielder with a strong and accurate arm, enabling him to record 16 assists from the garden. (*Asheville Citizen-Times* photograph.)

The Tourists went 83-57 in 1946 to finish in second place before losing four games to one to Knoxville in the first round of the playoffs. Pictured from left to right are (front row) Jim Cooksey, Cotton Myers, Veo Story, batboy Stub Lance, unidentified, Tom Lakos, Bill Glane, and Roy Whitaker; (back row) manager Bill Sayles and Sam Patton are on the left and right end, respectively. (*Asheville Citizen-Times* photograph.)

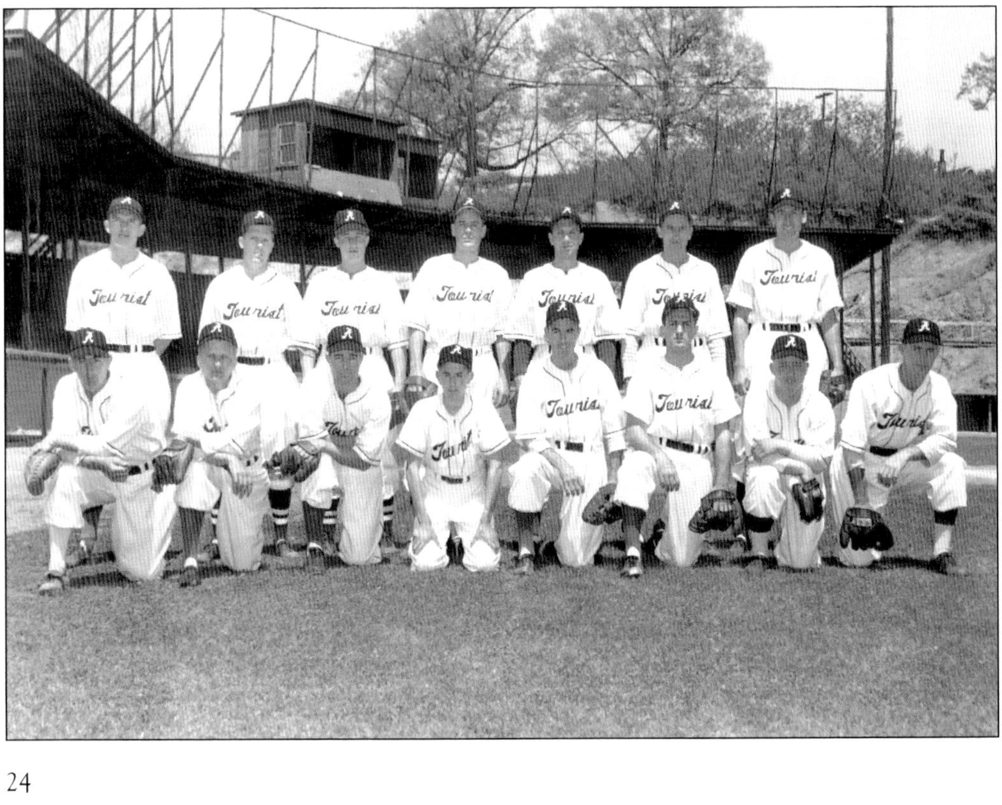

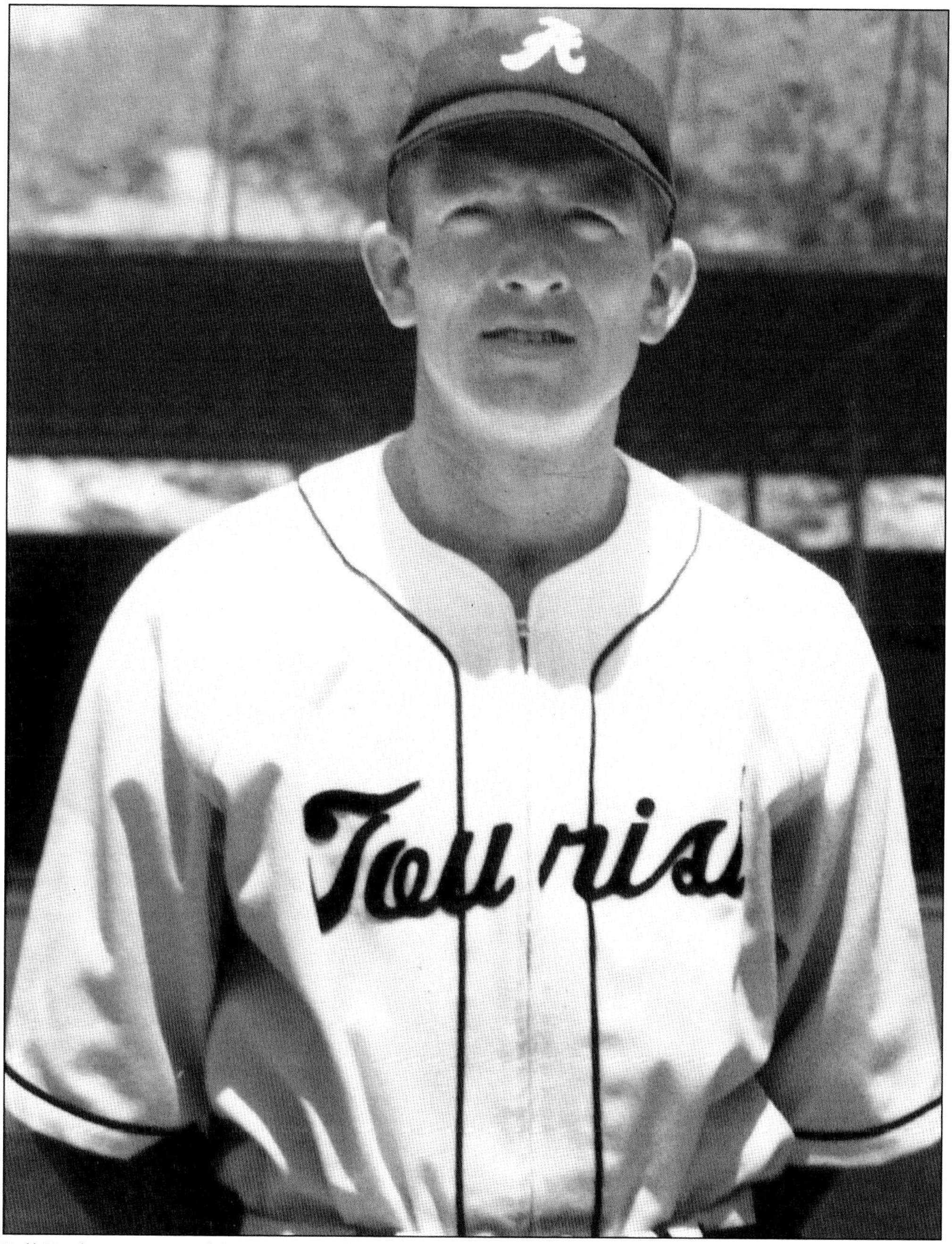

Bill Sayles was one of the premier players for the Tourists upon the return of professional baseball to Asheville in 1946. Sayles, who pitched in a demonstration game at the 1936 Berlin Olympics and went 1-3 with a 5.61 ERA in 28 games in the major leagues between 1939 and 1943, joined the Asheville nine as a player-manager in 1946, after serving two years in the military during World War II. Sayles topped the Class B Tri-State League with 105 RBIs and ranked ninth on the circuit with six home runs in 1946. In 1947, he tied teammate Ray Hickernell for fourth in the league with 12 long balls, placed fourth in the league with 174 hits, and ranked seventh in the league with 98 RBIs. (*Asheville Citizen-Times* photograph.)

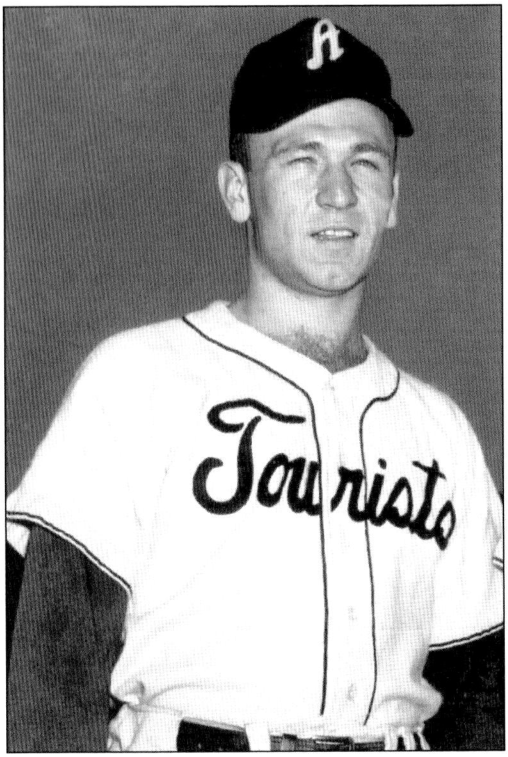

Left-hander Bill Glane went 9-9 with 11 complete games and a 4.07 ERA in 25 outings with the Tourists in 1947. (*Asheville Citizen-Times* photograph.)

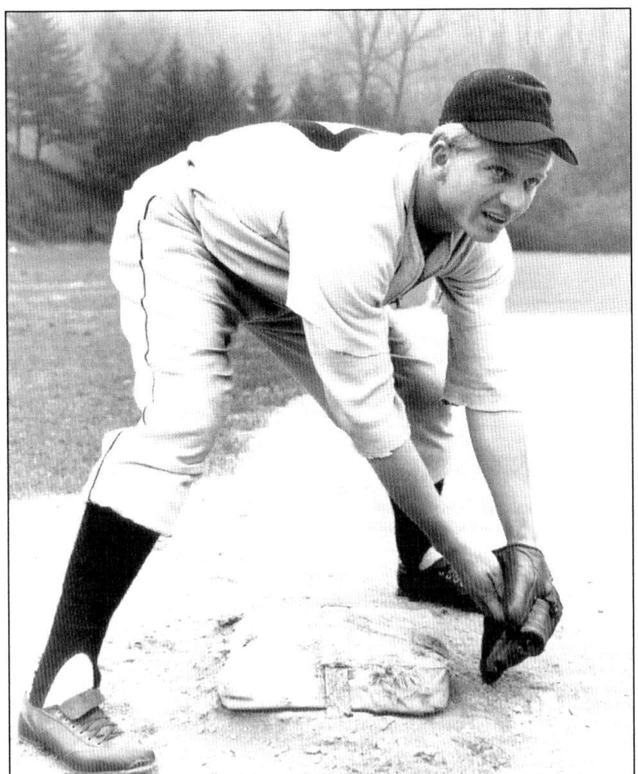

Richard "Cotton" Meyers handled third base for the Tourists in 1946 before moving to shortstop in 1947. Meyers was a target for the boo birds at McCormick Field after making 36 errors during his first season in Asheville. In 1946, he batted .237 with three home runs and 56 RBIs. (*Asheville Citizen-Times* photograph.)

Shortstop Billy "Kid" DeMars was one of the top offensive middle infielders in the Class B Tri-State League in 1947. DeMars batted .328, including five home runs and 88 RBIs. He also provided steady defense. He played 80 games in the major leagues from 1948 to 1951. (*Asheville Citizen-Times* photograph.)

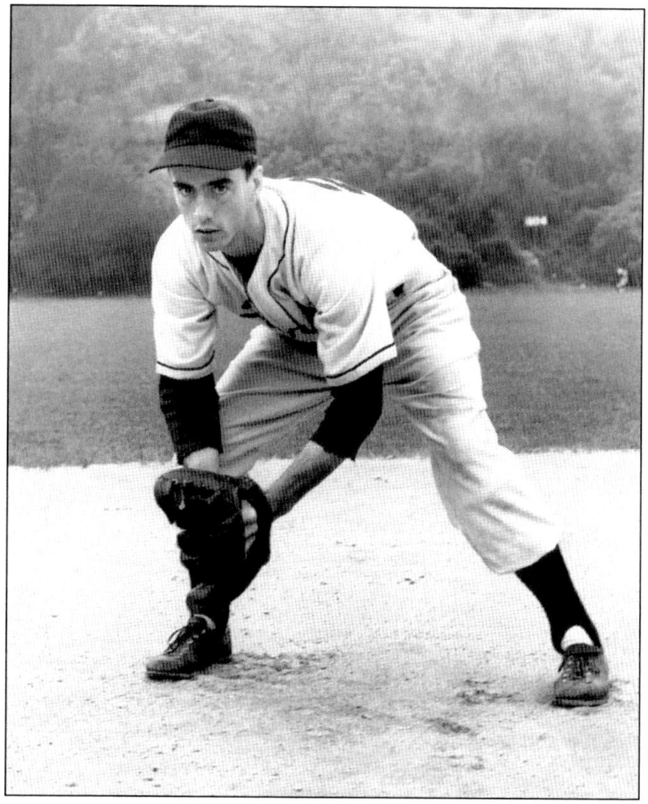

Fresco Thompson, George Mitchell, and C. Manley Llewellyn present Bill Sayles with the keys to a car at McCormick Field on August 31, 1947. In his two seasons as the Tourists' player-manager, Sayles guided the team to a 152-121 record in Tri-State League competition. (*Asheville Citizen-Times* photograph.)

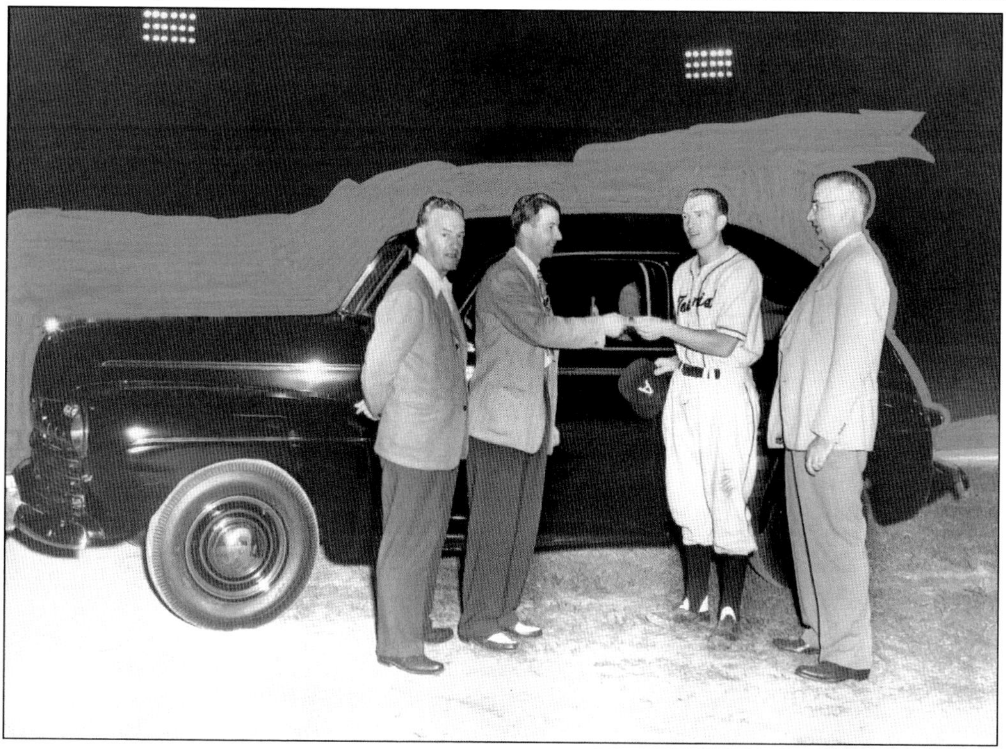

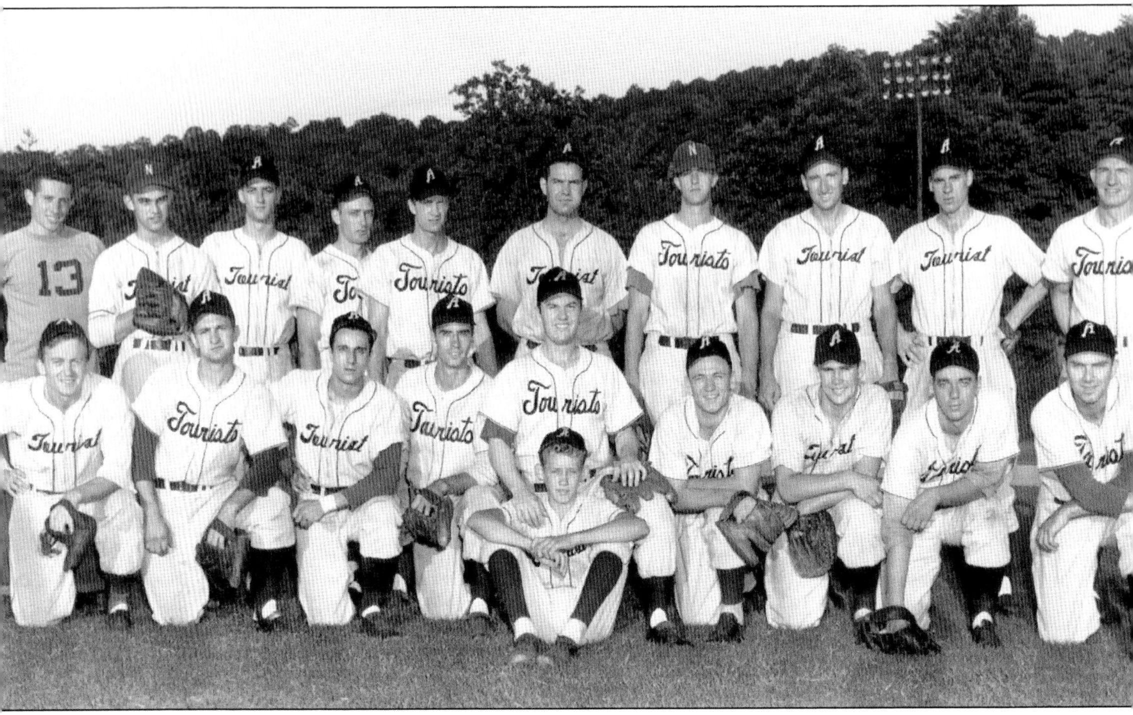

The 1947 Tourists went 65-74 and finished in sixth place in the Class B Tri-State League. The team was honored on August 31, 1947, when, according to the *Asheville Citizen-Times*, appreciative fans purchased homespun suits for each member of the club while various Asheville merchants presented each man with a gift. Pictured from left to right are (front row) Dick Bishop, Ben Stansky, Fred Pestolese, Billy DeMars, Jim MacFaden, Bill Glane, Leon Irwin, Stan Ogden, and Lyle Parkhurst; (back row) clubhouse boy Harry Bryson, Clem Labine, Dom Schmidt, Wayne Reside, Bud McBryde, Dick Bouknight, Ray Hickernell, Sam Patton, Frank Smith, and player-manager Bill Sayles. Seated in the front is batboy Tommy Huff. (*Asheville Citizen-Times* photograph.)

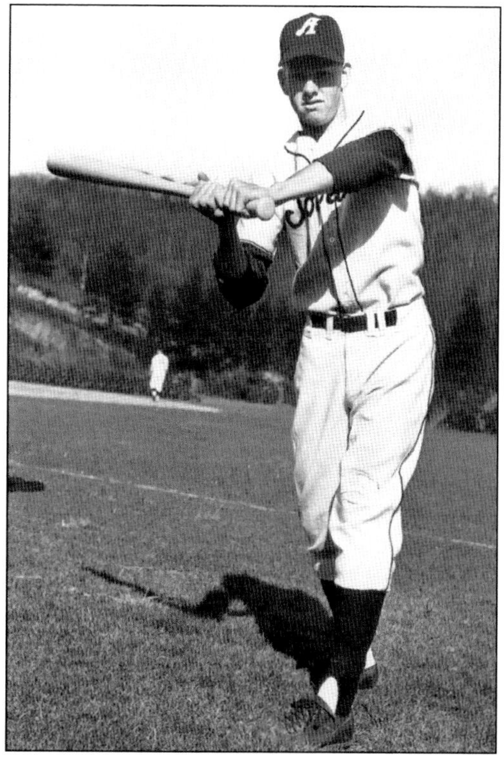

Russ Rose and Forrest "Spook" Jacobs formed the All-Star double-play combination in the Tri-State League in 1948. Rose was honored on the year-end club as the second baseman while Jacobs was recognized for his play at shortstop. Jacobs, who played three seasons in the major leagues from 1954 to 1956, batted .328 with 111 runs scored and 92 RBIs. Rose batted .274, allowing him to score 131 runs, including 12 triples and 73 RBIs. (*Asheville Citizen-Times* photograph.)

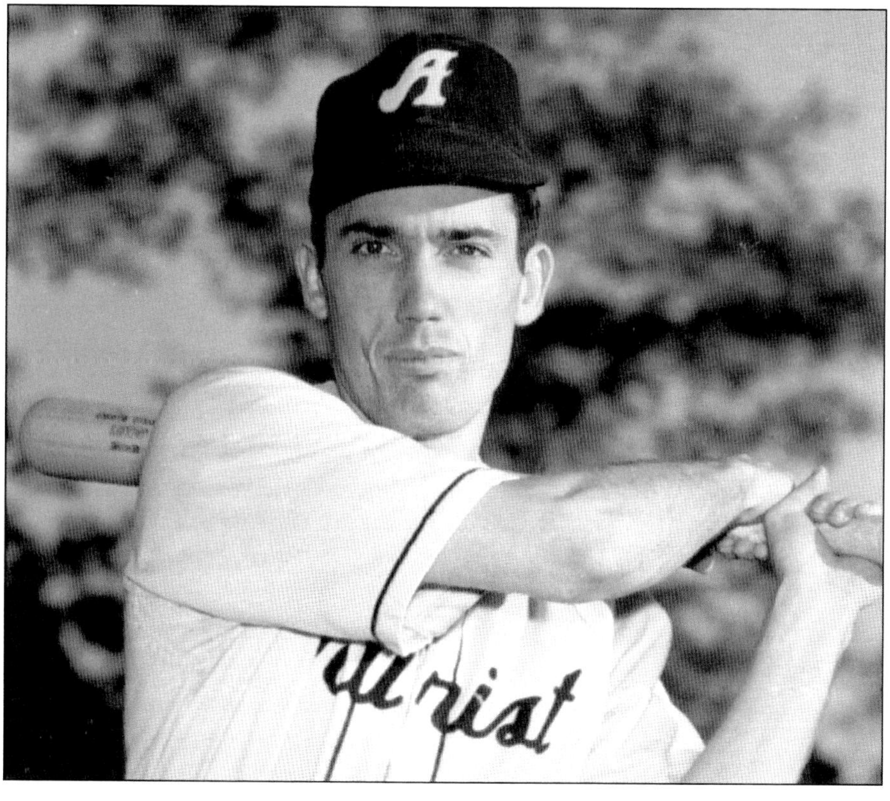

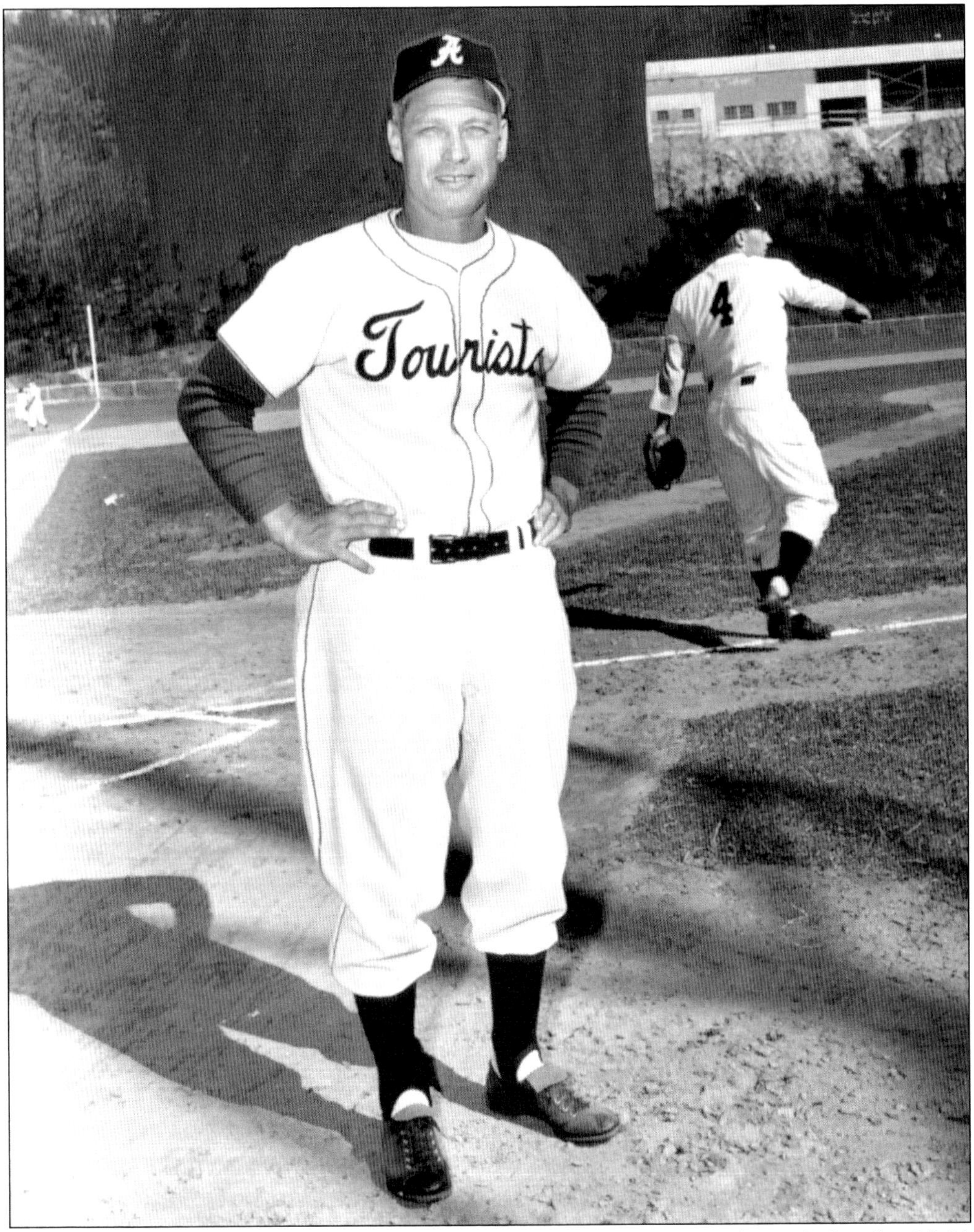

Manager Clay Bryant led the Tourists to the Class B Tri-State League title in 1948 with a 95-51 record to finish in first place, 17.5 games ahead of the second-place Anderson Rebels. The Tourists, however, were upset by the Rock Hill Chiefs in the first round of the playoffs, losing three games to one. An outstanding motivator, Bryant returned to manage Asheville again in 1950. The Tourists placed second in the Tri-State League with an 83-62 mark and swept the Spartanburg Peaches in three games in the first round of the playoffs before losing a seven-game championship series to Rock Hill. (*Asheville Citizen-Times* photograph.)

After going 3-2 in nine games with the Tourists in 1946, Tom Lakos returned to Asheville two years later and set the franchise standard for wins with a 21-8 record. In 39 starts during the 1948 campaign, Lakos completed 21 games and posted a 3.66 ERA to serve as the team's ace on the Tri-State League pennant-winning club. (*Asheville Citizen-Times* photograph.)

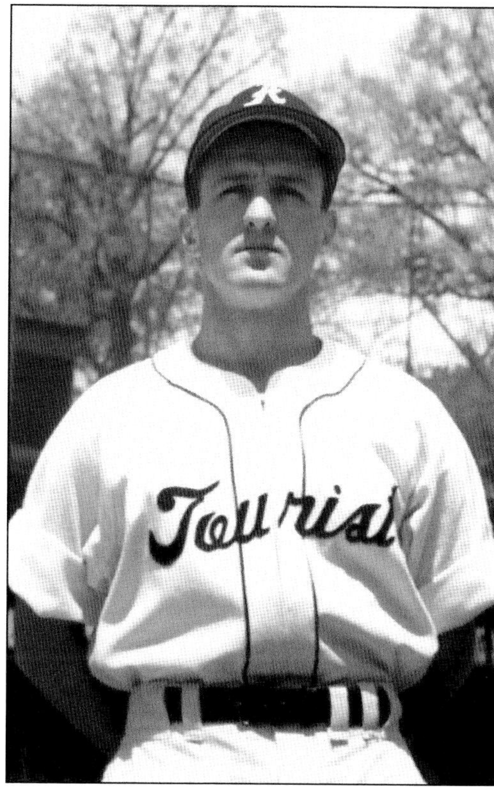

The Tourists walked away with the Tri-State League pennant in 1948, winning 95 games, the second-highest total in franchise history, behind an offense that scored 22 or more runs in no fewer than three contests. An example of Asheville's power was seen on May 1 when outfielder Bill Jekielek hit three home runs against Charlotte. While the Tourists lost three games to one to Rock Hill in the first round of the playoffs, owner E.C. Burleson (left) and general manager Paul S. Jones displayed the regular-season championship banner the following winter on the McCormick Field grandstands. (Asheville Tourists photograph.)

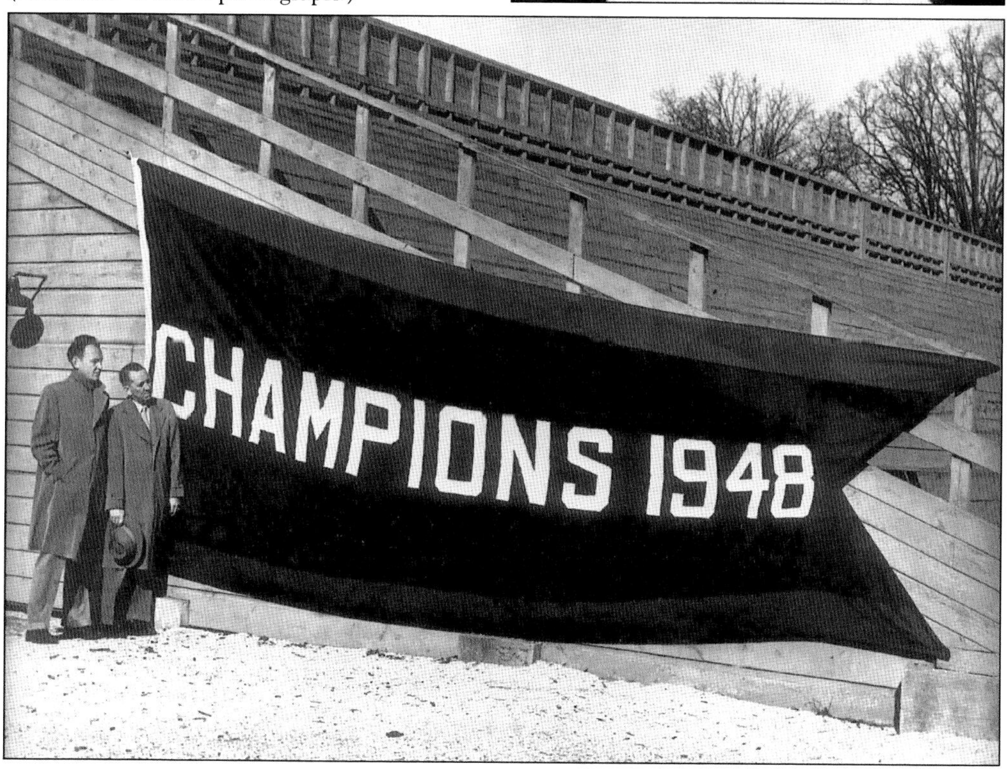

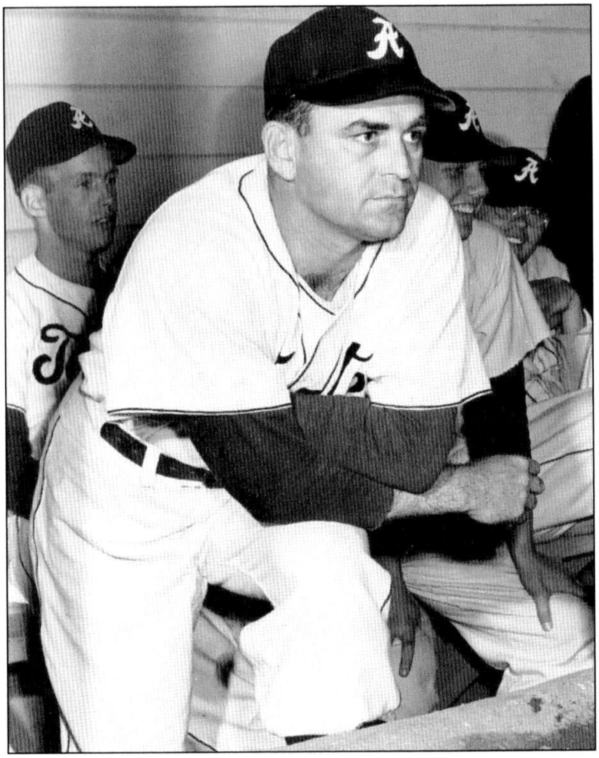

Ed Head managed the Tourists to a 76-71 record in the Tri-State League in 1949. Three years prior to guiding Asheville, the former pitcher tossed a no-hitter against the Boston Braves on April 23, 1946. (*Asheville Citizen-Times* photograph.)

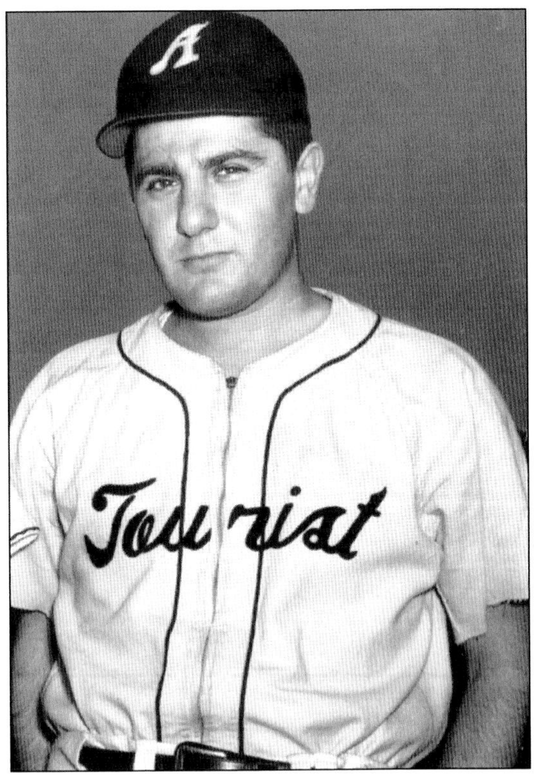

Joe DeStefano manned third base and filled in at second base for the Tourists in 1949. In 110 games, he batted .271 with 52 runs scored and 45 RBIs. (*Asheville Citizen-Times* photograph.)

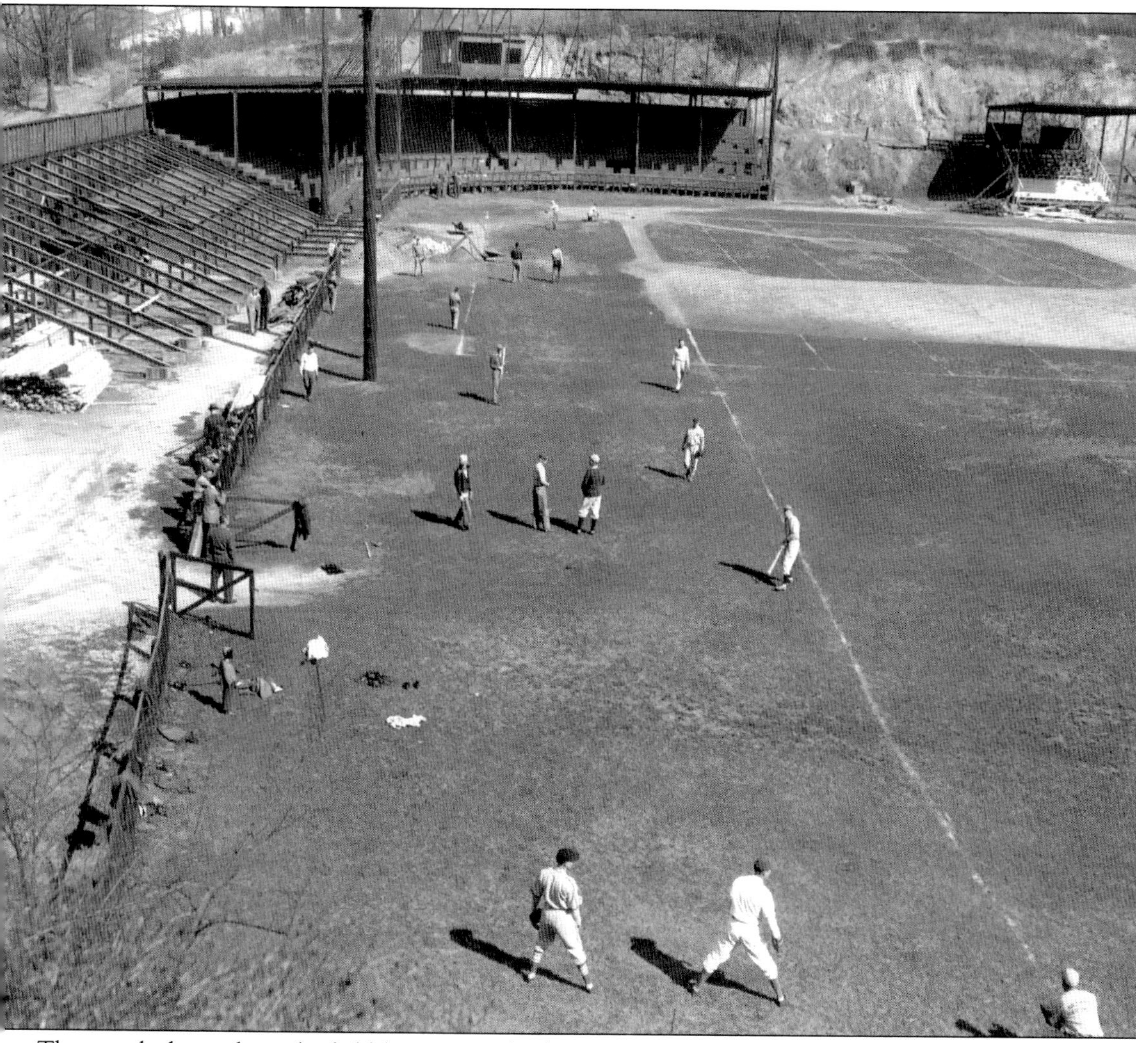

The stands down the right field line were rebuilt at McCormick Field approximately 20 years after the ballpark was initially constructed. (*Asheville Citizen-Times* photograph.)

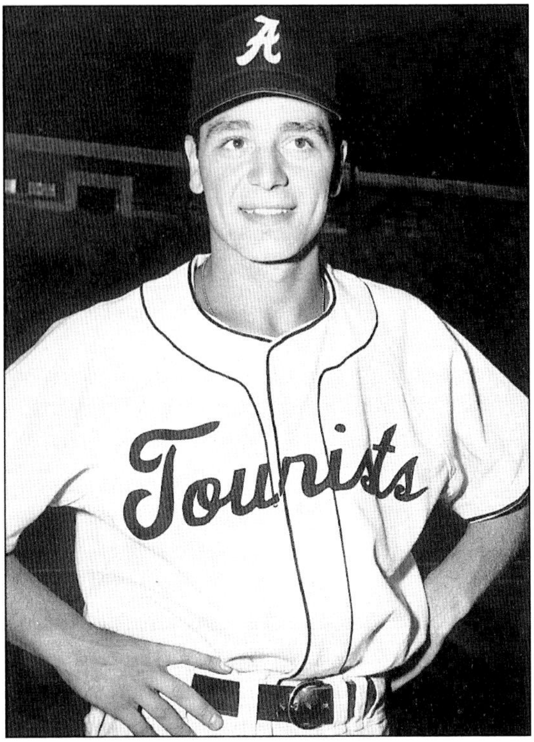

After hitting just .207 in 124 games with the Tourists in 1950, shortstop Chris Kitsos earned All-Star recognition in the Tri-State League for the 1951 season in which he led the Class B circuit with 134 runs scored. Kitsos also drew 137 walks and batted .334 while posting in 49 RBIs. (*Asheville Citizen-Times* photograph.)

Red Hawkins (left) and Yogi Prestamo handled much of the Tourists' catching chores during the 1951 season. Hawkins hit .286 with 29 RBIs in 42 games, while Prestamo batted .277 with 39 RBIs in 80 outings. (*Asheville Citizen-Times* photograph.)

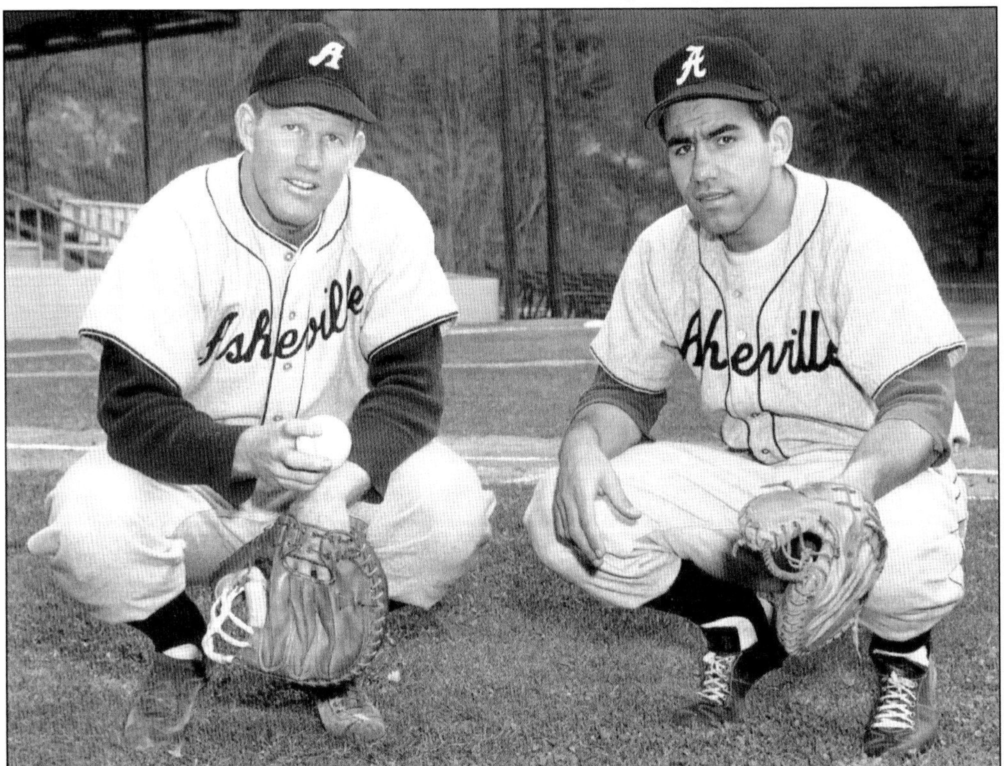

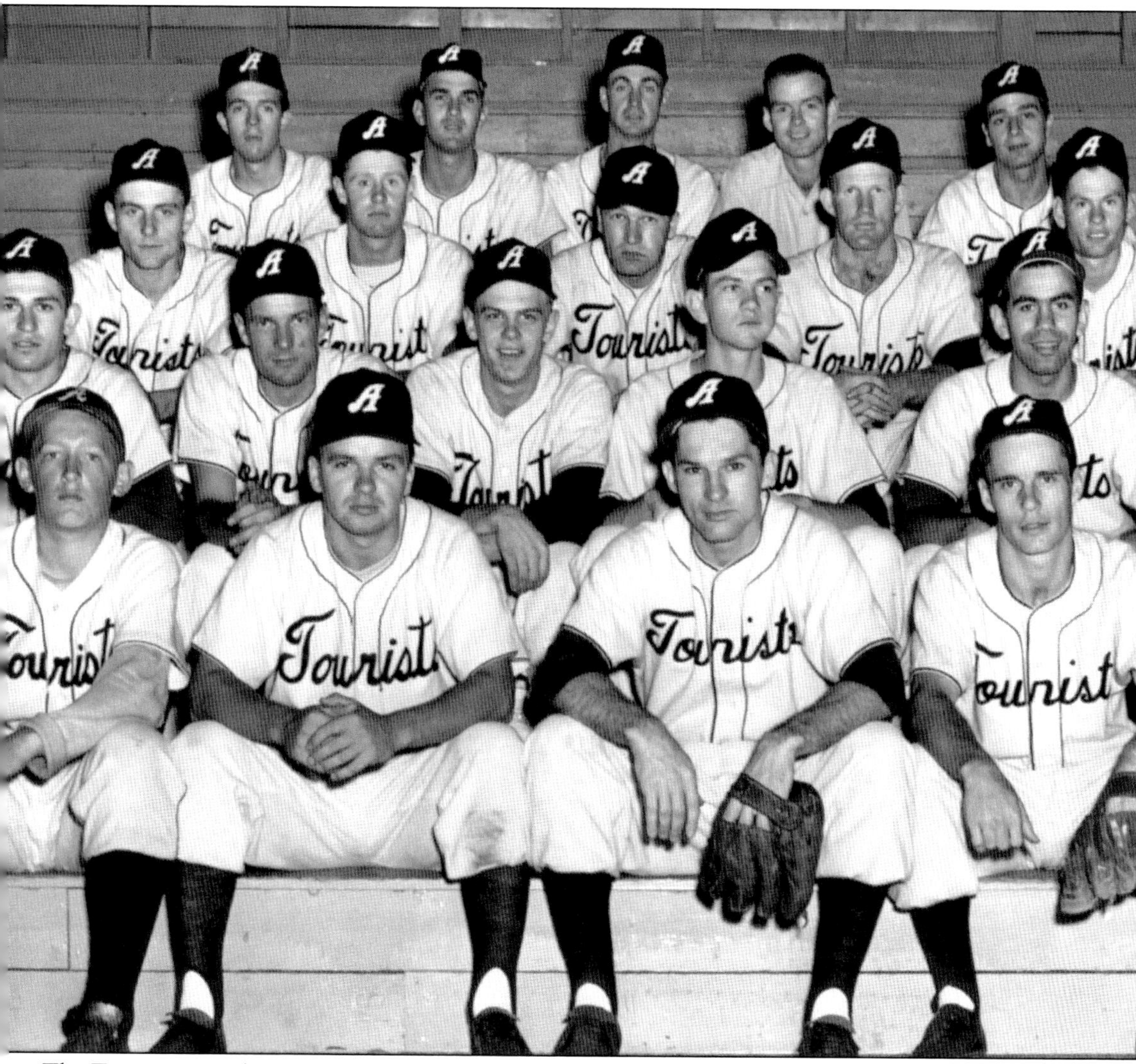

The Tourists posted an 85-55 record in the Class B Tri-State League in 1951 to finish in second place, 15 games behind Charlotte. Asheville proceeded to oust Rock Hill from the playoffs, three games to two, before getting swept in four games by Spartanburg in the championship series. (*Asheville Citizen-Times* photograph.)

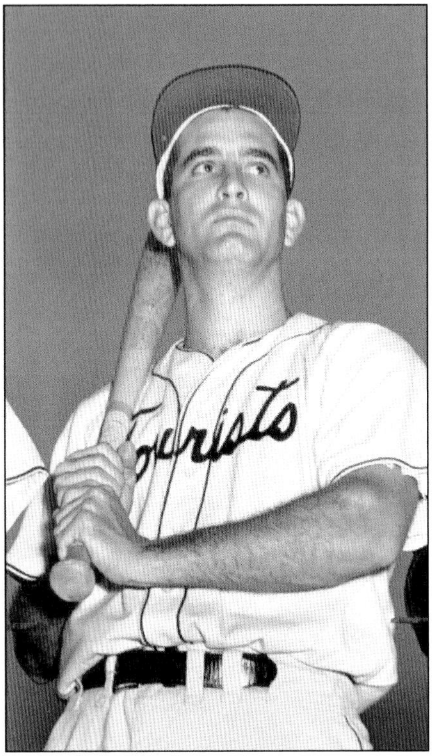

Oscar Sierra led the Tri-State League with 104 RBIs and placed seventh with 11 home runs in 1954. The first baseman/outfielder added a team-high 36 doubles and 97 walks along with a .290 batting average. (*Asheville Citizen-Times* photograph.)

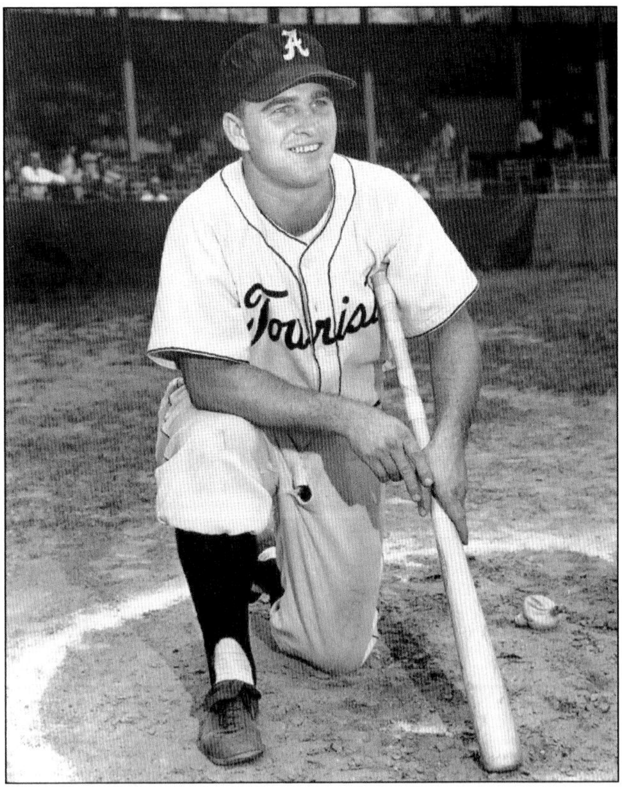

Catcher Ken Worley ranked among the Tri-State League's leading hitters in 1954 with a .324 batting average. In 81 games, Worley contributed 15 doubles, 7 triples, 3 home runs, and 42 RBIs, yet committed 20 errors behind the plate. (*Asheville Citizen-Times* photograph.)

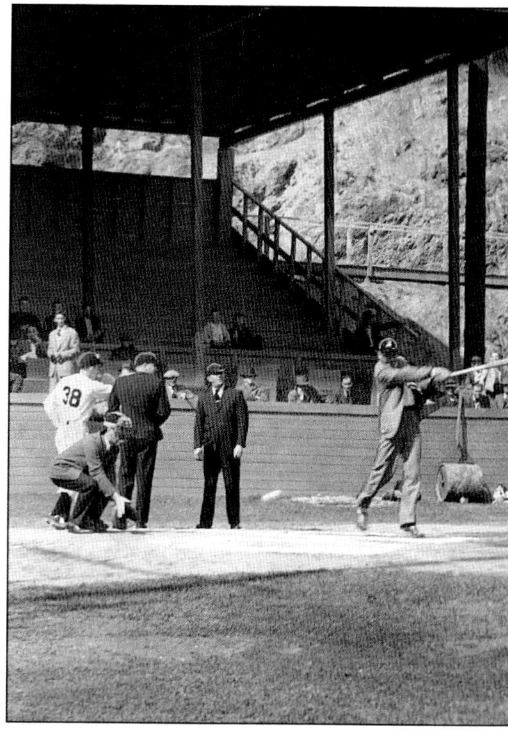

Festivities on Opening Day were commonplace in the early 1950s. In the top picture, a ceremonial first pitch, complete with a batter and catcher, takes place while the managers meet with the game's umpires. The bottom photograph shows a high school marching band playing the national anthem. It also shows the segregated stands; the black fans were relegated to seats down the left field line. (*Asheville Citizen-Times* photograph.)

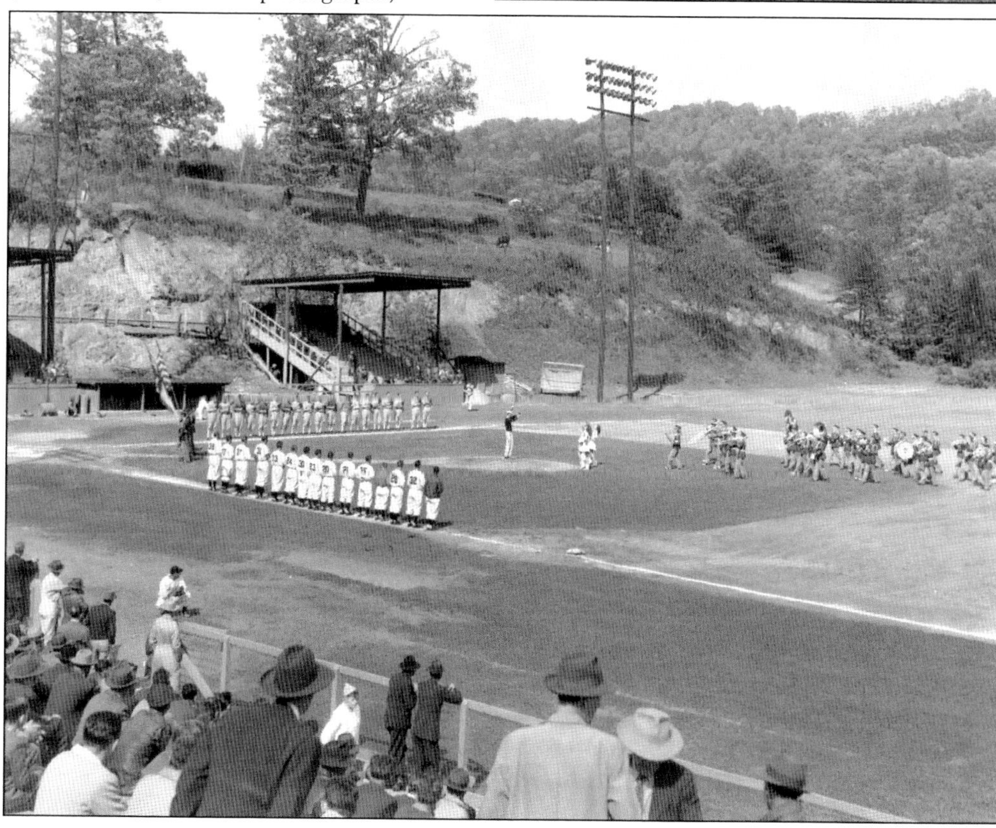

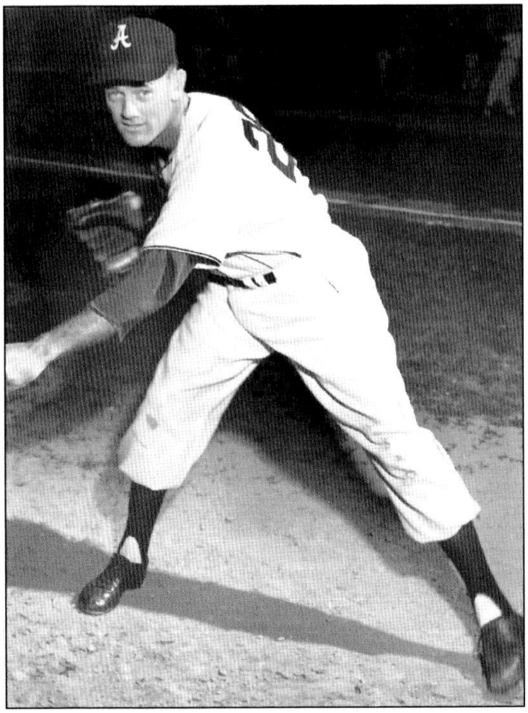

Left-hander Roy Whitaker became a familiar face at McCormick Field during the 1940s and 1950s. He went 12-9 with 11 complete games for the Tourists in 1946 before returning in 1952 and posting a 13-12 mark with 16 complete games. Whitaker's last stand in Asheville came in 1954 when he served as a swingman on the pitching staff and earned a 9-4 record. (*Asheville Citizen-Times* photograph.)

The Tourists celebrate in the McCormick Field clubhouse after winning the Class B Tri-State League regular season title in 1954. Manager Ray Hathaway won his first championship as the Asheville skipper by guiding the team to an 86-54 record. The Tourists defeated Greenville three games to two in the first round of the playoffs before falling three games to one to Knoxville in the finals. (*Asheville Citizen-Times* photograph.)

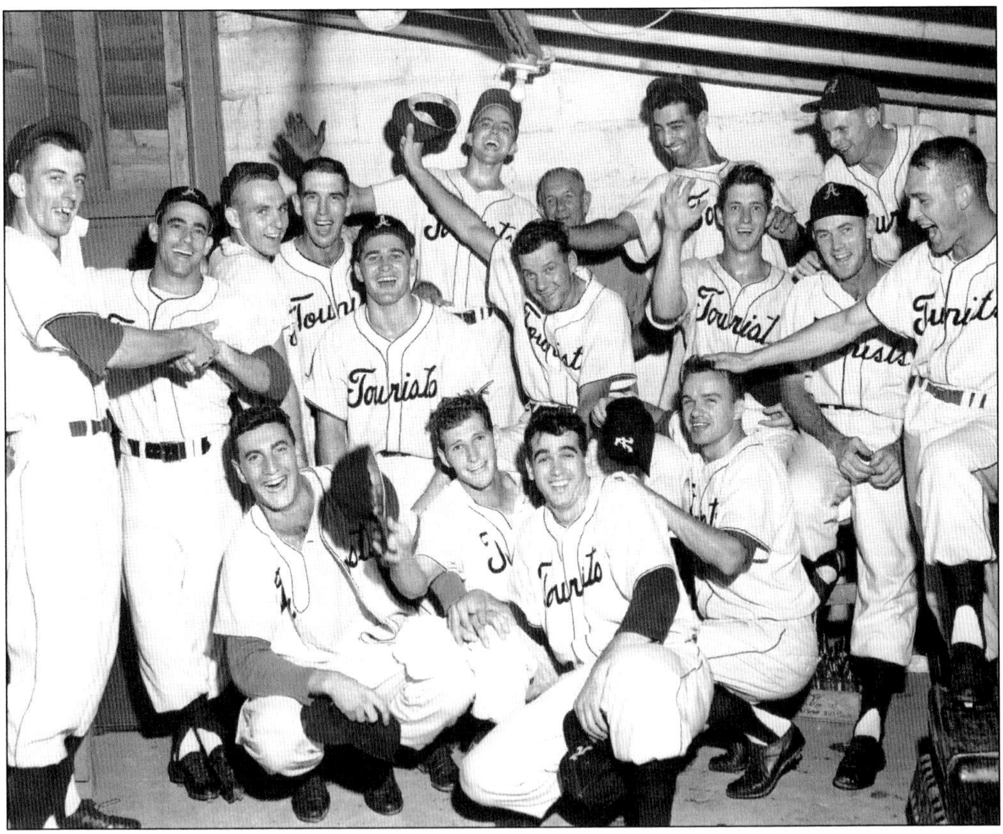

THREE

Baseball's Back

The demise of the Tri-State League after the 1955 season left Asheville without baseball for the next three years. The professional game had struggled for much of the decade, kept afloat primarily by donations from a non-profit corporation called Community Baseball, Inc. Weekly stockcar races kept McCormick Field operational while the city courted another baseball league.

Through the efforts of businessman W. Fleming Talman and Community Baseball, the Tourists returned to McCormick Field in 1959 in the South Atlantic League. Asheville had served as a St. Louis Cardinals' farm club from 1935 to 1942 and a Brooklyn Dodgers' affiliate from 1946 to 1955. After receiving players from the Philadelphia Phillies and several other clubs in 1959, the Tourists were a Phillies' farm club in 1960 before serving as the Class AA affiliate of the Pittsburgh Pirates from 1961 to 1966. The Pirates sent numerous future major leaguers to Asheville, as did the Cincinnati Reds from 1968 to 1970, the Chicago White Sox in 1971, and the Baltimore Orioles from 1972 to 1975.

As a Class AA team, just two short steps from the game's top level, Asheville proved to be a gateway to the major leagues. That scenario changed after the 1975 season when the team's management became frustrated with Baltimore over the lack of talent provided during the previous two years. That led the Tourists to drop down to Class A ball, beginning with a six-year run with the Texas Rangers in the Western Carolinas League (later renamed the present-day South Atlantic League) in 1976.

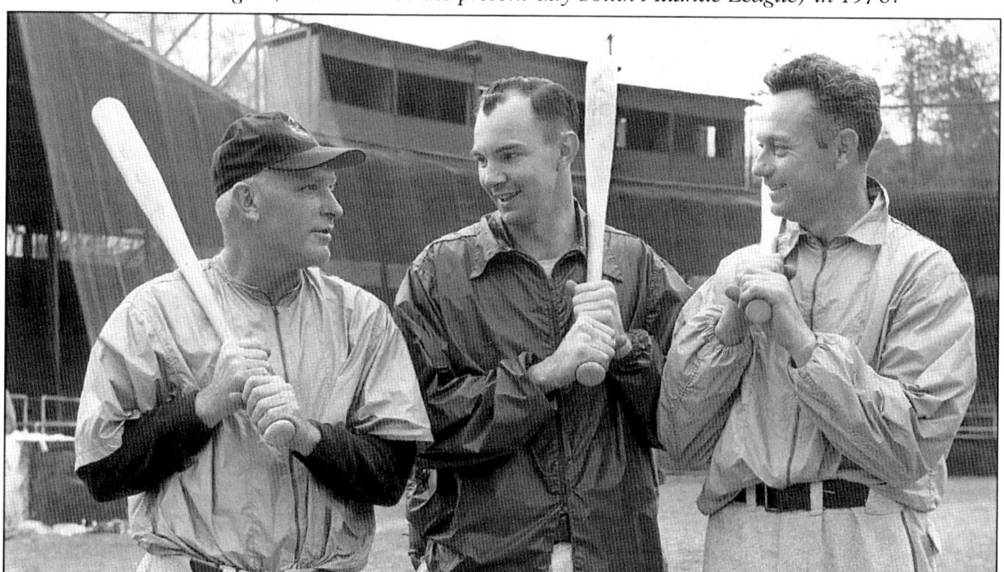

Without a major league affiliation, the Tourists and manager Clyde McCullough (far left) had to scour the waiver wire and beg, borrow, and plead with other teams in order to build a roster. The first two players signed were veterans Danny Keith (middle) and Al Gettel. Gettel was 41 years old and pitched seven seasons in the major leagues between 1945 and 1955. Neither player spent much time with Asheville; Gettel went 1-1 in five games while Keith went hitless in three at-bats. (Bob Terrell collection.)

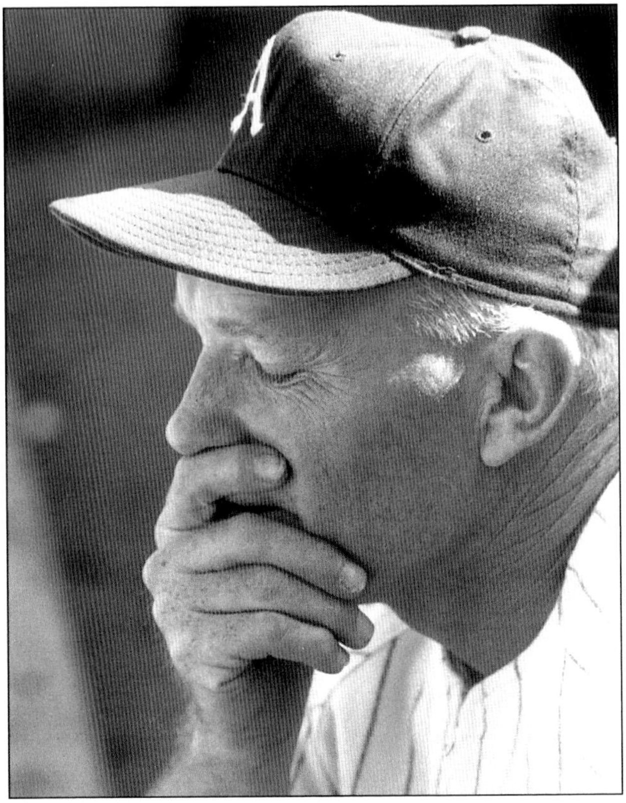

Clyde McCullough experienced occasional frustration while managing a Tourist team with no major league affiliation to a 70-70 record during the 1959 season. A former catcher with the Chicago Cubs, McCullough received players on loan from several organizations and molded the motley crew into a competitive club with the help of the skipper's demanding style. (Bob Terrell collection.)

The 1959 Tourists finished the season with a respectable 70-70 record, earning fifth place in the eight-team South Atlantic League. Asheville was only eight games behind the first-place Knoxville Smokies. Art Perkins, the team's general manager in 1959 and 1960, is pictured to the far right on the back row. (Bob Terrell collection.)

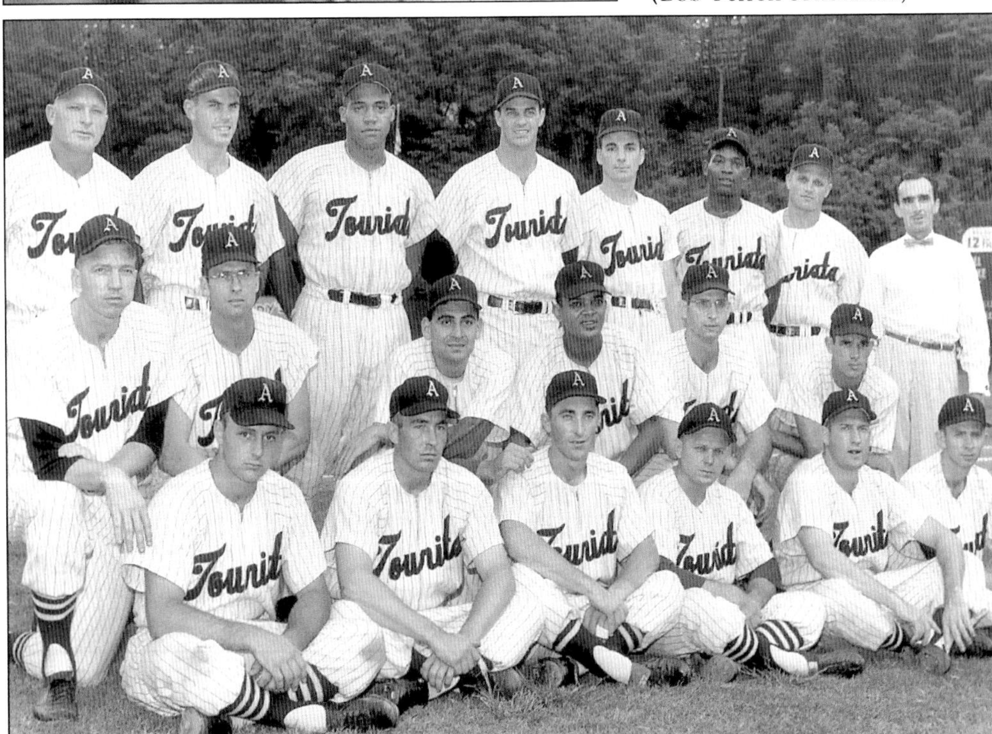

Manager Clyde McCullough (center) offers some encouragement to Chico Fernandez and Jack Whited during the early days of the 1959 season. Both players are wearing the Tourists' road uniforms from the campaign. As was the case with many Tourists during the 1959 slate, neither Fernandez nor Whited remained with the team for an extended period. Fernandez was traded to Knoxville during the season after playing in 35 contests, while Whited appeared in only 17 games with Asheville. (Bob Terrell collection.)

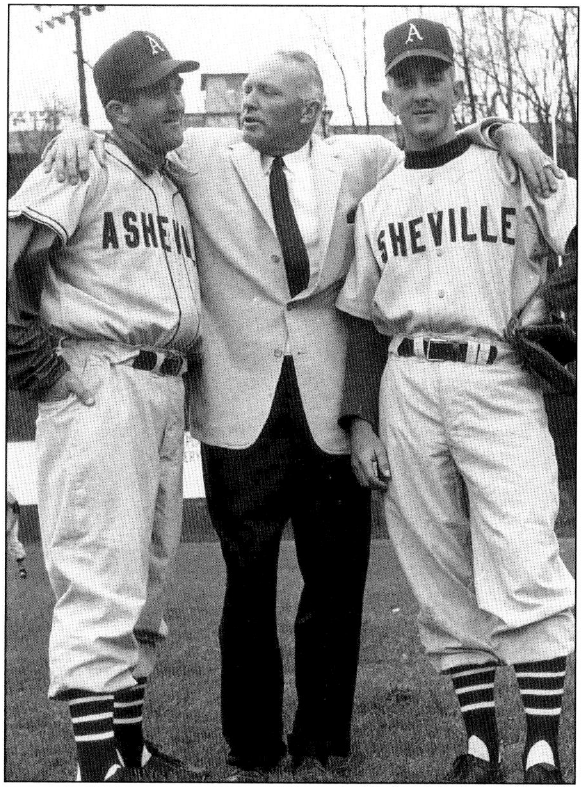

Baseball fever swept through Asheville with the return of the Tourists in 1959. On June 23, 1959, Enka Night packed a paying crowd of 2,939 fans into McCormick Field. The Tourists attracted 113,001 fans during the 1959 campaign. (*Asheville Citizen-Times* photograph.)

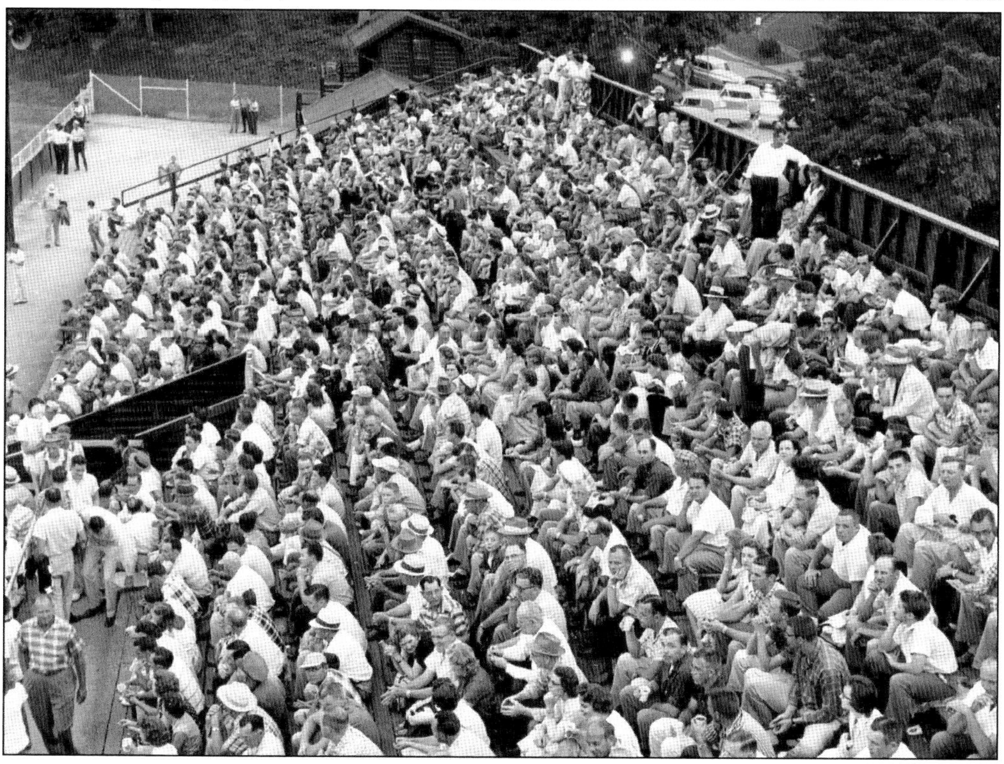

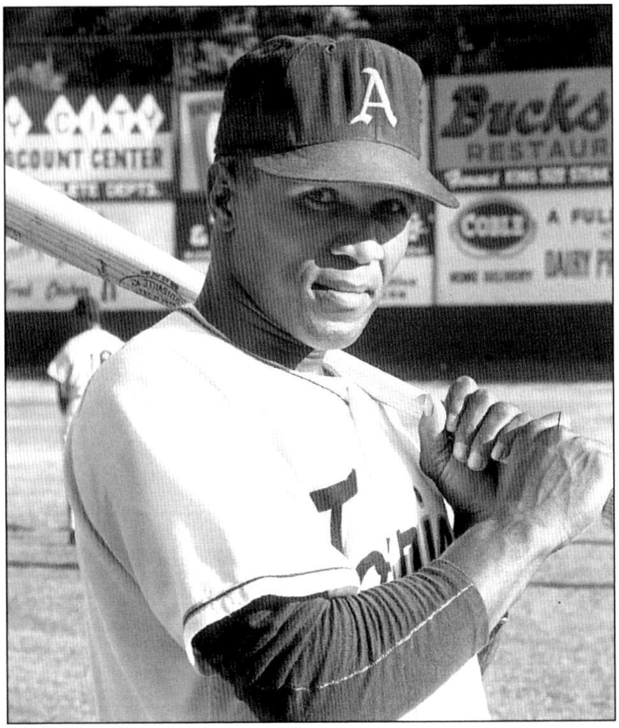

Nathan Dickerson led the South Atlantic League with a .362 batting average in 1959. The left-handed-hitting first baseman did not produce much power, swatting only eight home runs with 50 RBIs, but found his niche by driving balls between first and second base. The result was 112 singles among his 141 hits, tying for third in the league. (Bob Terrell collection.)

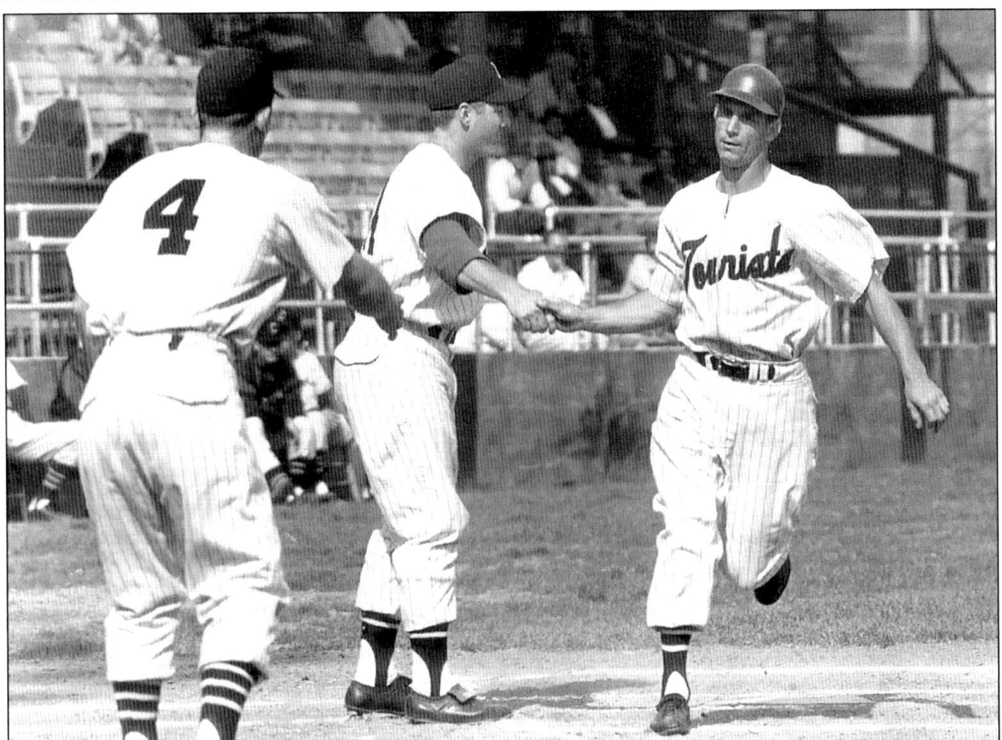

Pitcher Billy Joe Dashner shakes hands with Paul Leslie after the outfielder hit one of his 11 home runs during the 1959 season at McCormick Field. Leslie batted .264 with 28 RBIs in 76 games with the Tourists. (Bob Terrell collection.)

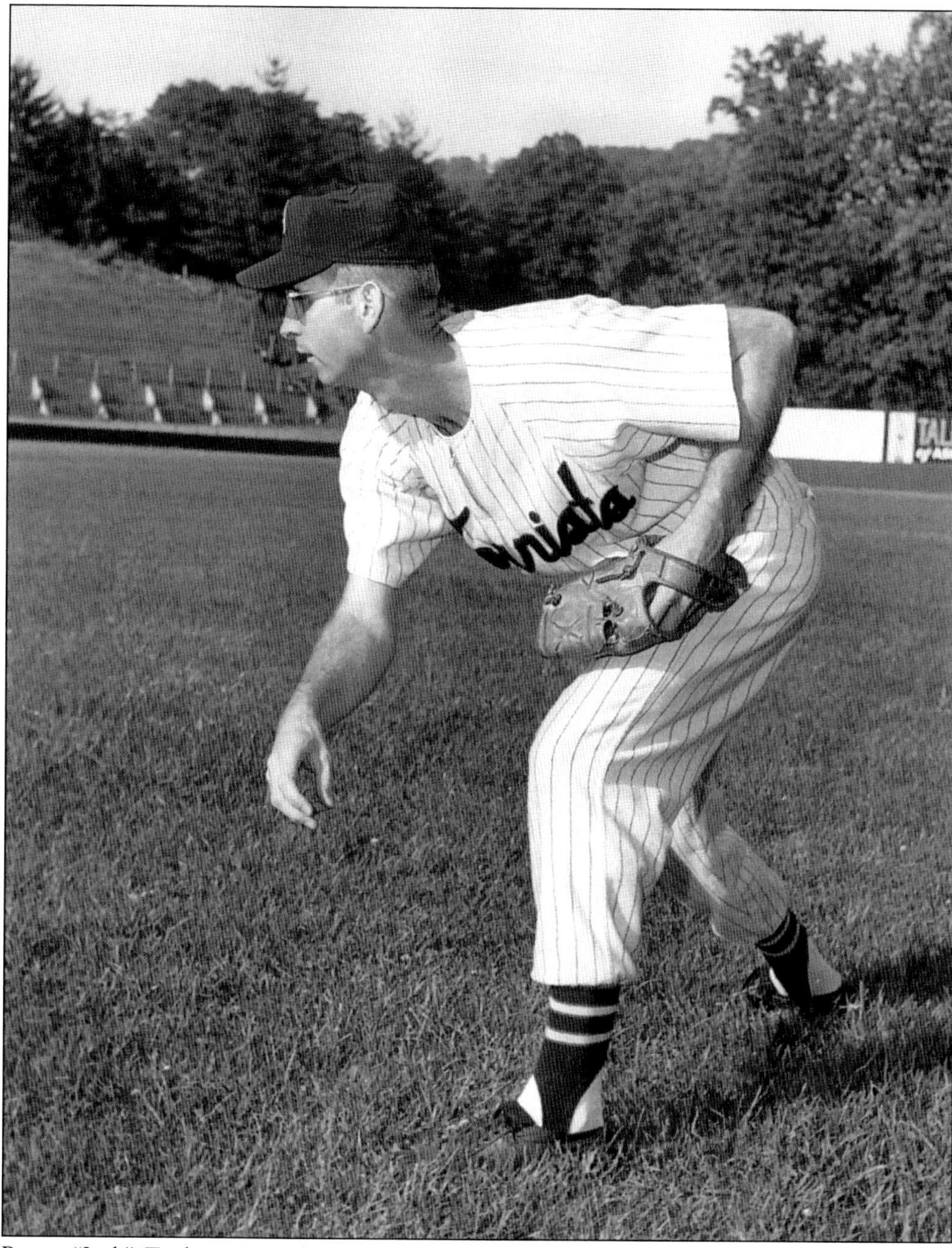

Byron "Jack" Taylor emerged as the Tourists' ace during the 1959 and 1960 seasons. The right-hander led the South Atlantic League with 18 victories during his first campaign in Asheville. In addition to his 28 starts, Taylor relieved 16 other contests and concluded the slate with a 3.46 ERA and 220 innings pitched. In 1960, Taylor went 11-14 with a 3.66 ERA. (Bob Terrell collection.)

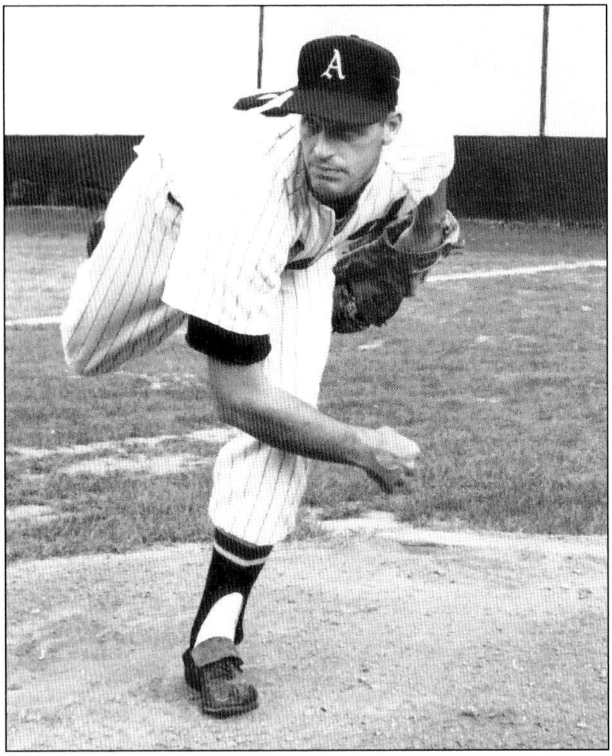

Bob Greenwood combined with Byron Taylor to give the Tourists a solid one-two punch at the top of the rotation in 1959. The right-hander tossed 12 complete games on his way to an 11-13 record with a 3.80 ERA in 28 games, including 25 starts. (Bob Terrell collection.)

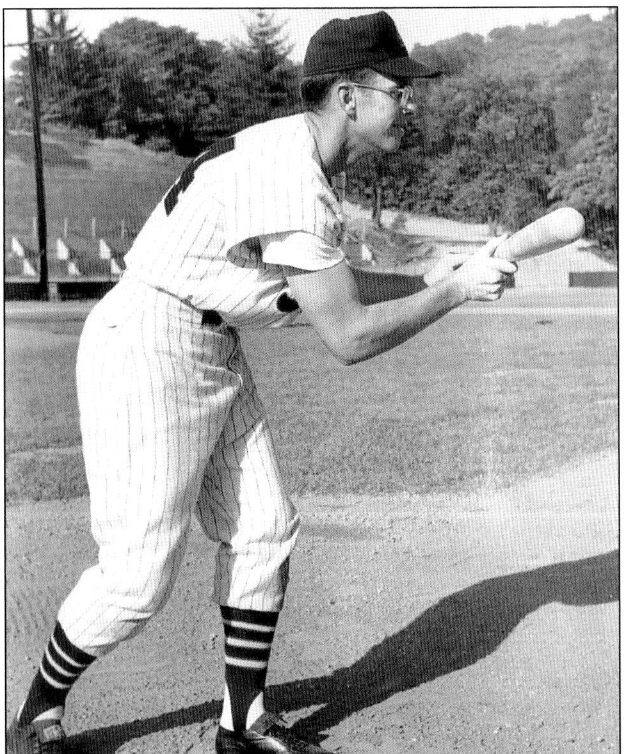

Ben Tompkins served as a key component to the Tourists' lineup during the 1959 campaign. Tompkins led the South Atlantic League with 30 doubles and ranked eighth with a .282 batting average. The right-handed hitter added 10 home runs and 59 RBIs to his record. (Bob Terrell collection.)

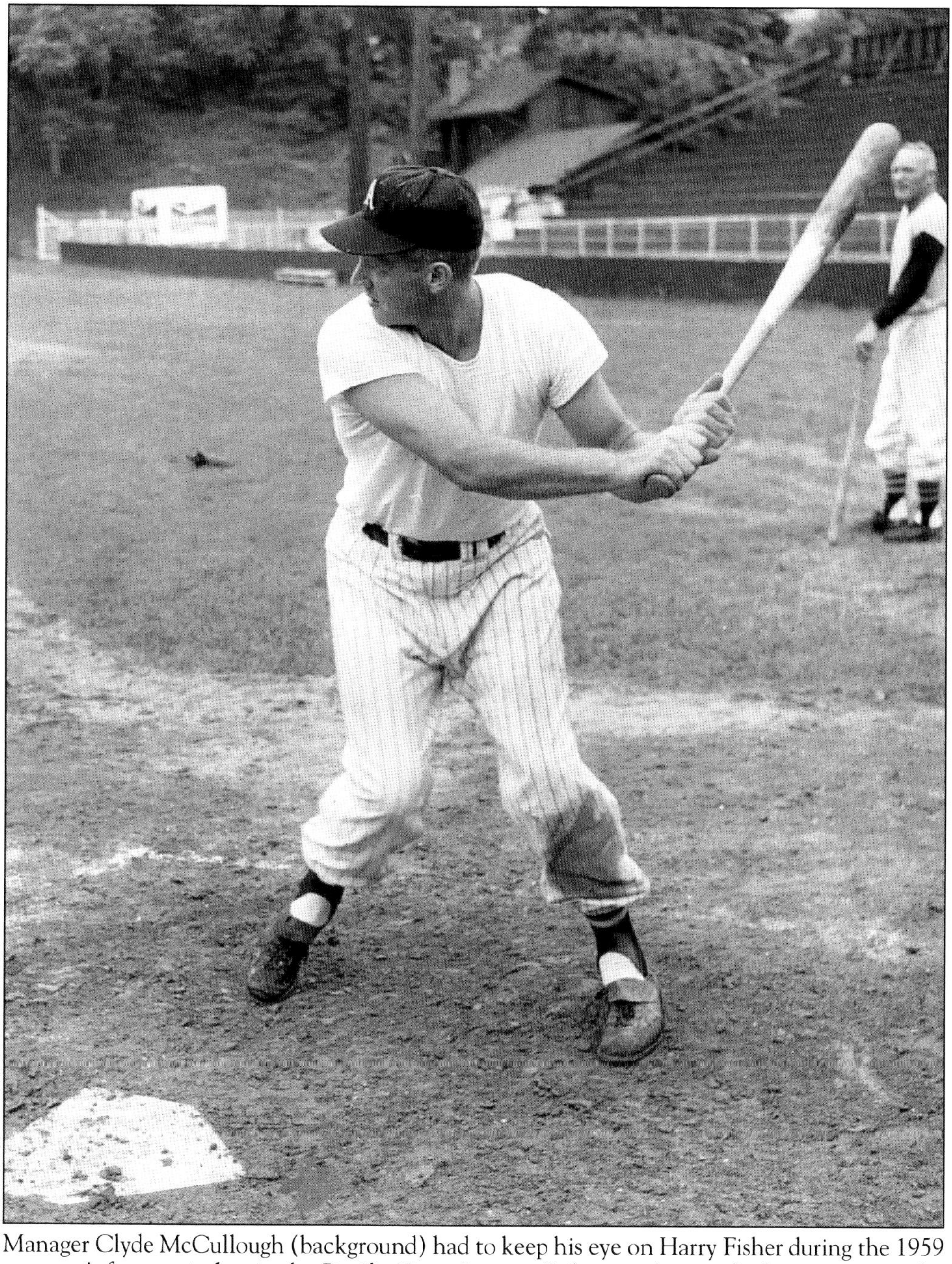

Manager Clyde McCullough (background) had to keep his eye on Harry Fisher during the 1959 season. A former pitcher in the Pacific Coast League, Fisher was known for his extracurricular activities. He played outfield for the Tourists, yet was released following a Sunday afternoon game at McCormick Field during which he made five errors. The Tourists re-signed him two days later as a pitcher due to a sudden shortage of moundsmen. For the season, Fisher batted .261 with 15 home runs and 57 RBIs and went 4-4 with a 2.71 ERA in 21 games on the hill. (Bob Terrell collection.)

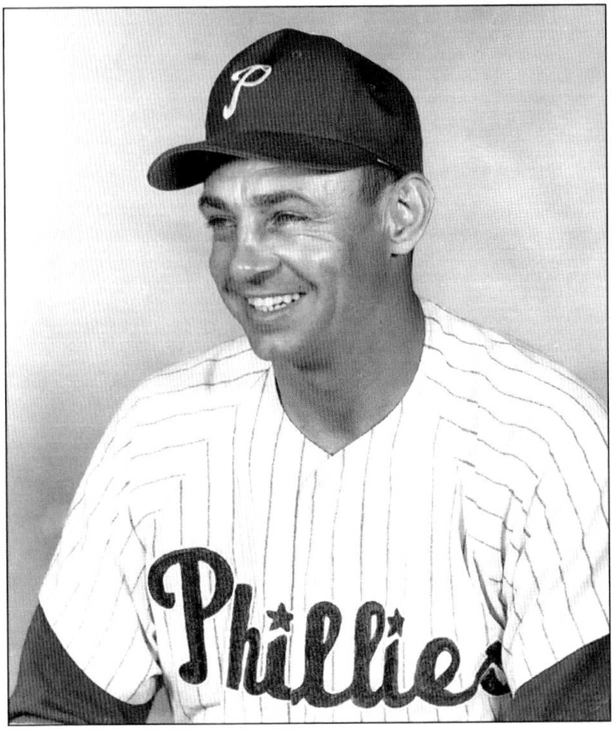

Chuck Kress, a former first baseman who played four years in the major leagues with four teams from 1947 to 1954, was named the Asheville manager for the 1960 season after the Tourists entered into a working agreement with the Philadelphia Phillies. (Bob Terrell collection.)

Members of the 1960 Tourists stepped off the Greyhound bus and got their first look at McCormick Field. From left to right are pitcher Ed Radzevich, pitcher Lou DeBole, pitcher Ed Hughes, outfielder Paul Price, shortstop Jim Williamson, and pitcher Mike Urrizola. (Bob Terrell collection.)

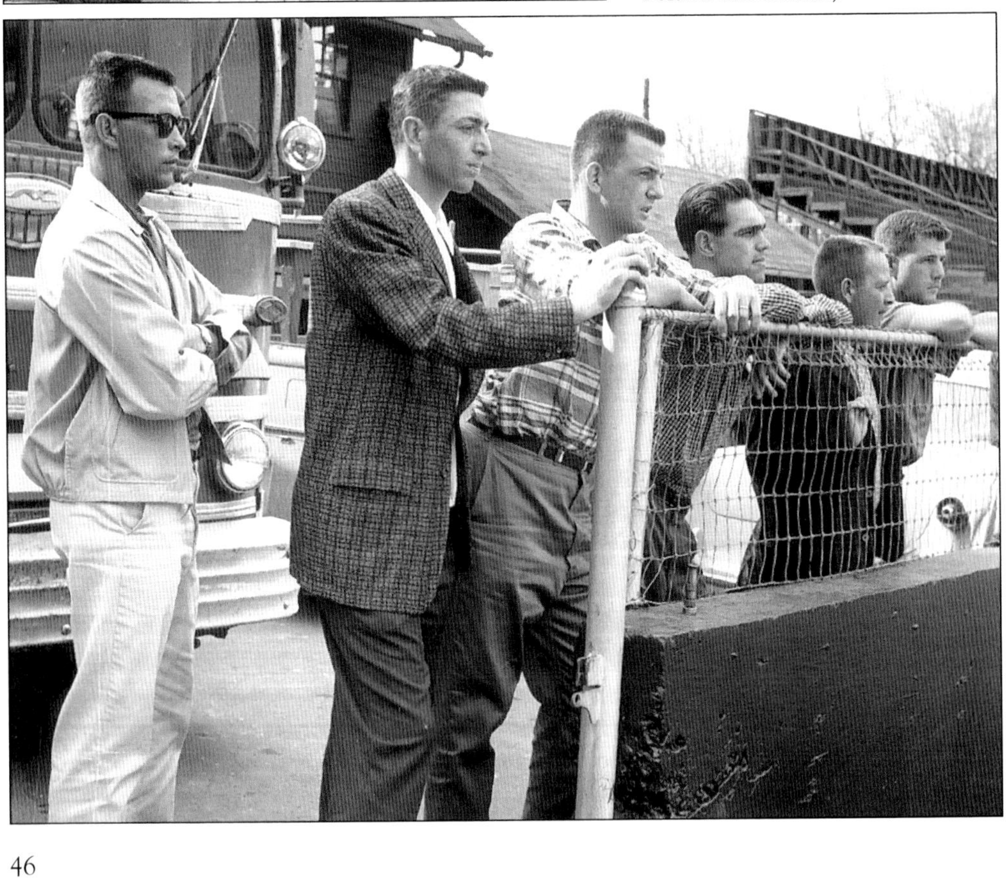

First baseman Herbert "Glen" Merklen arrived in Asheville with the reputation as a smooth first baseman with a big stick from the left side. While the would-be slugger liked what he saw during his first glance at the right field wall, Merklen wound up batting .278 with eight home runs in 50 games with the Tourists in 1960. (Bob Terrell collection.)

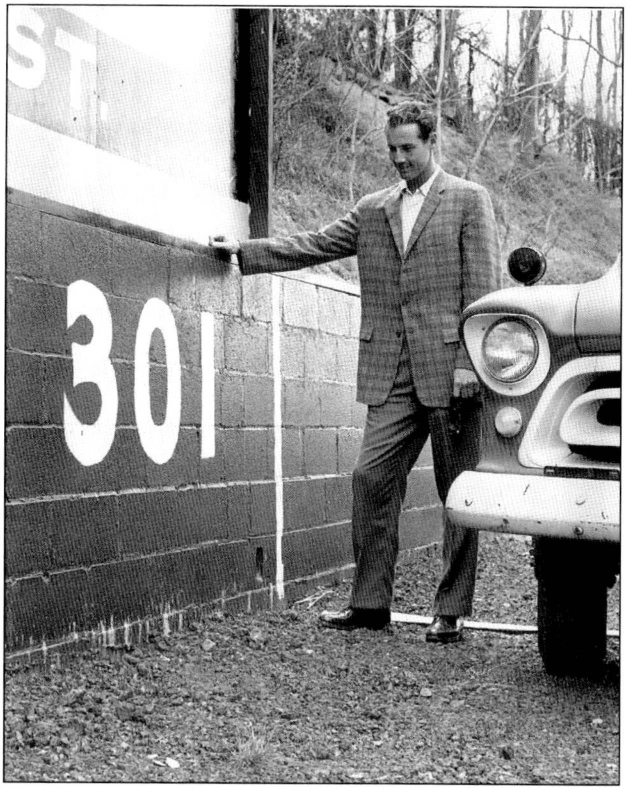

The Tourists finished in sixth place in the eight-team South Atlantic League during the 1960 season, posting a 62-77 record, 21 games behind the first-place Columbia Reds. No member of the team was named to the league's year-end All-Star squad. (Bob Terrell collection.)

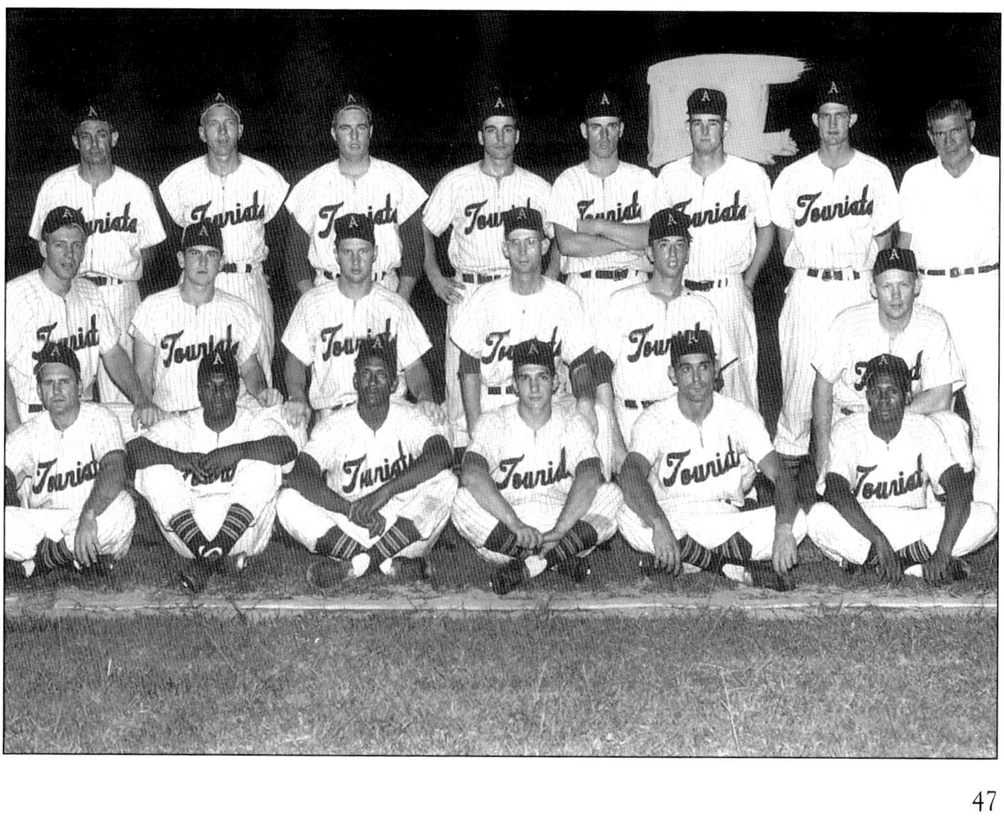

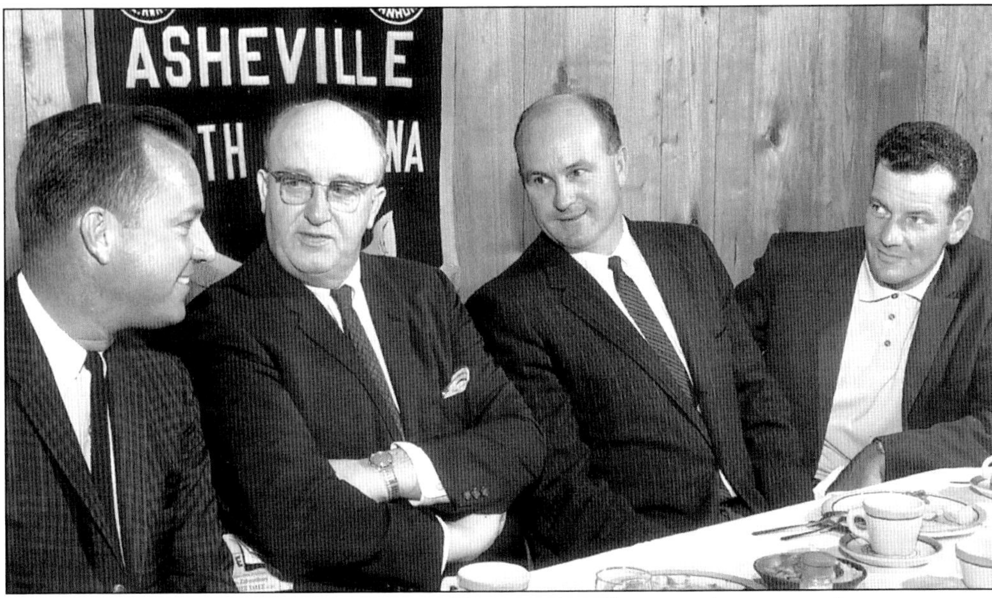

After a one-year stint as a Philadelphia affiliate, Asheville entered into a working agreement with the Pittsburgh Pirates prior to the 1961 campaign. The cogs of the Tourists' engine met with numerous civic organizations leading up to the season. From left to right are Pittsburgh general manager Joe L. Brown; W. Fleming Talman, president of Asheville's Community Baseball; Tourists general manager Jim Mills; and Asheville manager Ray Hathaway. (Bob Terrell collection.)

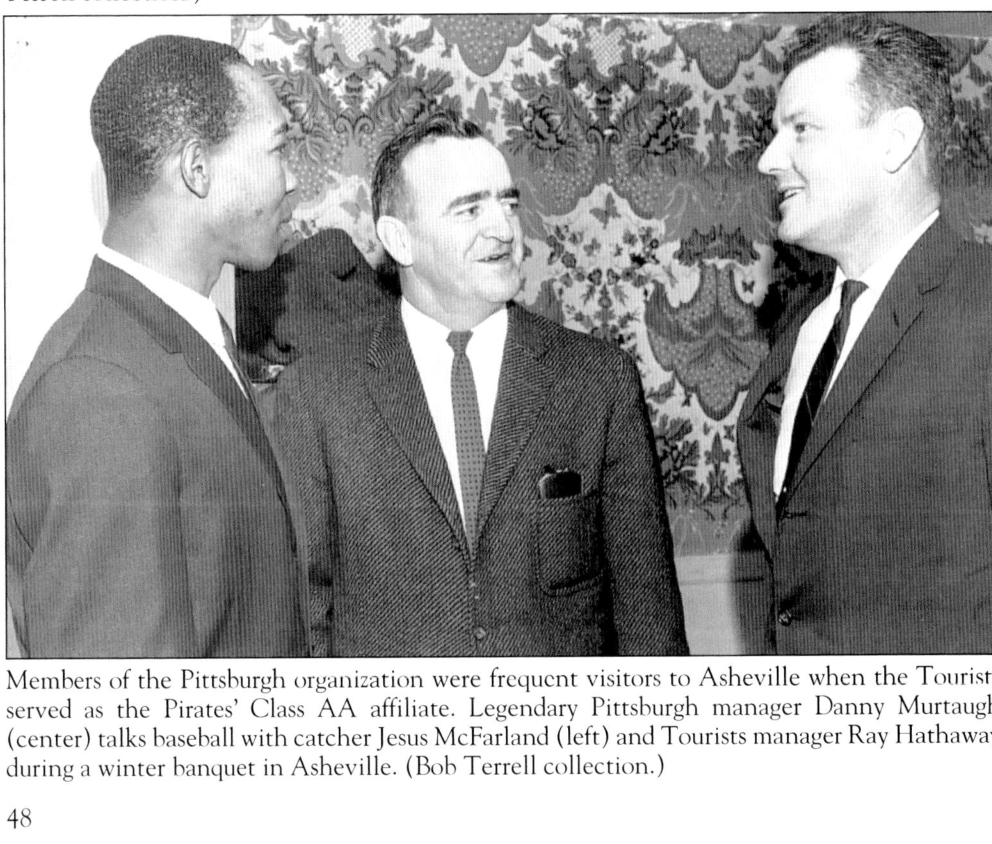

Members of the Pittsburgh organization were frequent visitors to Asheville when the Tourists served as the Pirates' Class AA affiliate. Legendary Pittsburgh manager Danny Murtaugh (center) talks baseball with catcher Jesus McFarland (left) and Tourists manager Ray Hathaway during a winter banquet in Asheville. (Bob Terrell collection.)

Bob Priddy, a husky right-hander, started the home opener for the Tourists in 1961 before earning his first win at Knoxville on April 16. Priddy, who pitched nine years in the major leagues, beginning in 1962 with the Pirates, went 2-1 in five games with Asheville prior to joining Burlington in the Three-I League in May. (Bob Terrell collection.)

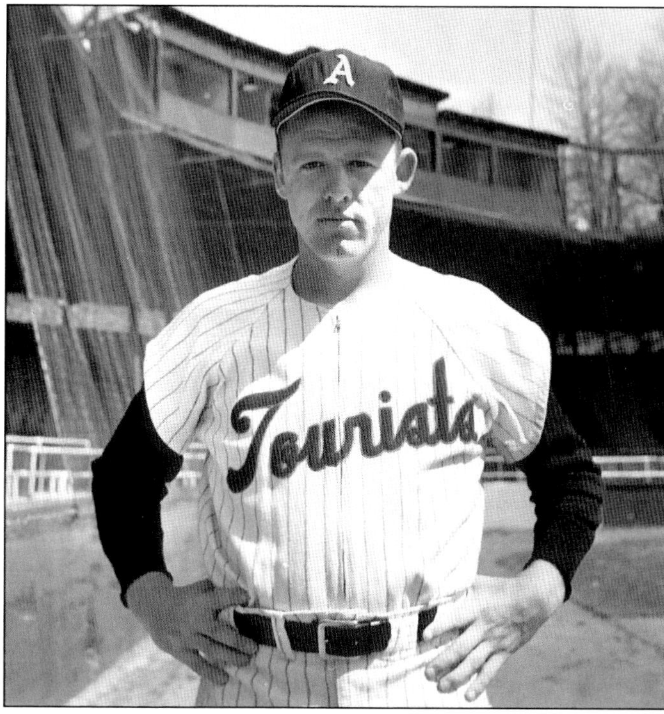

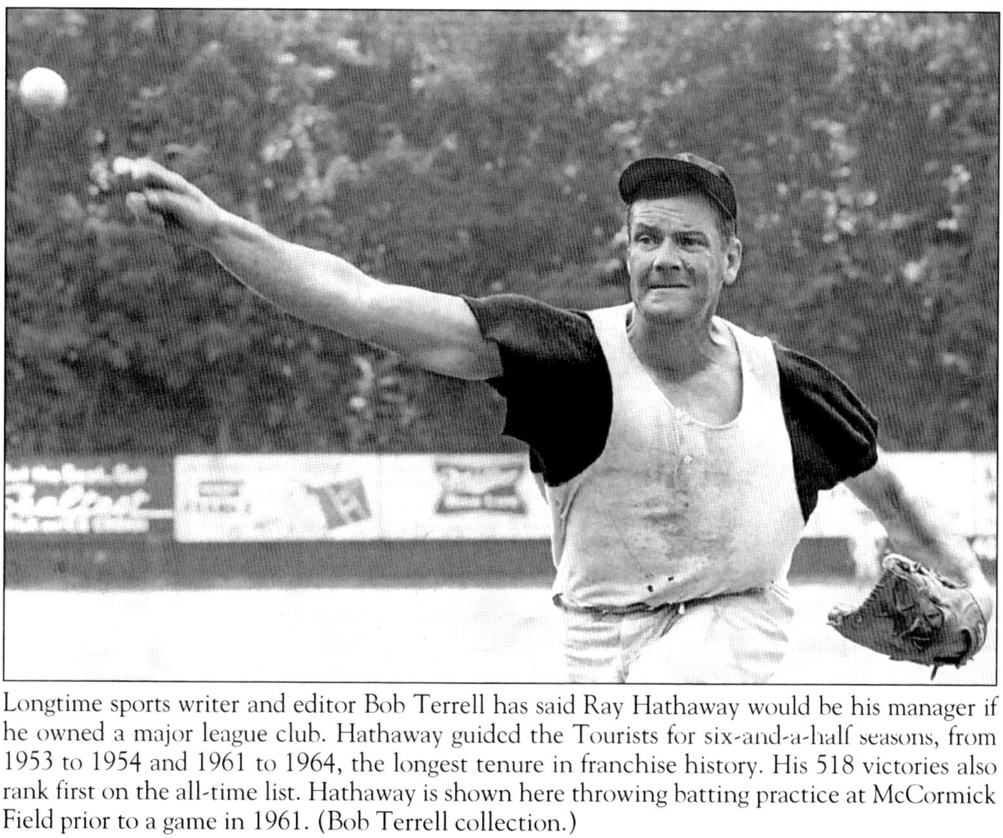

Longtime sports writer and editor Bob Terrell has said Ray Hathaway would be his manager if he owned a major league club. Hathaway guided the Tourists for six-and-a-half seasons, from 1953 to 1954 and 1961 to 1964, the longest tenure in franchise history. His 518 victories also rank first on the all-time list. Hathaway is shown here throwing batting practice at McCormick Field prior to a game in 1961. (Bob Terrell collection.)

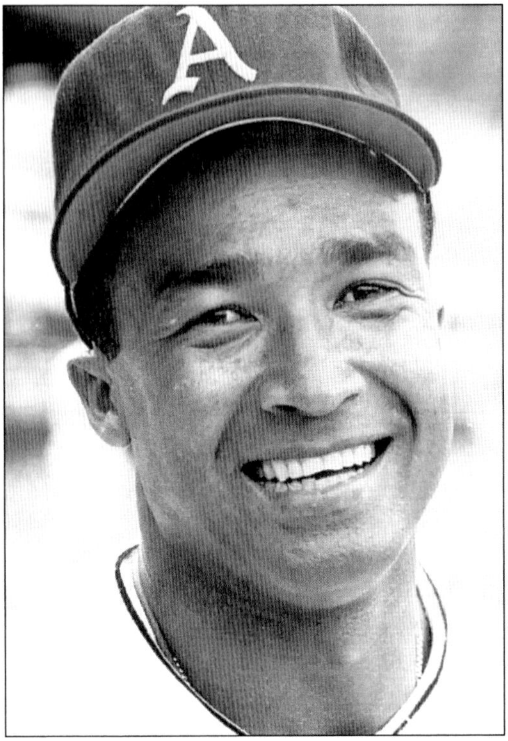

Duncan Campbell was a chunky, hustling Nicaraguan with a canon for an arm at third base. Deemed the best third baseman in Asheville history by most franchise followers, Campbell was promoted to the Class AAA Columbus Jets in early August after hitting at a .292 clip with the Tourists in 1961. (Bob Terrell collection.)

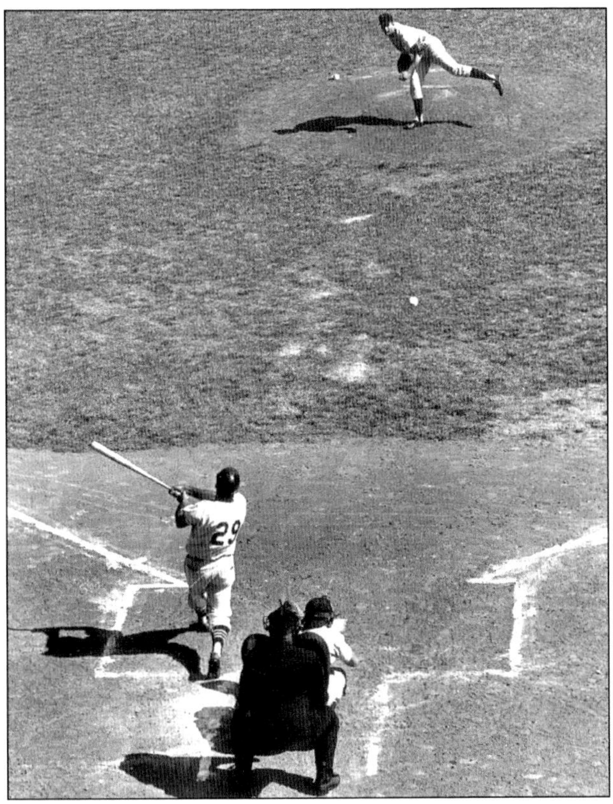

Duncan Campbell hit two home runs and drove in six runs in a 15-11 win at Knoxville on April 16, 1961. For the season, the third baseman swatted 16 home runs with 75 RBIs in 106 games. Campbell returned to the Tourists in 1962 and hit 27 homers and batted .311 in 140 contests. (Bob Terrell collection.)

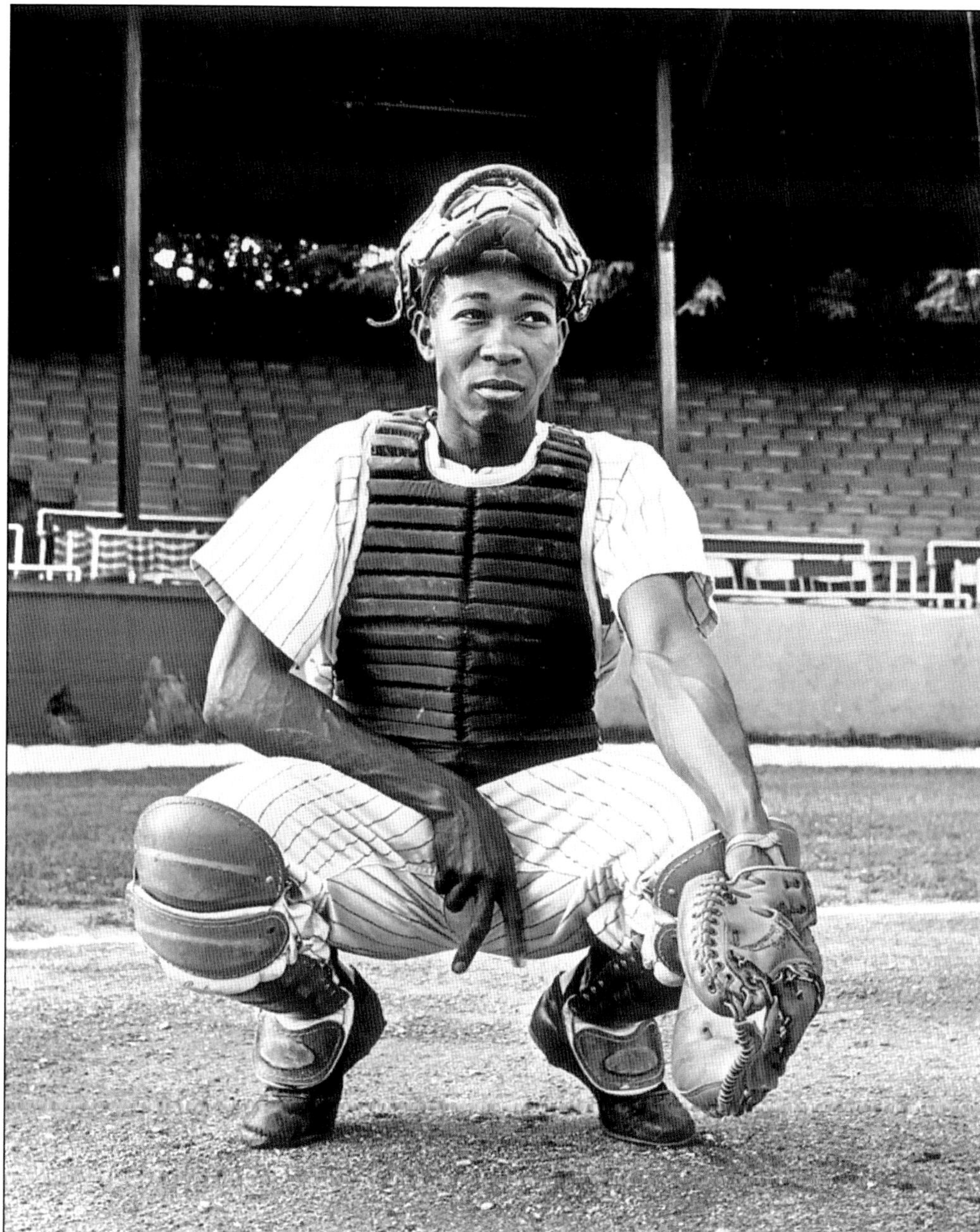

Jesus McFarland's biggest game as a Tourist came on May 4, 1961, when he crushed three home runs, beginning with a 450-foot shot over the left field fence in the first inning during a 12-10 win over Columbia. McFarland was considered the best major league prospect among the Sally League's position players during the 1961 season, and Pittsburgh skipper Danny Murtaugh said McFarland "was the best catcher I ever saw . . . from the neck down." McFarland was rewarded for his performance with a promotion to Pittsburgh in early September, yet returned to Asheville for the 1962 and 1965 seasons, the latter in which he led the Southern League with 22 home runs. (Bob Terrell collection.)

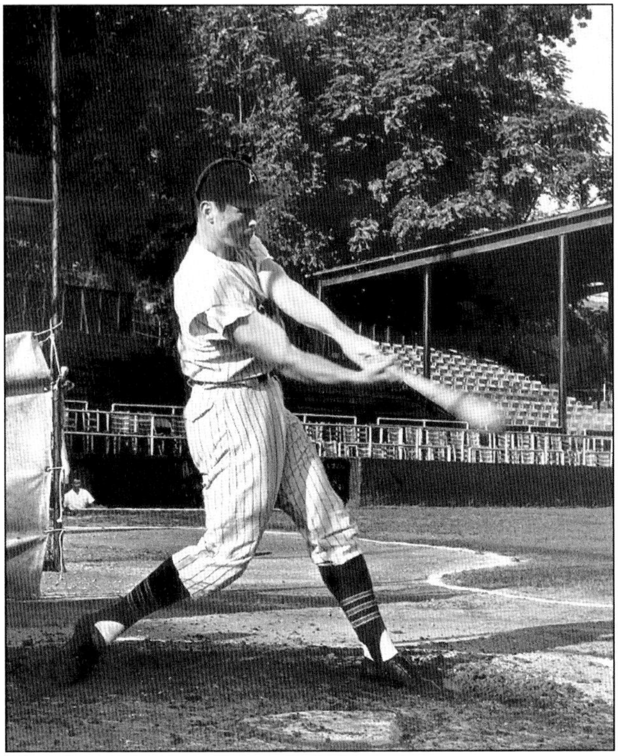

Clutch-hitting Gary Rushing, described in the *Asheville Times* as "an affable, freckled-faced young giant," was rated the best power hitter in the Sally League in 1961 when he led the league with 25 home runs and 99 RBIs and ranked second with a .311 batting average. Rushing moved from first base to the outfield at midseason to make room for veteran Charlie Leonard. (Bob Terrell collection.)

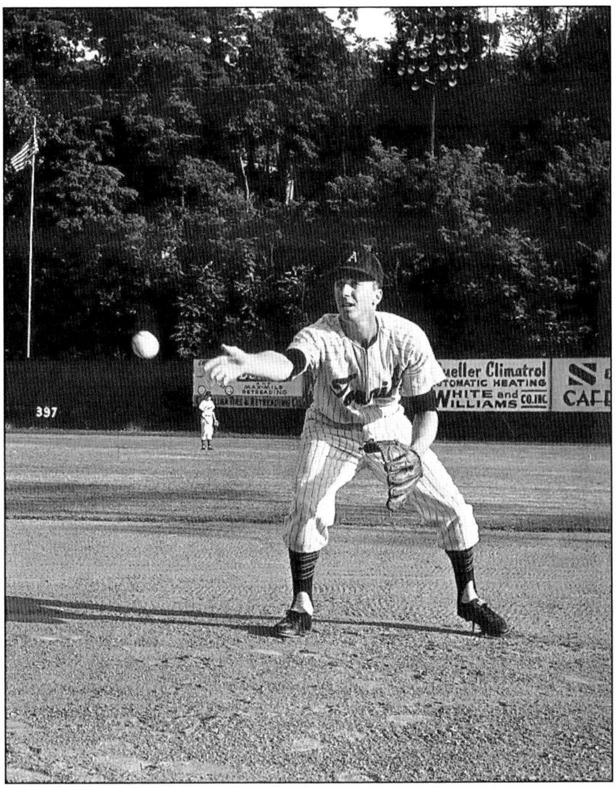

Gene Alley was the best defensive second baseman in Tourists history. The leader of the infield who came through with numerous key hits, Alley emerged as one of the catalysts for the 1961 Tourists. He hit a single and two home runs while driving in four runs in a 7-3 win over Charleston on June 9; he had two of Asheville's three hits with three RBIs in the Sally League All-Star game at McCormick Field. In 135 games in 1961, Alley clubbed 23 doubles and 14 home runs while driving in 61 runs. He returned to Asheville for half of the 1962 campaign and had 18 doubles, 10 home runs, and 35 RBIs before reaching Pittsburgh as a rookie in 1963. (Bob Terrell collection.)

Asheville general manager Jim Mills picks up Jim Hardison at the Asheville Regional Airport after the pitcher was sent from Macon in the Southern Association during the first two days of June in 1961. Hardison marveled at the Tourists' lineup upon his arrival at McCormick Field and said, "I might not lose a game here." He was nearly correct. (Bob Terrell collection.)

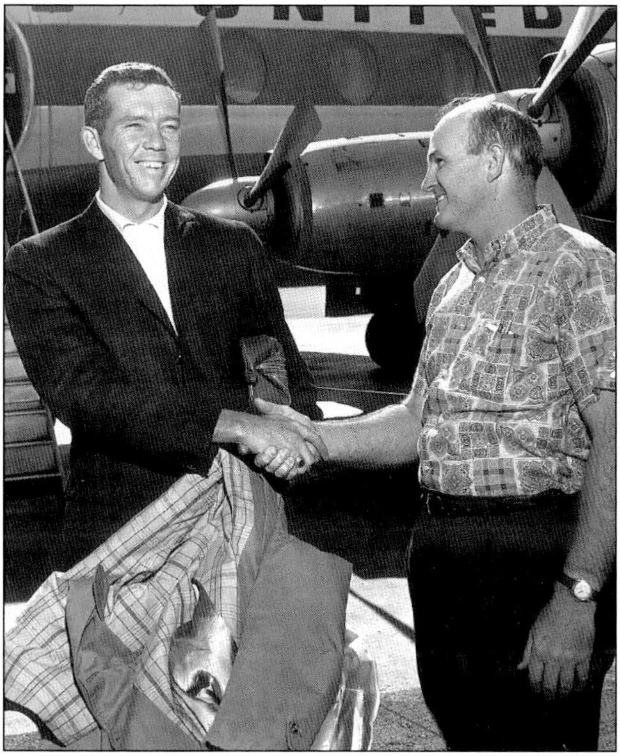

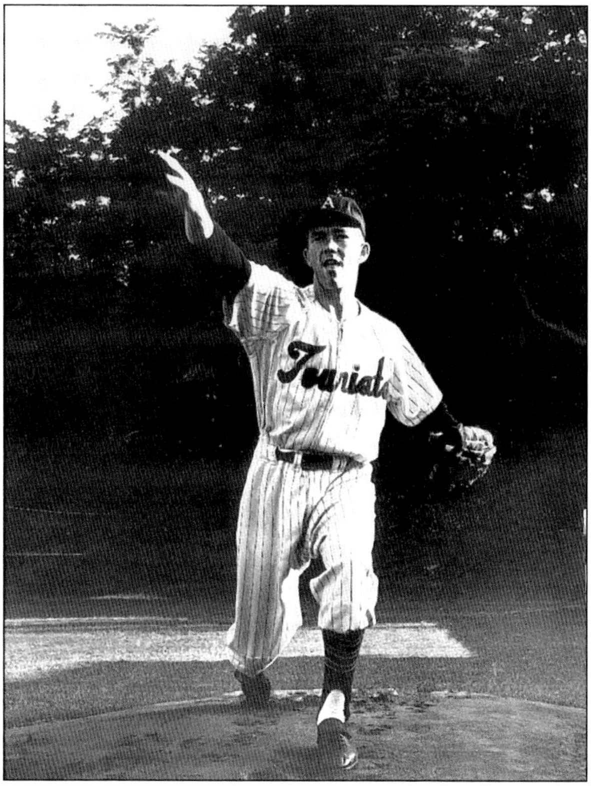

A crafty right-hander from North Carolina State University with a wicked curveball and an effective changeup, pitcher Jim Hardison emerged as one of the Tourists' aces during the 1961 season's last three months, posting a 16-2 record and 2.75 ERA with 13 complete games in 18 starts. He returned to Asheville a year later and found the going a little rougher, registering a 7-12 mark in 27 contests. (Bob Terrell collection.)

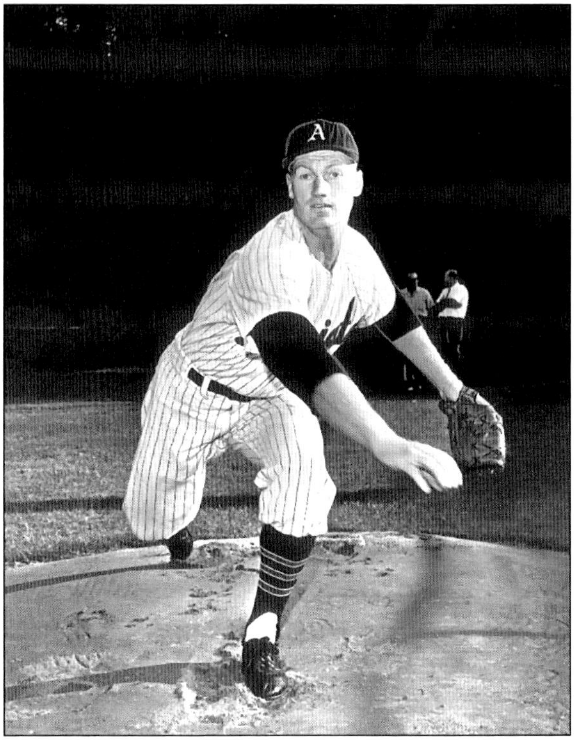

One of the first big "bonus babies" to report to Asheville, Larry Foss was a hard-throwing right-hander who had pitched well for manager Ray Hathaway at Savannah in 1960. He had one of the best fastballs in the Sally League in 1961, enabling him to post a 10-3 record, including six straight victories and two shutouts during the season's second half. He led the Asheville staff with a 2.34 ERA, earning a promotion to Pittsburgh in early September. (Bob Terrell collection.)

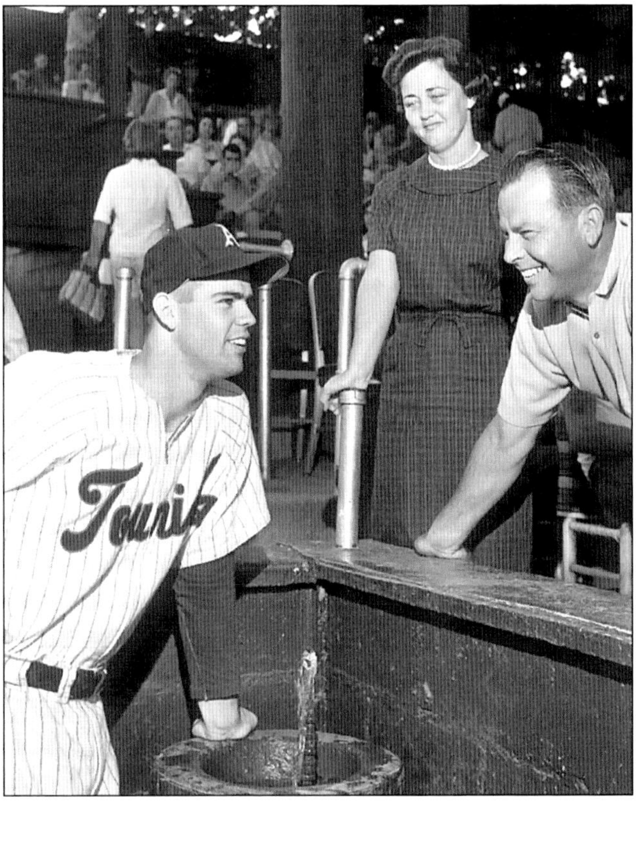

Bob Bailey's reputation preceded his arrival in Asheville in mid-June. A shortstop from Long Beach, California, Bailey was known as baseball's biggest bonus player after receiving $175,000 from the Pittsburgh Pirates in 1961. He proved his worth in his first pro game in front of his parents on July 4, when he singled with the bases loaded to break a 2-2 tie at McCormick Field and lead the Tourists to an 8-2 win over Knoxville. Bailey is pictured leaning on the fountain that was tapped into a natural spring that ran under the ballpark—it produced some of the purest drinking water ever found in Asheville. (Bob Terrell collection.)

First baseman Charlie Leonard arrived in Asheville on June 25 after getting caught up in a numbers game at Class AAA Columbus. While Leonard batted just .240 in 67 games with the Tourists in 1961, he came through with numerous big hits, including 13 home runs and 38 RBIs to help lead the team to the South Atlantic League crown. (Bob Terrell collection.)

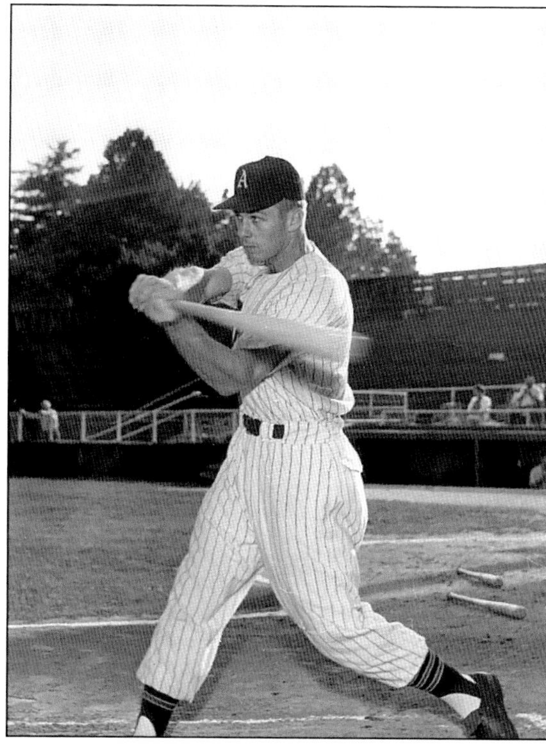

Jim Mills served as the Tourists' general manager from 1961 until 1968, a tenure that included the franchise's entire six-year relationship with the Pirates and one season with the Astros. A three-sport athlete at North Carolina State University and a former minor league player and manager prior to his tour of duty in Asheville, Mills's Tourists teams won three pennants. A native of Apex, Mills spent more than 50 years in professional baseball and was elected to the North Carolina Hall of Fame in 1997. (Bob Terrell collection.)

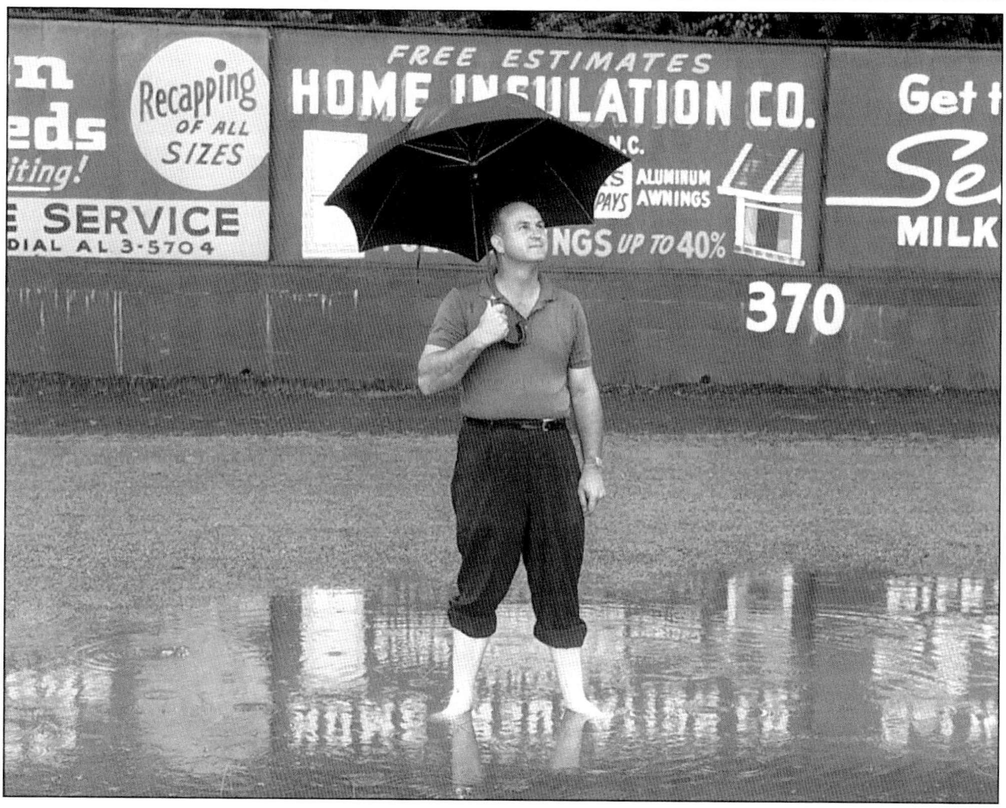

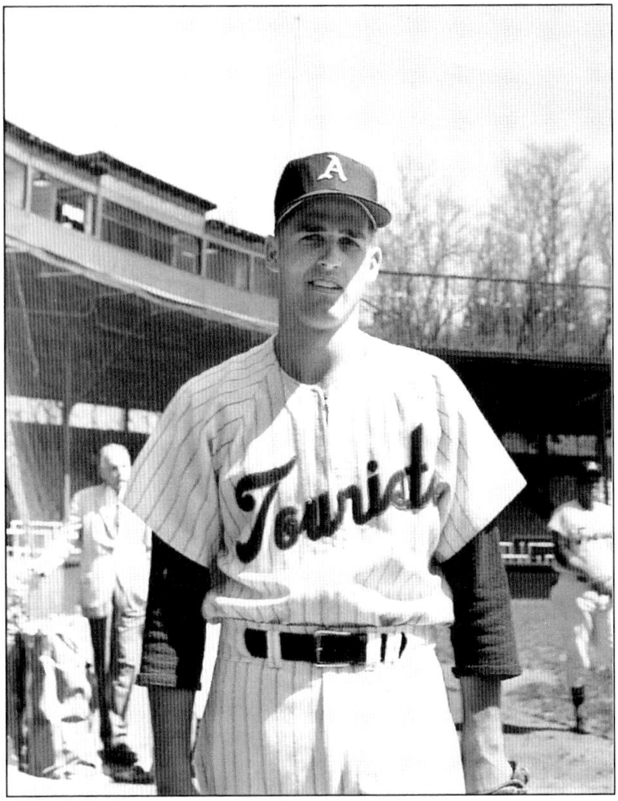

Right-hander Dick Doepker was a key reliever and spot starter for the Tourists during the 1961 campaign, his first of three seasons with Asheville. Doepker went 8-4 with a 2.47 ERA in 25 games with the Tourists his first year before posting a 2-3 record in 1962 and a 5-4 mark in 1963. (Bob Terrell collection.)

Tourists manager Ray Hathaway (far left) and third baseman Duncan Campbell talk baseball in the McCormick Field home dugout during the 1961 season. Pittsburgh general manager Joe L. Brown listens to the conversation while Asheville general manager Jim Mills (far right) sits in on the discussion. (Bob Terrell collection.)

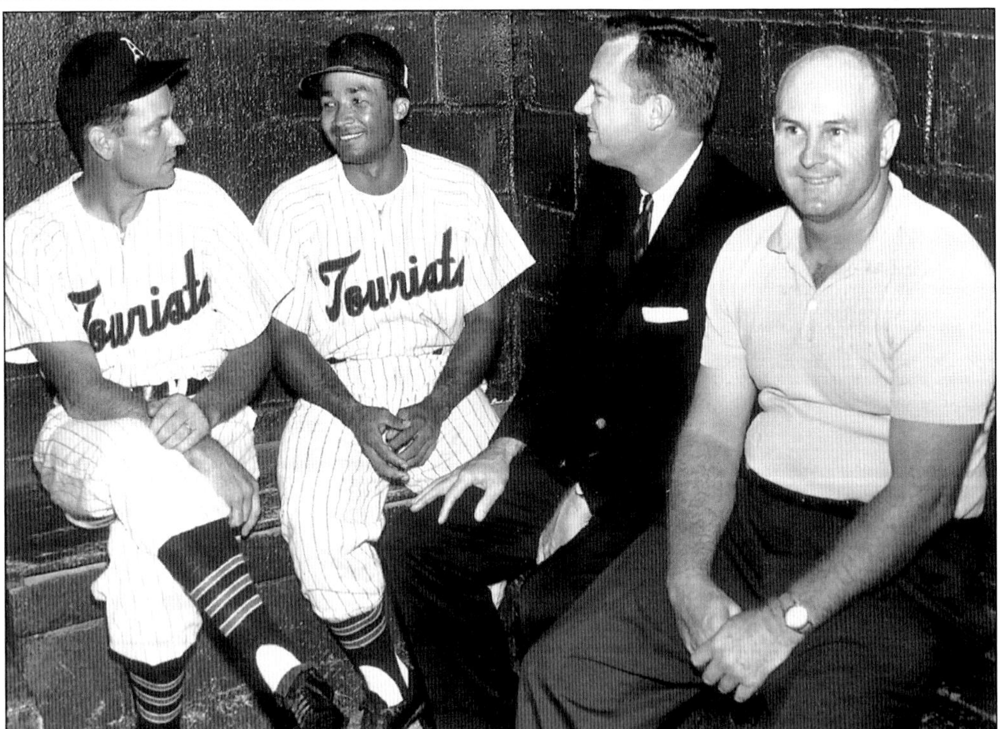

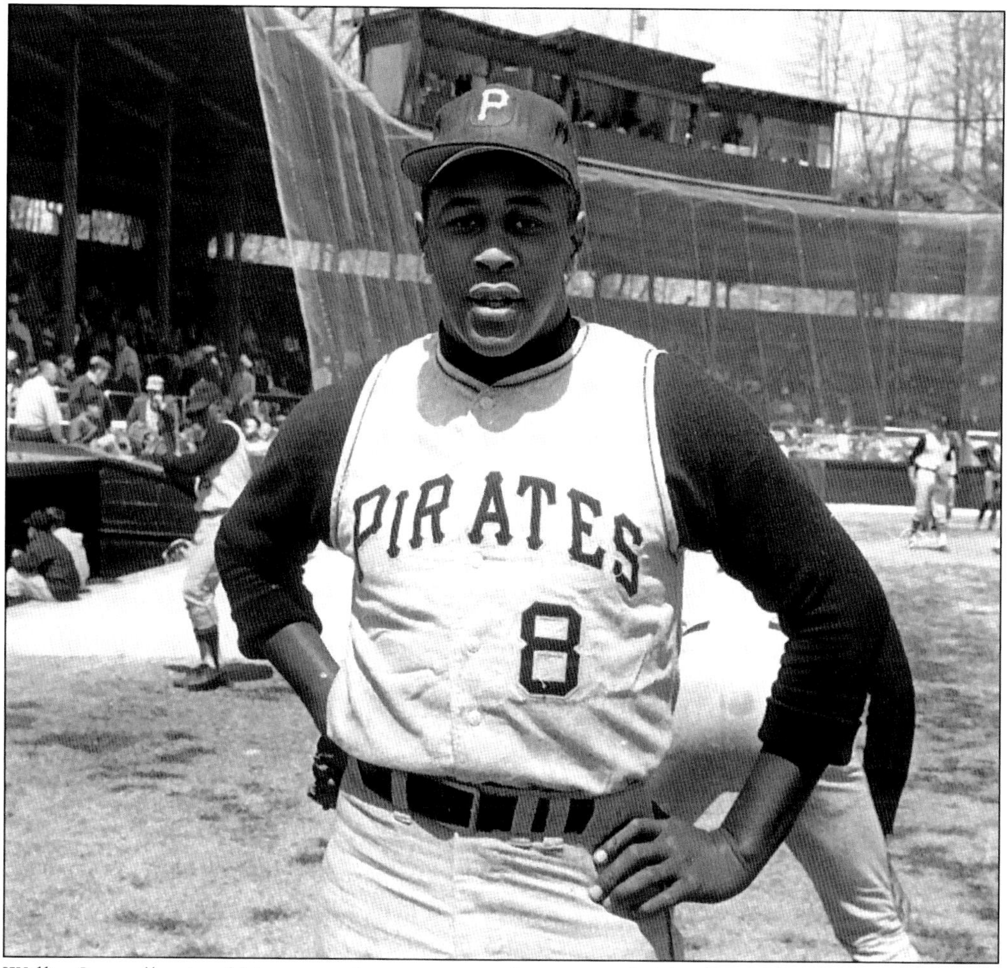

Willie Stargell gained his reputation as a power-hitting outfielder during his days in Asheville. Nicknamed "On the Hill Will," Stargell deposited the majority of his 22 home runs in 1961 on the banks beyond the outfield wall at McCormick Field. Stargell, who became the first former Tourist to earn induction to the Baseball Hall of Fame in Cooperstown, New York, was rated by the Sally League managers as having the strongest throwing arm among circuit flycatchers in 1961. Stargell is pictured at McCormick Field prior to an exhibition game in 1964. (Bob Terrell collection.)

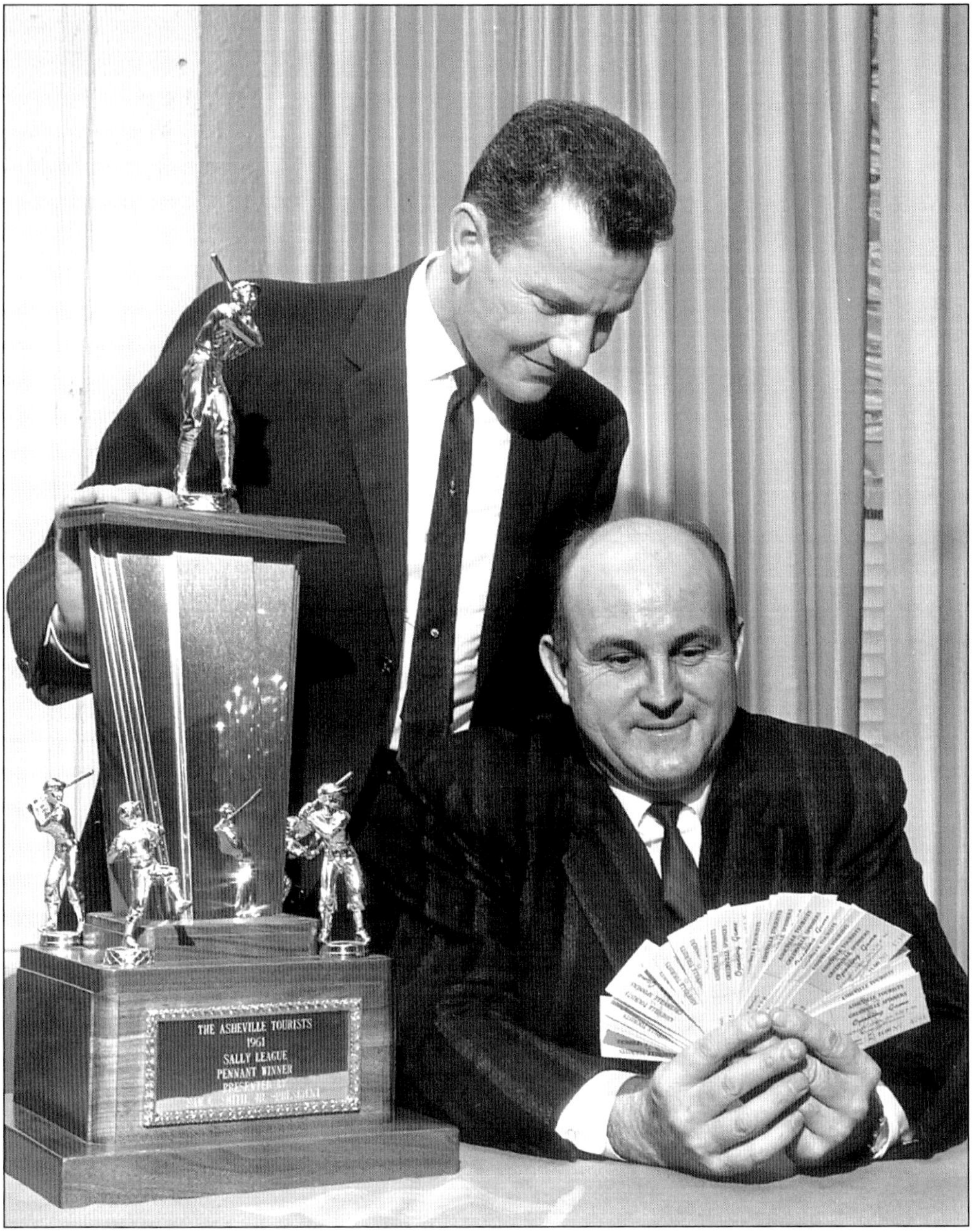

Asheville skipper Ray Hathaway looks over Tourists general manager Jim Mills's shoulder after accepting the South Atlantic League championship trophy for the 1961 campaign. Mills holds what he believes will be a hot ticket—ducats to the 1962 home opener against the Greenville Spinners. (Bob Terrell collection.)

Elmo Plaskett topped Charlotte's Tony Oliva by .0005 to claim the South Atlantic League batting crown with a .3498 average in 1962. The hard-hitting Plaskett, who hailed from the Virgin Islands, also tied for second in the South Atlantic League with 96 RBIs, placed fourth with 170 hits, and clubbed 27 home runs. (Bob Terrell Collection.)

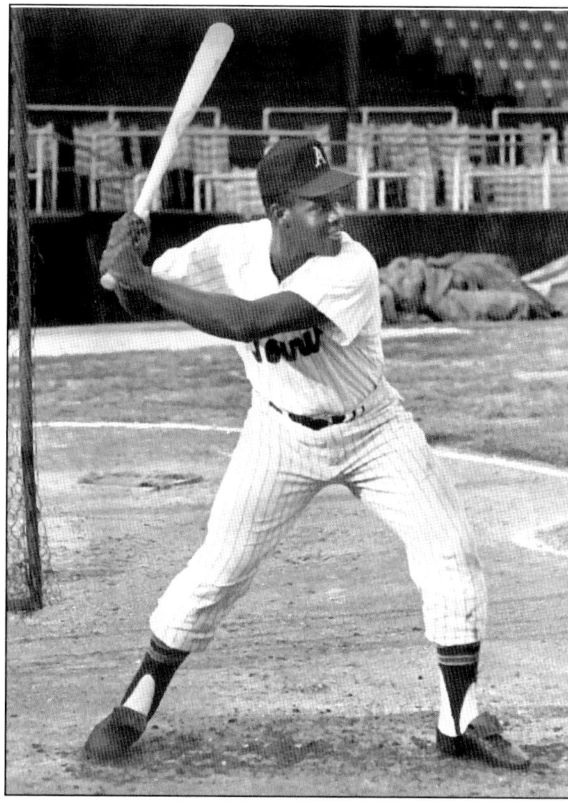

Tourists manager Ray Hathaway (far right) kneels with his starting lineup for the home opener at McCormick Field for the 1962 season. Asheville produced a 70-70 record to finish in fourth place in the South Atlantic League before losing to Knoxville in the first round of the playoffs, three games to one. (Bob Terrell collection.)

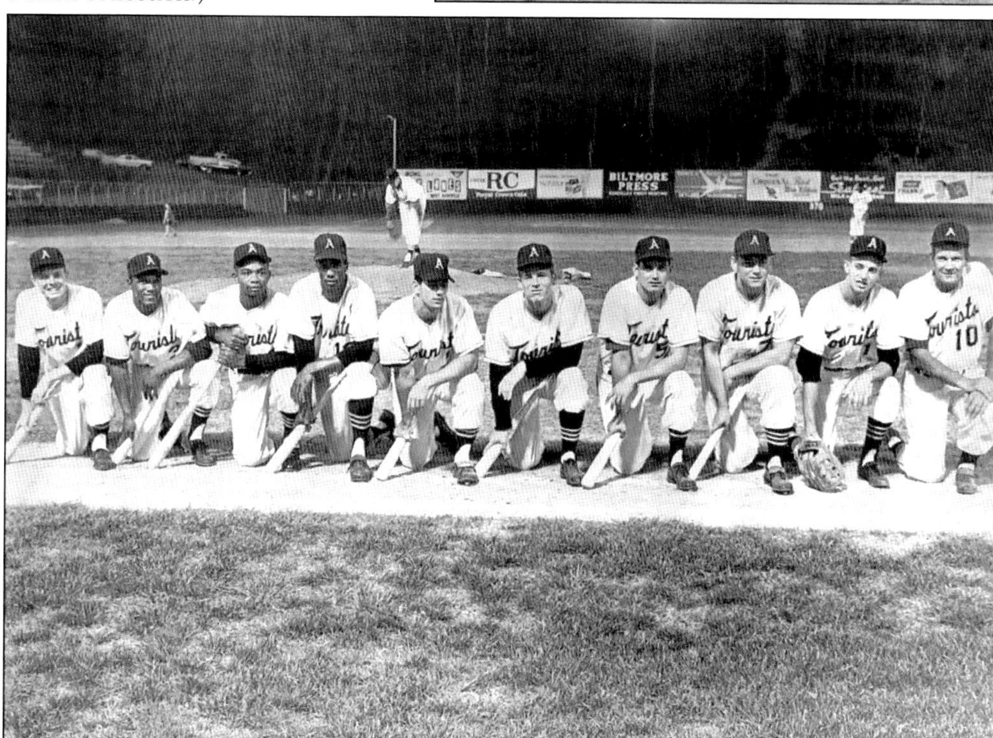

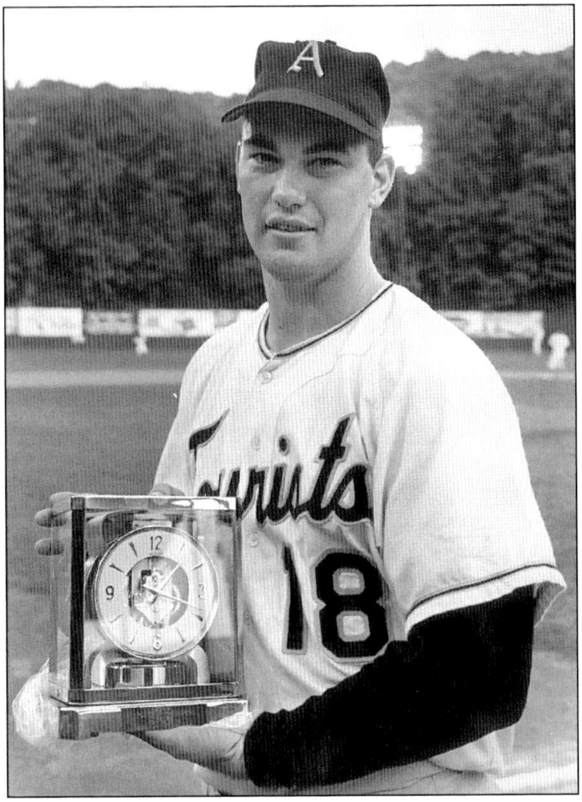

Troy Giles holds his clock after being honored as Player of the Month in the South Atlantic League during the 1963 season. The ambidextrous Giles led the Class AA circuit with 159 strikeouts and equaled Lynchburg's Fred Talbot with 18 wins. Giles also was named to the South Atlantic League year-end All-Star team. (Bob Terrell collection.)

Crowds remained strong at McCormick Field during the early 1960s, with 97,065 patrons entering the turnstiles in 1961 and more than 70,000 fans taking in a baseball game in 1962 and 1963. Attendance fell to 41,086 in 1964 and rebounded to 68,490 in 1965 before the Tourists welcomed 51,704 fans in 1966. The team, however, did not draw more than 50,000 fans in a single season again until 1981. (Bob Terrell collection.)

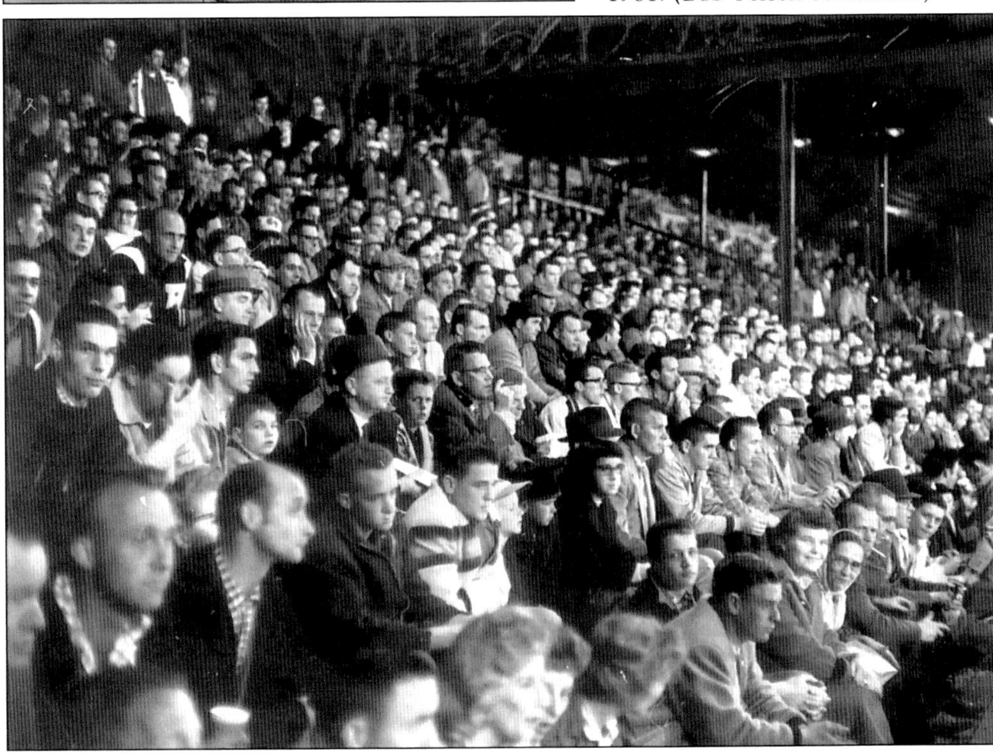

Pittsburgh featured many former Asheville players during the 1964 exhibition game with the Phillies at McCormick Field, including 1961 Tourists (from left to right) Rex Johnston, Gene Alley, and Bob Bailey. Johnston was considered the best left fielder in the South Atlantic League in 1961. (Bob Terrell collection.)

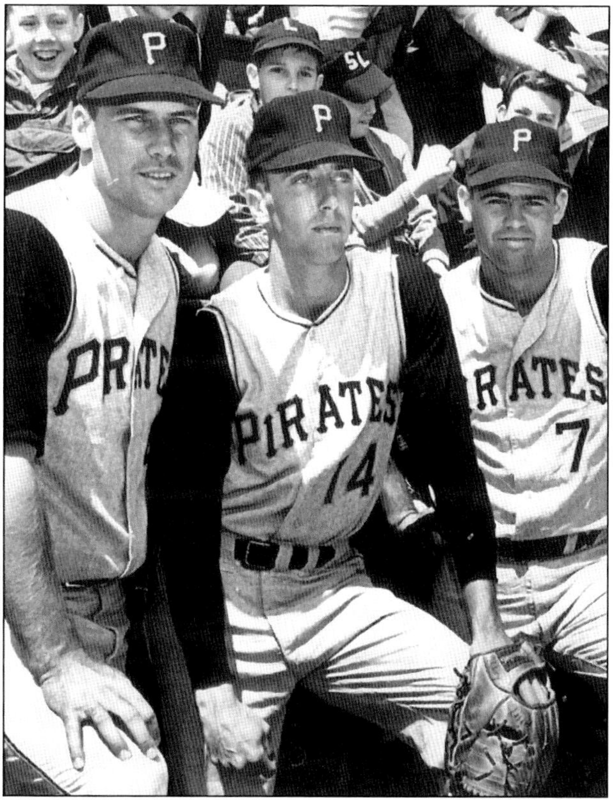

Fans clamor to obtain autographs from members of the Pittsburgh Pirates prior to an exhibition game against the Philadelphia Phillies on April 11, 1964. McCormick Field hosted 5,315 fans to the afternoon tilt that saw the Pirates defeat the Phillies, 16-3. (Bob Terrell collection.)

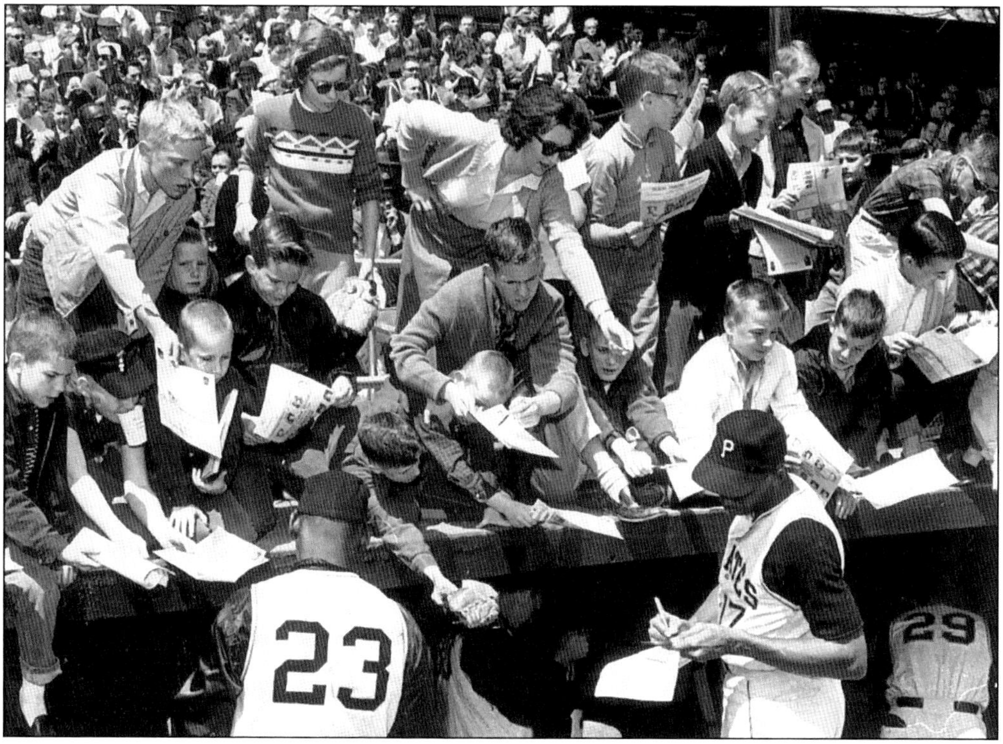

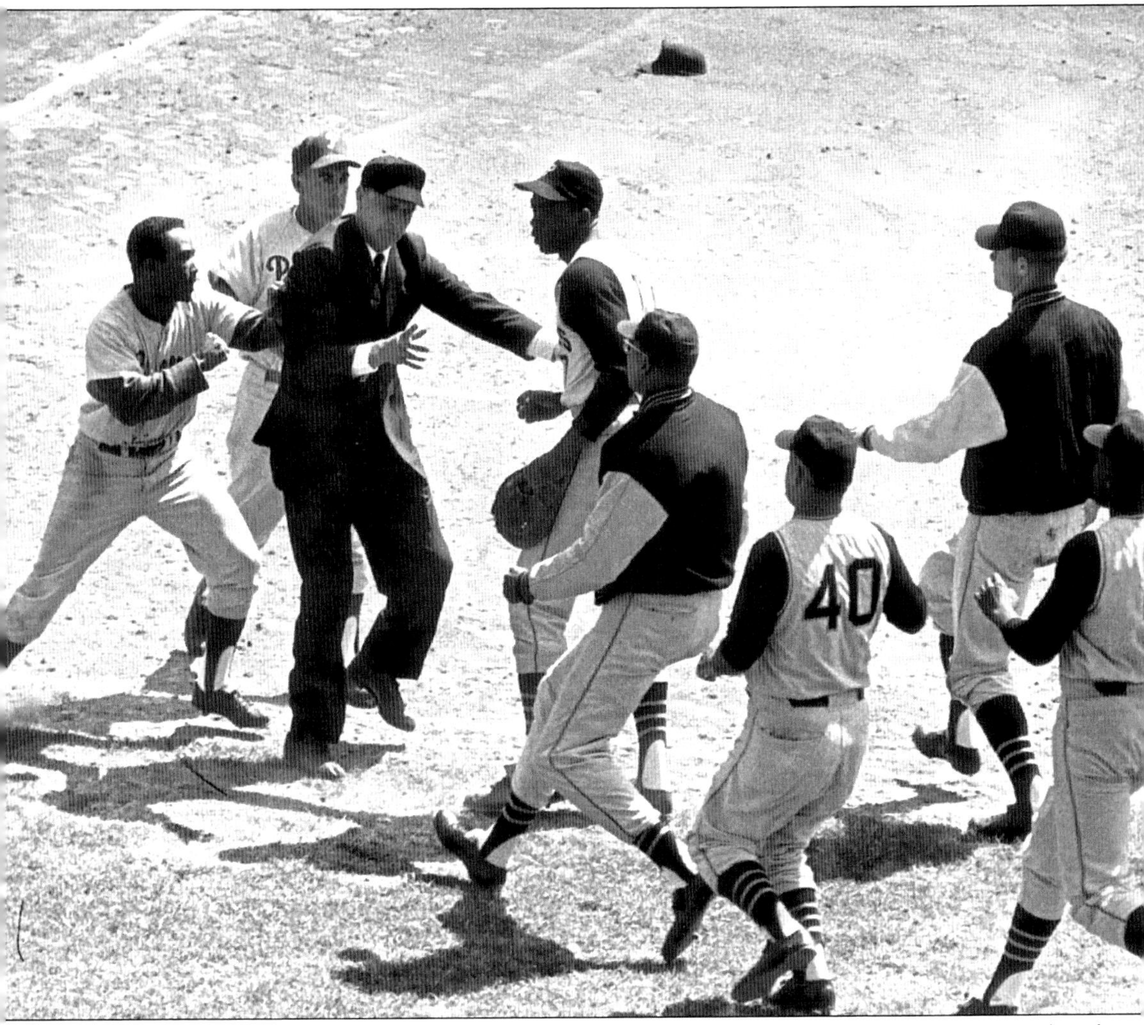

The game prior to the 1964 season may have been an exhibition, but the two teams displayed their fighting spirit at McCormick Field. The Pirates and Phillies nearly engaged in a brawl when umpire Ken Burkhardt (third from left) tossed Pirates first baseman Donn Clendenon (center, with glove) from the game after applying an aggressive tag to Philadelphia's Tony Taylor (far left). (Bob Terrell collection.)

After a stellar performance with the Tourists in 1962, Elmo Plaskett returned to Asheville for parts of the 1964 and 1966 campaigns; he hit .284 with 18 home runs during his second season with the Tourists and .243 with seven home runs during his last stint with the team. Plaskett played parts of the 1962 and 1963 seasons in the major leagues with the Pirates. (Bob Terrell collection.)

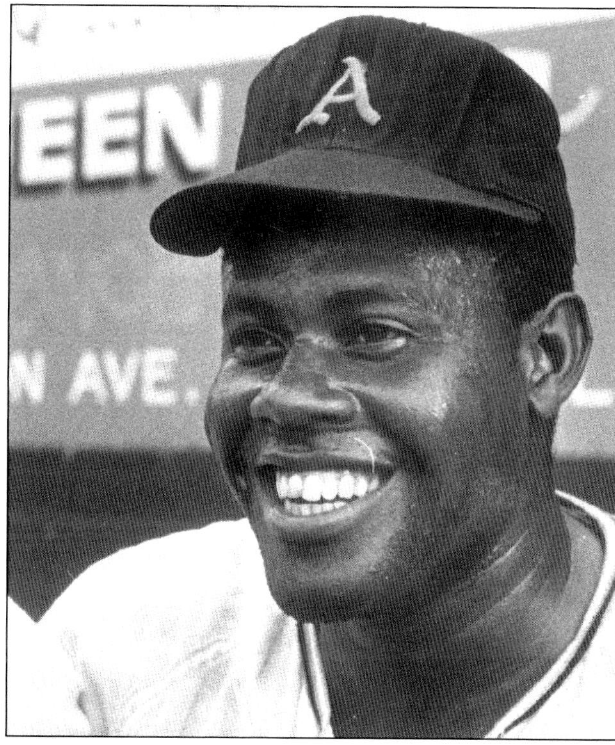

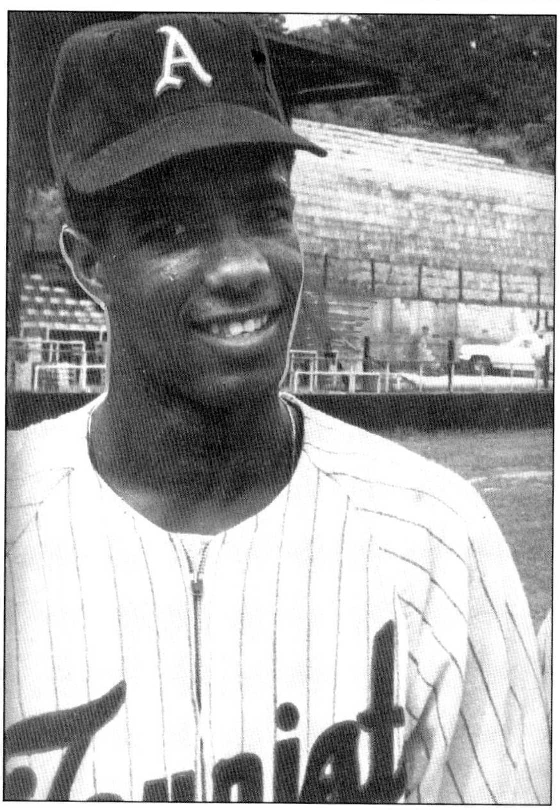

Jose Martinez tied for fifth in the Southern League with 78 RBIs and paced the Tourists with 20 home runs in 1964. Martinez played parts of the 1969 and 1970 seasons with Pittsburgh before becoming the first base coach for the Chicago Cubs from 1988 to 1994. (Bob Terrell collection.)

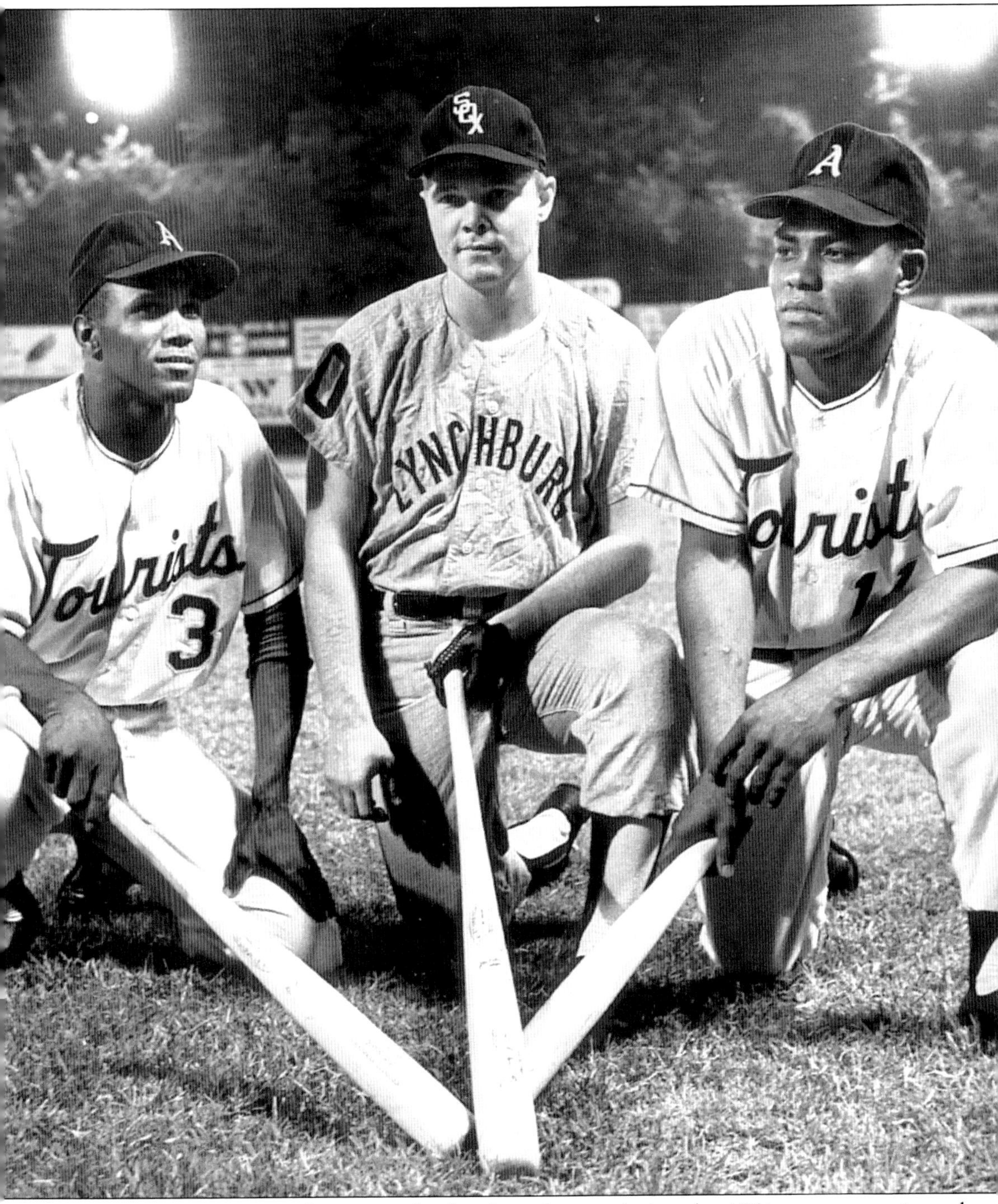

Three of the premier hitters in the Southern League during the 1964 season are pictured at McCormick Field. All-Star outfielder George Spriggs, who ranked second in the Southern League with a .322 batting average, and Bobby Pena, who tied for seventh in the Southern League with a .303 batting average, flank Lynchburg's Dick Kenworthy. Despite the hitting prowess of Spriggs and Pena, the Tourists finished in last place with a 52-86 record. (Bob Terrell collection.)

Luke Walker twirled two seasons in Asheville, compiling a combined record of 20-21 with a 2.99 ERA in 56 games. The left-hander led the Southern League with a 2.26 ERA in 1965 and posted a 12-7 record to earn All-Star recognition. He later pitched in 243 games in the major leagues, going 45-47 with a 3.64 ERA. (Bob Terrell collection.)

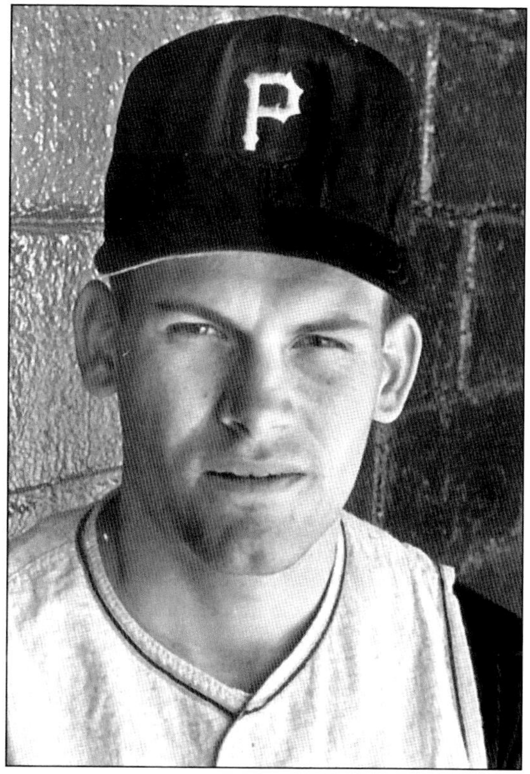

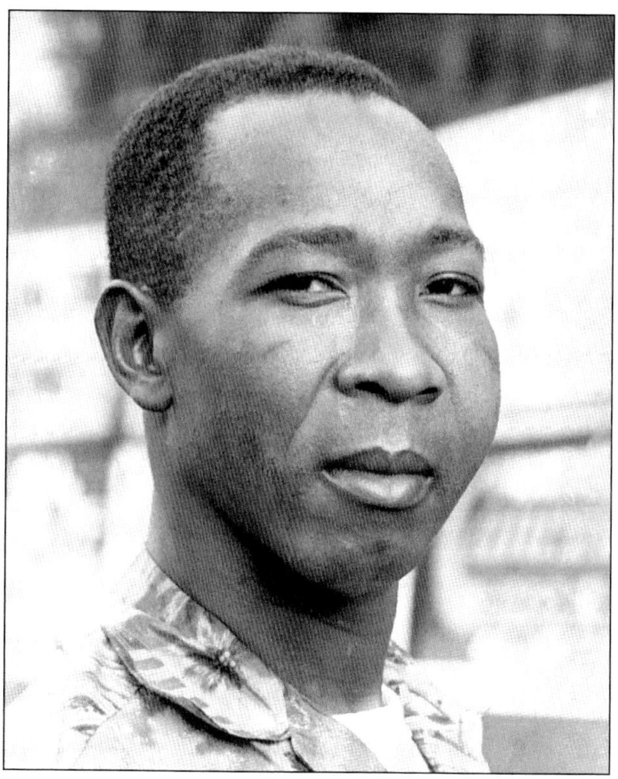

An imprint of the baseball's stitches is obvious on Jesus McFarland's swollen face several months after he was struck by a pitch. McFarland, who batted .301 with 21 home runs and 74 RBIs in 1961, spent most of the 1965 season in Asheville and hit at a .292 clip with 22 home runs and 69 RBIs. (Bob Terrell collection.)

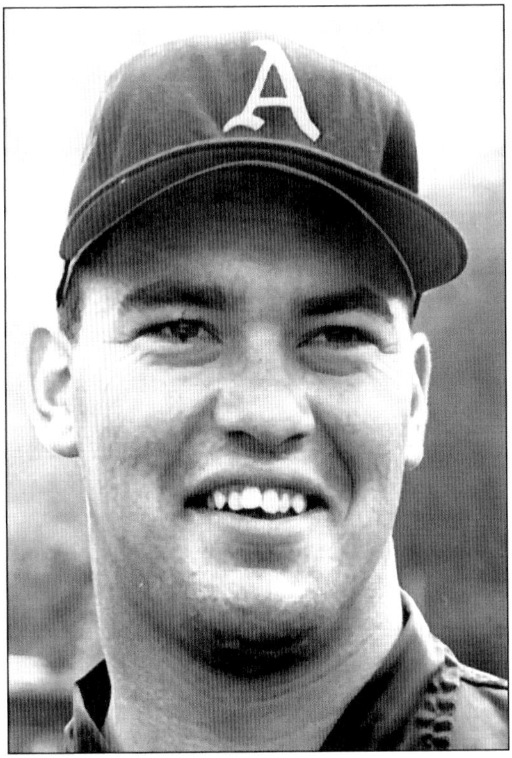

Troy Giles joined Jesus McFarland in 1965 as a former Tourist trying to rediscover the magic he possessed in Asheville. Giles was not as productive as his batterymate, going 4-7 with a 3.88 ERA in 28 games, including 19 starts, during his second stint in the Land of the Sky. (Bob Terrell collection.)

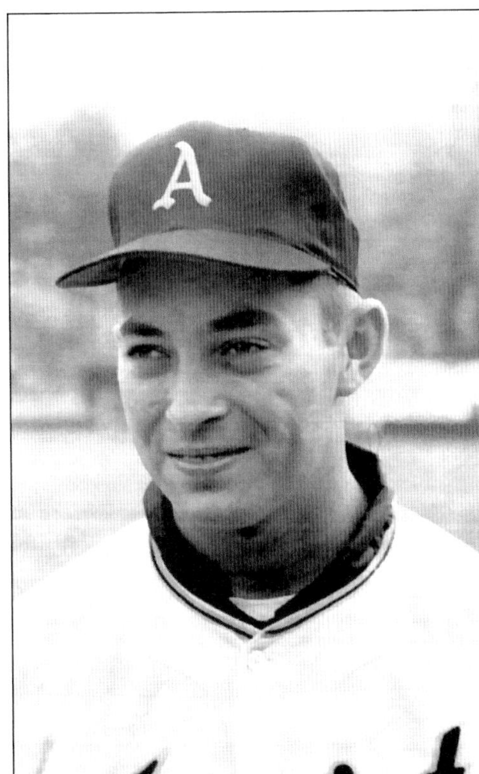

Left-hander Asa Small was a productive relief pitcher who tied for third on the Tourists with 10 victories during the 1965 season. Small also ranked second with 47 appearances in Asheville and posted a 3.16 ERA. Shortly after his tenure with the Tourists, Small was killed in a house fire. (Bob Terrell collection.)

Long-time observers at McCormick Field claim Bob Robertson hit some of the longest home runs in the ballpark's storied history. The third baseman clubbed a Southern League-best 32 homers in 1966, including one that reportedly landed above the ballpark, in Memorial Stadium. Robertson also led the Southern League with 99 RBIs and batted .287. He played 11 seasons in the major leagues, from 1967 to 1979. (Bob Terrell collection.)

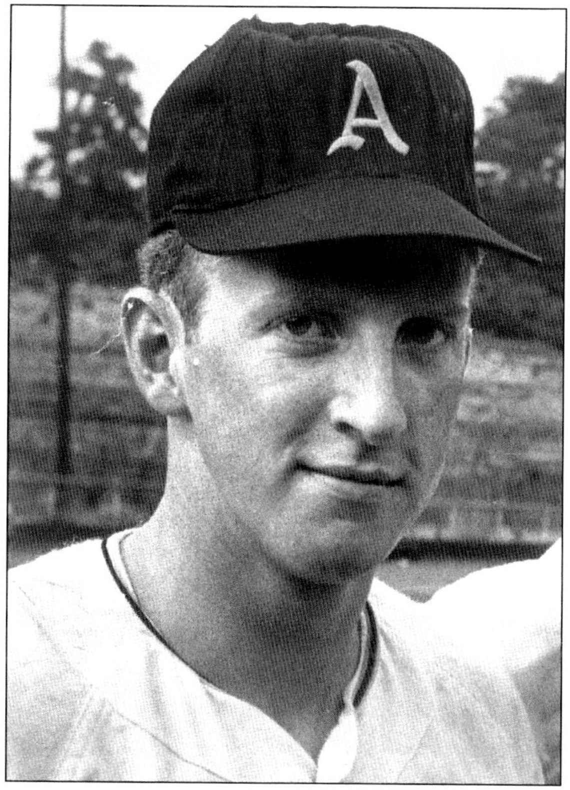

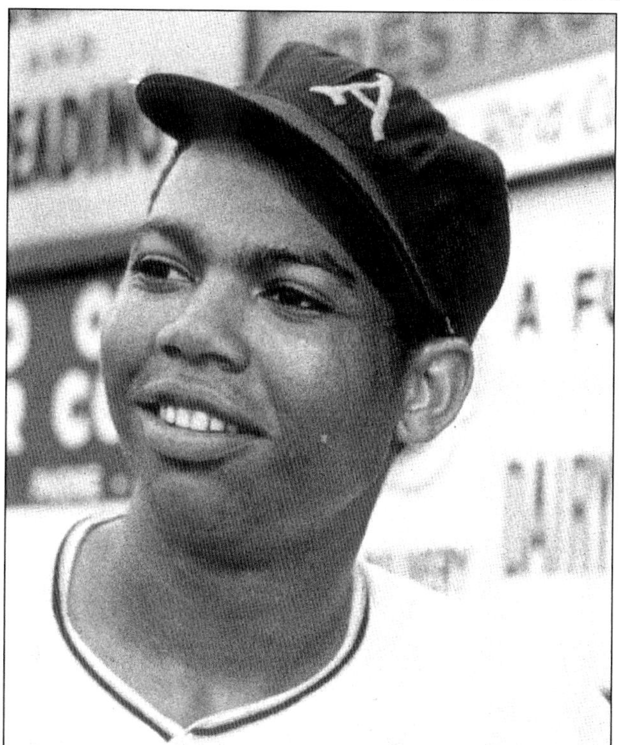

Dock Ellis completed 13 of his 24 starts with the Tourists in 1966 while registering a 10-9 record and a 2.76 ERA. Ellis became one of the most effective right-handers in the National League during the early 1970s and started the 1971 All-Star game as a member of the Pittsburgh Pirates. (Bob Terrell collection.)

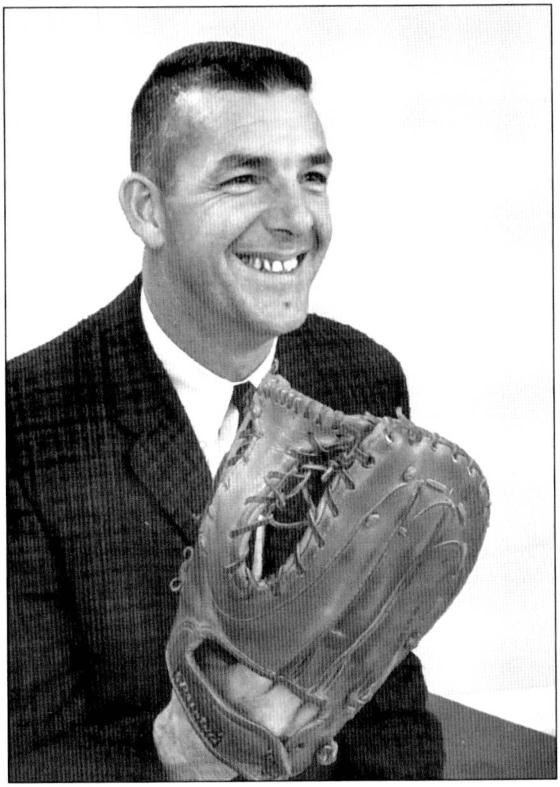

Chuck Churn served as the Tourists' manager in 1967 in the team's lone season as a Carolina League affiliate of the Houston Astros. A major league pitcher with the Dodgers, Pirates, and Indians, Churn led Asheville to a 64-74 record and finished in sixth place in the loop's West Division. (Bob Terrell collection.)

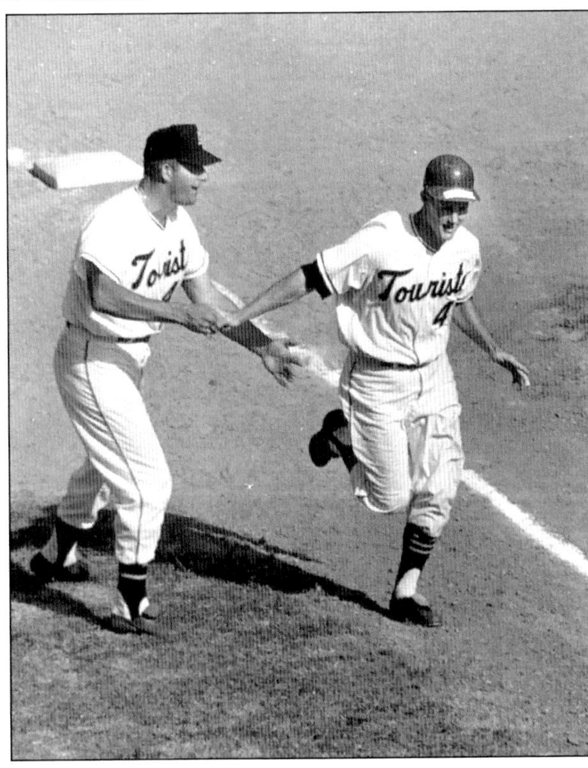

Asheville manager Chuck Churn congratulates Alex Barrett while rounding third base after Barrett hit one of his six home runs during the 1967 campaign. (Bob Terrell collection.)

Hall of Fame manager George "Sparky" Anderson led the Tourists to the Southern League championship in his lone season at the Asheville dugout helm. Less than two years later, prior to the 1970 season, Anderson was named skipper of the Cincinnati Reds and guided the team to the World Series in his first major league season. Inducted into the Cooperstown shrine in 2000, Anderson won 2,194 games during his 26 seasons as manager of the Reds and Tigers. (*Asheville Citizen-Times* photograph.)

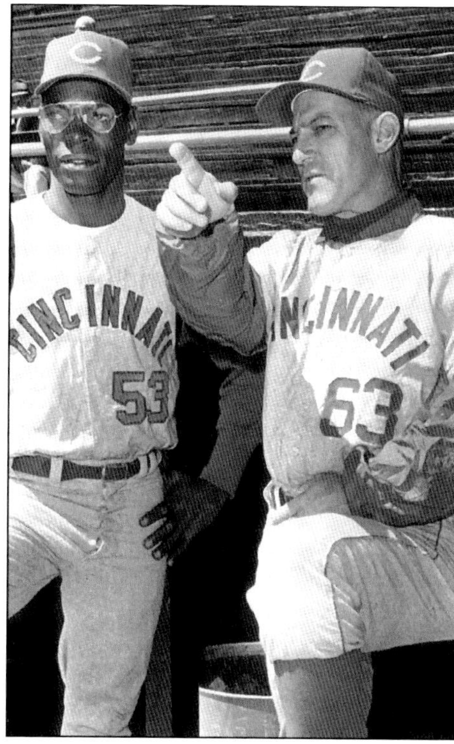

The Tourists won the 1968 Southern League title with an 86-54 record. From left to right are (front row) DeGold Francis, Sherman Minster, Wayne Meadows, Arlie Burge, Bernie Carbo, George Lattera, manager Sparky Anderson, Grover Powell, Jake Martinez, and Billy Henry; (back row) pitcher/coach Bunky Warren, Don Anderson, Fred Kendall, Dan McGinn, Steve Blateric, Darrel Chaney, Scott Seger, Wayne Simpson, John Noriega, and Archie Moore. George Anderson Jr. is the batboy, front and center. (Asheville Tourists photograph.)

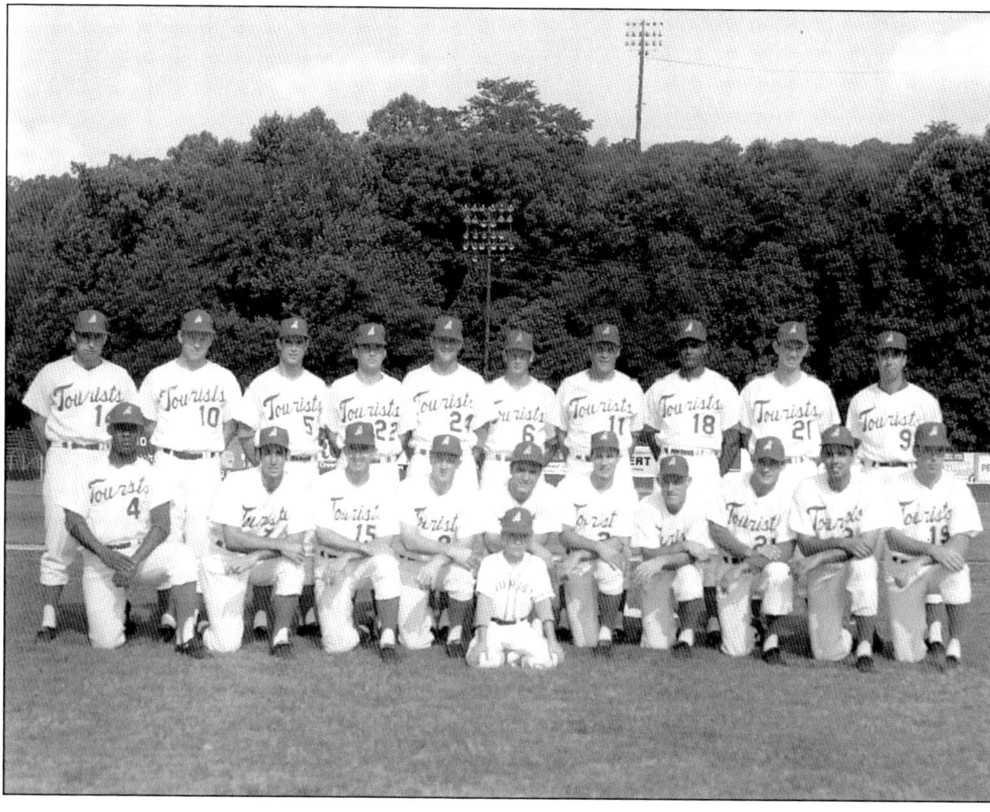

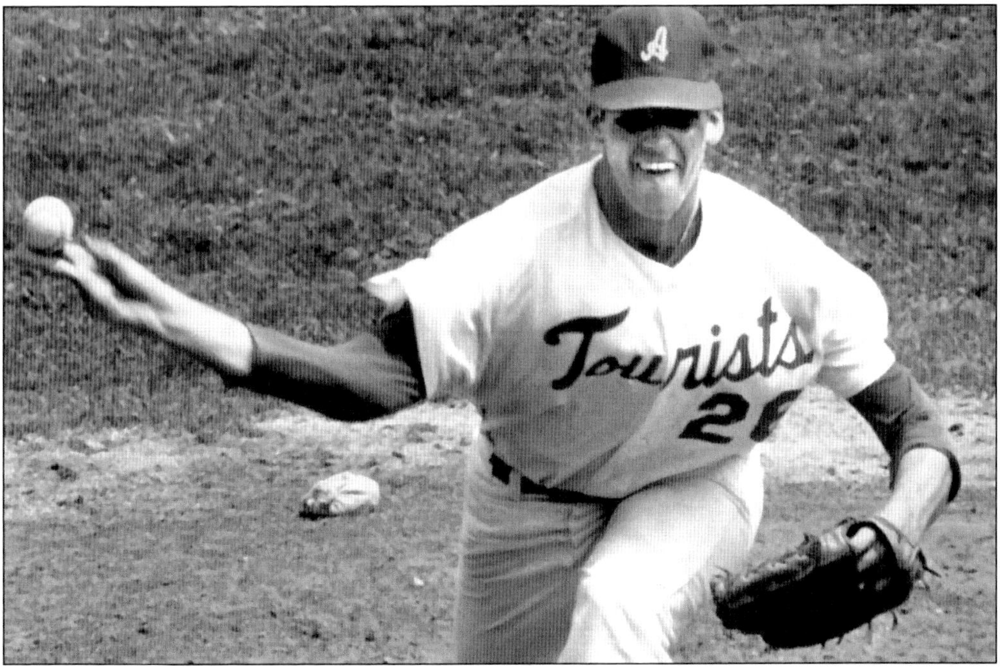

Tom Frandorf did an excellent job of relieving and spot starting for the Tourists in 1968. The right-hander registered a 9-4 record and a 3.88 ERA with three complete games and a shutout. (Asheville Tourists photograph.)

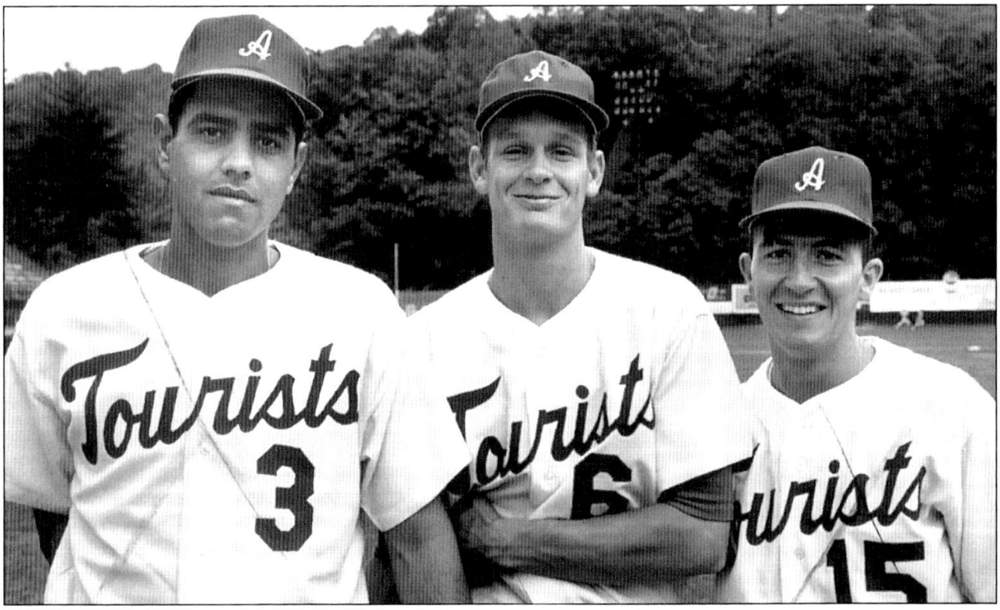

Darrel Chaney, pictured here between teammates Jake Martinez (left) and Wayne Meadows (right), was a slick-fielding shortstop with surprising power. Chaney placed second in the Southern League in 1968 with 23 home runs, just three behind Montgomery's Wayne Redmond. Chaney's home runs helped guide Asheville to the Southern League championship. In 11 major league seasons with Cincinnati and Atlanta, Chaney went deep a total of 14 times. (*Asheville Citizen-Times* photograph.)

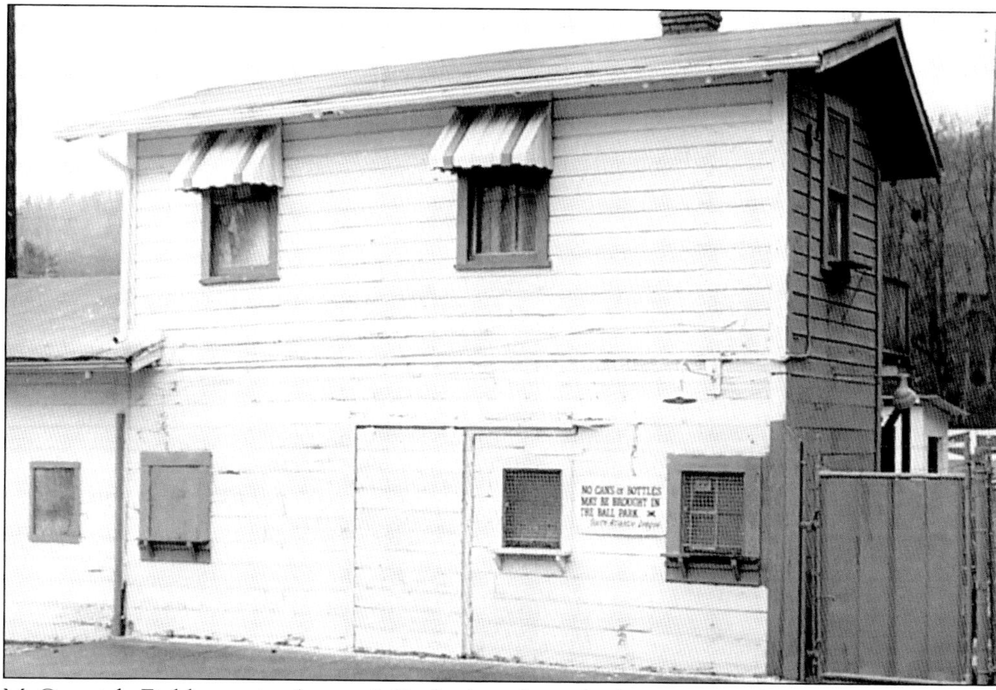

McCormick Field remained a no-frills facility through the 1960s and into the 1970s. This photograph, taken around 1970, shows the ticket windows and the Tourists offices, which were located on the second floor. (Bob Terrell collection.)

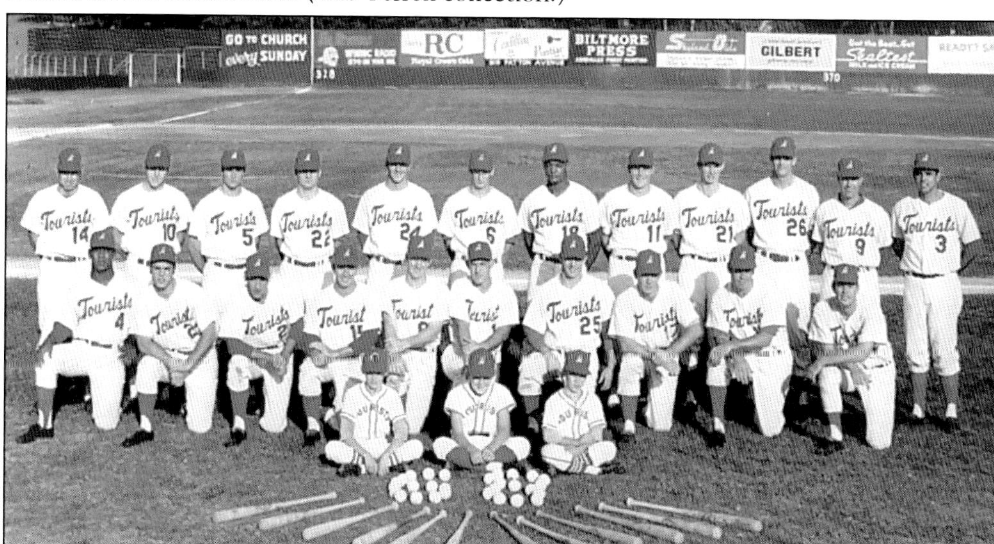

The Tourists finished third with a 69-69 record in the six-team Southern League during the 1969 season. The following are pictured from left to right: (front row) trainer John Moyer, Virgilio Mata, Joe Hamende, Arlie Burge, Sheldon Andrens, manager Alex Cosmidis, Frank Portera, James Hibbs, Al Crawford, Frank Ferro, and Kurt Bevacqua; (back row) Steve Blateric, Daryl Hallmark, George Runk, Jack Camacho, Marv Branscomb, George Shoemaker, Rick Sires, Bruce Von Hoff, Ken Myette, Ron Crook, Mel Behney, Don Anderson, Bill Henry, and general manager Marvin Lorenz. (Asheville Tourists photograph.)

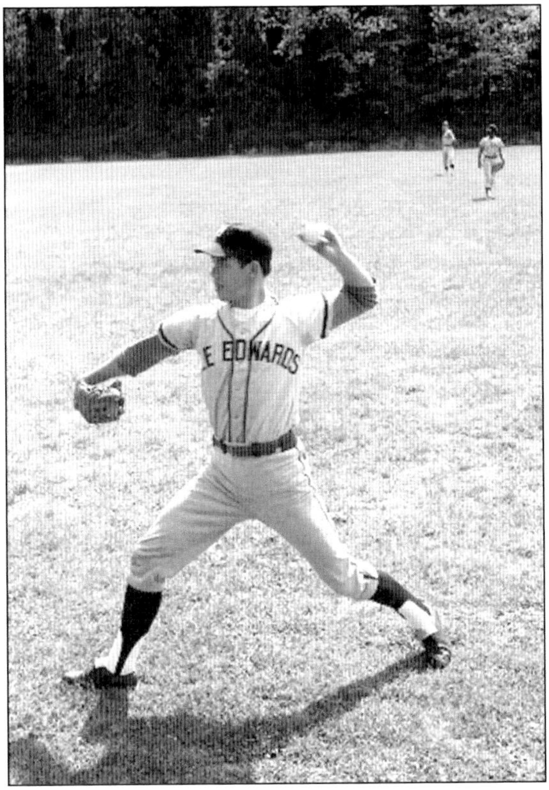

Asheville High School (known as Lee Edwards High School prior to 1970) standout Dave Cheadle became the highest-drafted player in Western North Carolina history when the New York Yankees nabbed the pitcher with the 11th overall pick of the 1970 draft. Cheadle went 10-1 with four no-hitters and a 0.16 ERA during his senior season. The left-hander had 119 strikeouts and his only loss came in the state finals. (Dave Cheadle photograph.)

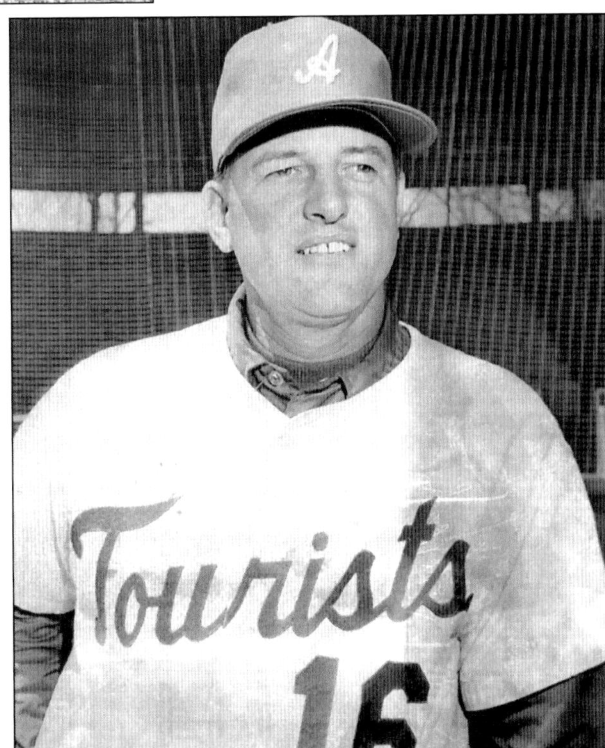

Jim Snyder, who played in the major leagues with the Minnesota Twins from 1961 to 1964, managed the Tourists in 1970. In what proved to be the franchise's last season as the Reds' Class AA affiliate, Snyder's squad was one of the weaker in Asheville history, going 59-80 for a .424 winning percentage. Snyder later managed the Seattle Mariners during the 1988 campaign. (Asheville Tourists photograph.)

Former major league catcher Russ Nixon served as a coach with the Tourists during the first half of the 1970 slate before reporting to Sioux Falls to manage in the short-season Northern League. Nixon later managed Cincinnati from 1982 to 1983 and Atlanta from 1988 to 1990. He returned to McCormick Field as manager of the Lexington Legends in 2003. (Asheville Tourists photograph.)

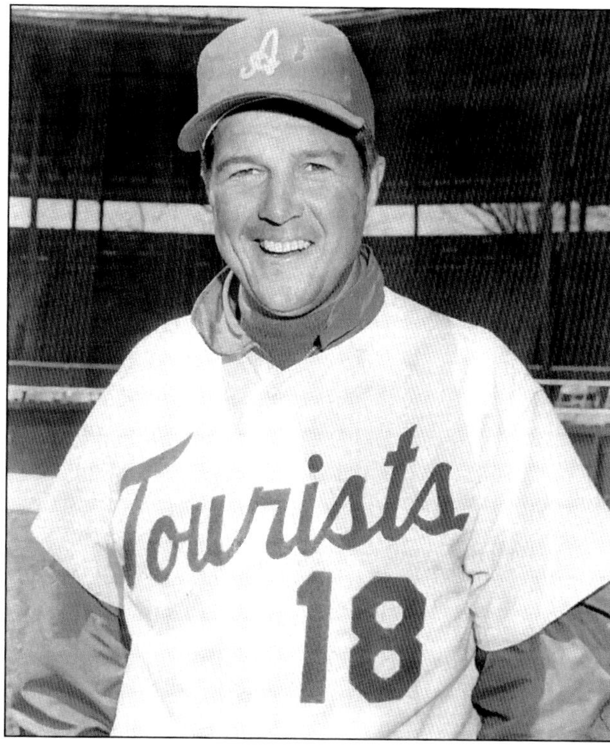

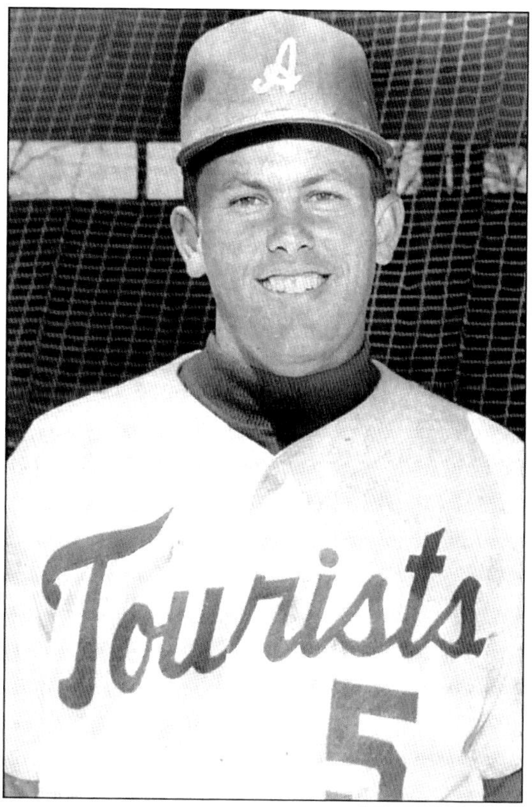

Ironically, three members of the 1970 Tourists later managed at the major league level. Third baseman Greg Riddoch, who hit .205 with one home run and 22 RBIs in 132 games with Asheville, managed the San Diego Padres from 1990 to 1992. (Asheville Tourists photograph.)

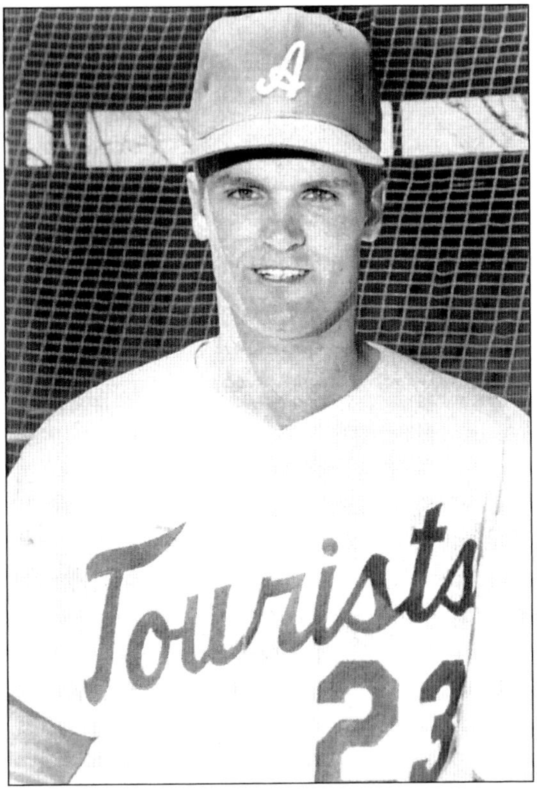

Dave Tomlin went 6-10 with a 3.11 ERA in 25 games with the Tourists in 1970. The left-hander emerged as a steady reliever at the major league level while pitching for Cincinnati, San Diego, and Pittsburgh from 1972 to 1986. Tomlin returned to McCormick Field in 2002 and 2003 as pitching coach of the Augusta GreenJackets. (Asheville Tourists photograph.)

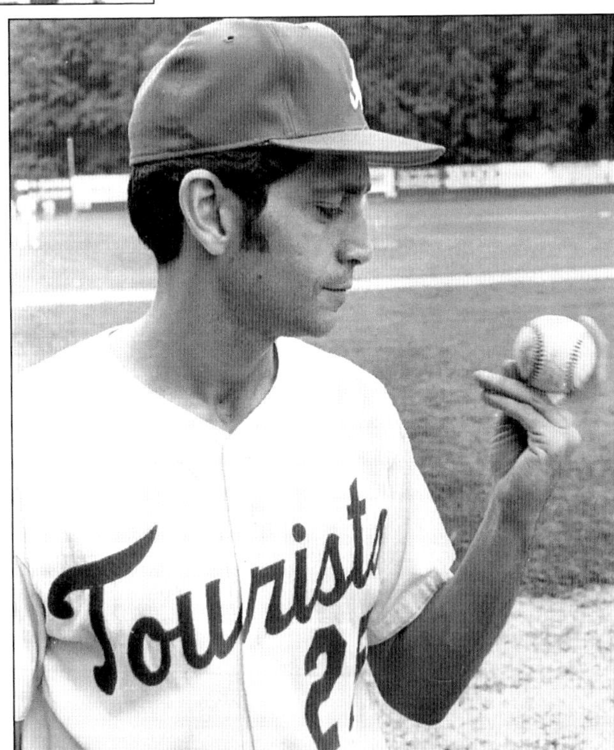

Screwball pitcher Bo Belinsky made a rehab visit to Asheville during the 1970 season and went 0-2 with a 2.88 ERA in five outings. Belinsky was as noted for his exploits off the field with some of Hollywood's most attractive women as he was for his talents on the diamond. He threw a no-hitter against Baltimore in 1962 and posted a 28-51 record in the big leagues before pursuing a career in acting. (Bob Terrell collection.)

In 1971, their lone season as an affiliate of the Chicago White Sox, the Tourists won 90 games, which ties for the fourth-highest total in franchise history, and posted a .638 winning percentage, which ranks sixth in Asheville annals. Pictured here is the game program sold that year at McCormick Field. (Author's collection.)

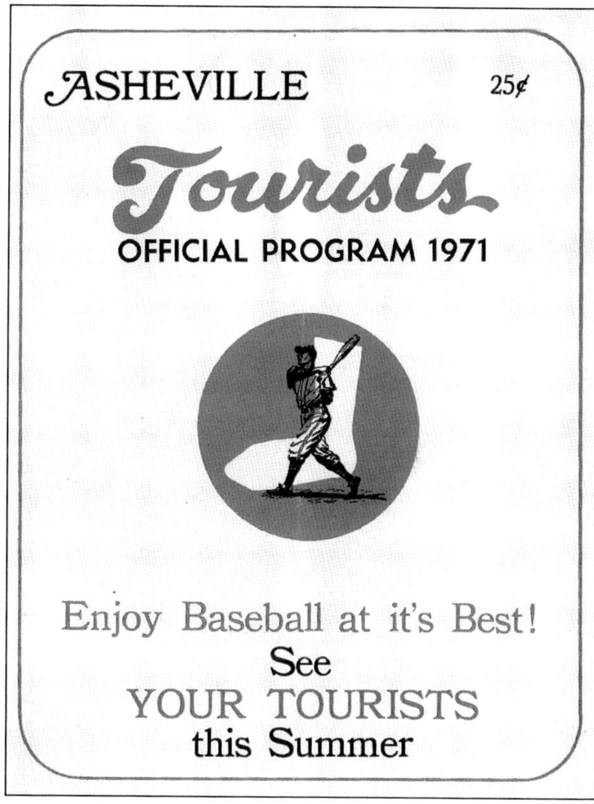

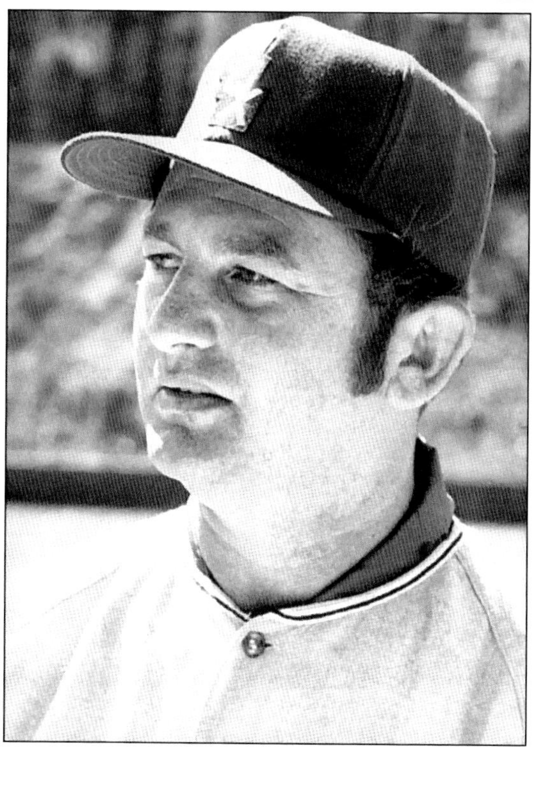

Larry Sherry managed the Tourists to a 90-51 record in 1971. Sherry, who pitched in the major leagues for Los Angeles and Detroit, owns the third-highest winning percentage at .638 among Asheville skippers. He was named the Southern League's Manager of the Year during his lone season with the Tourists. (Asheville Tourists photograph.)

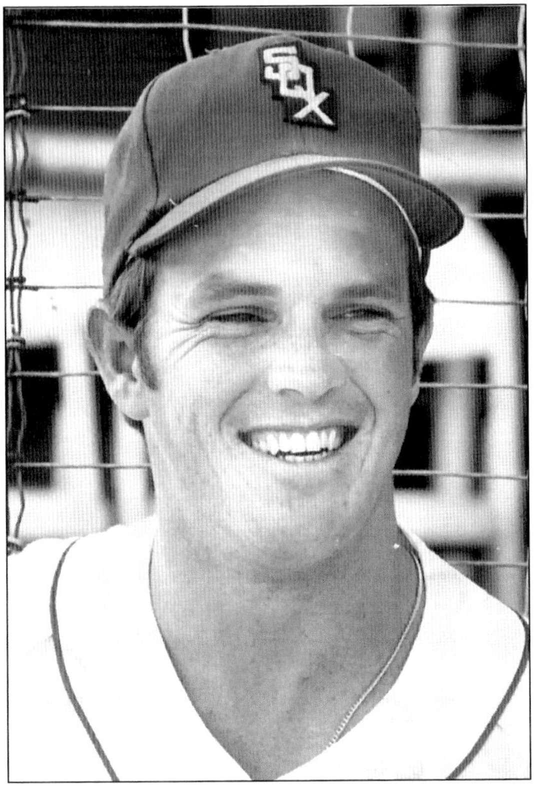

Vic Correll handled the majority of the catching chores for the Tourists during the 1971 season and batted .273 with 22 home runs and 58 RBIs. Correll played in the major leagues for eight seasons with Boston, Atlanta, and Cincinnati. (Asheville Tourists photograph.)

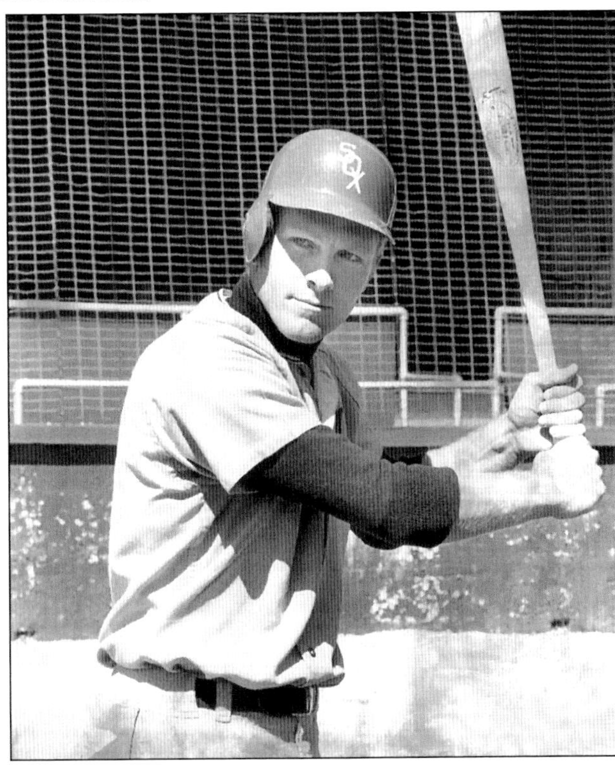

Don Anderson played three seasons in Asheville, beginning in 1968, continuing in 1969, and concluding in 1971. His best season with the Tourists was his second campaign, when he made a strong run at the Southern League's Triple Crown. Anderson topped the team with 18 home runs, good for seventh in the Southern League, while pacing the Class AA circuit with a .324 batting average and tying for top honors with Birmingham's Bobby Brooks by driving in 100 runs. He also ranked third in the Southern League with a .305 batting average in 1971. (Asheville Tourists photograph.)

Asheville led the Southern League in fielding during the 1971 season. Sure-handed second baseman Glenn Redmon steadied the infield for Asheville while contributing a .267 batting average with seven home runs and 62 RBIs in 133 games. Redmon had four RBIs in seven games with the San Francisco Giants in 1974. (Asheville Tourists photograph.)

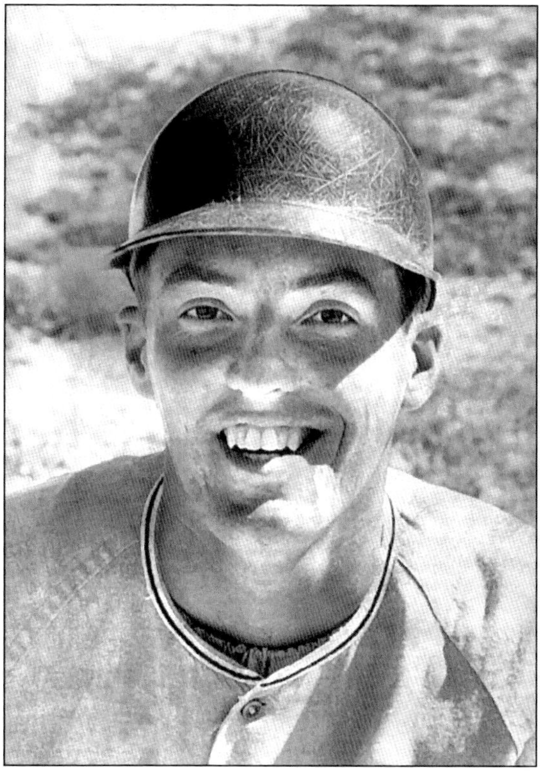

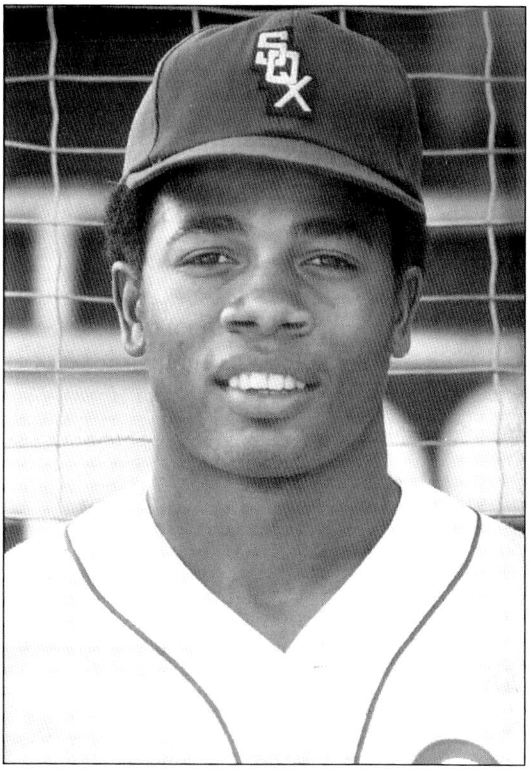

Hugh Yancy ranked ninth in the Southern League by producing a .276 batting average during the 1971 campaign. The third baseman provided much of the speed in a power-laden lineup by leading the Tourists with 19 stolen bases. Yancy played seven games with the Chicago White Sox from 1972 to 1976. (Asheville Tourists photograph.)

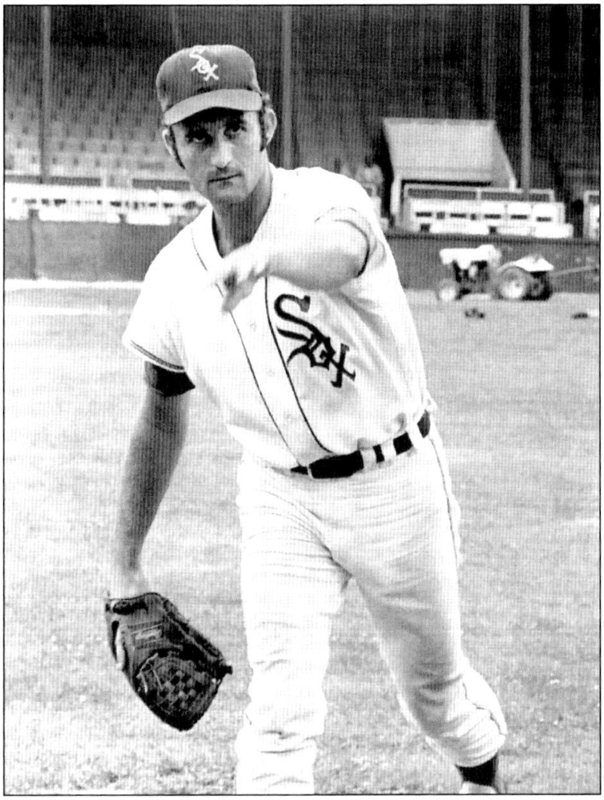

Left-hander John Bauer was second on the Tourists with eight saves and tied for third on the club with 11 wins despite relieving in all of his team-high 42 appearances during the 1971 season. (*Asheville Citizen-Times* photograph.)

High winter winds not only left a dusting of snow at McCormick Field, but also cost the facility its scoreboard during the early 1970s. (*Asheville Citizen-Times* photograph.)

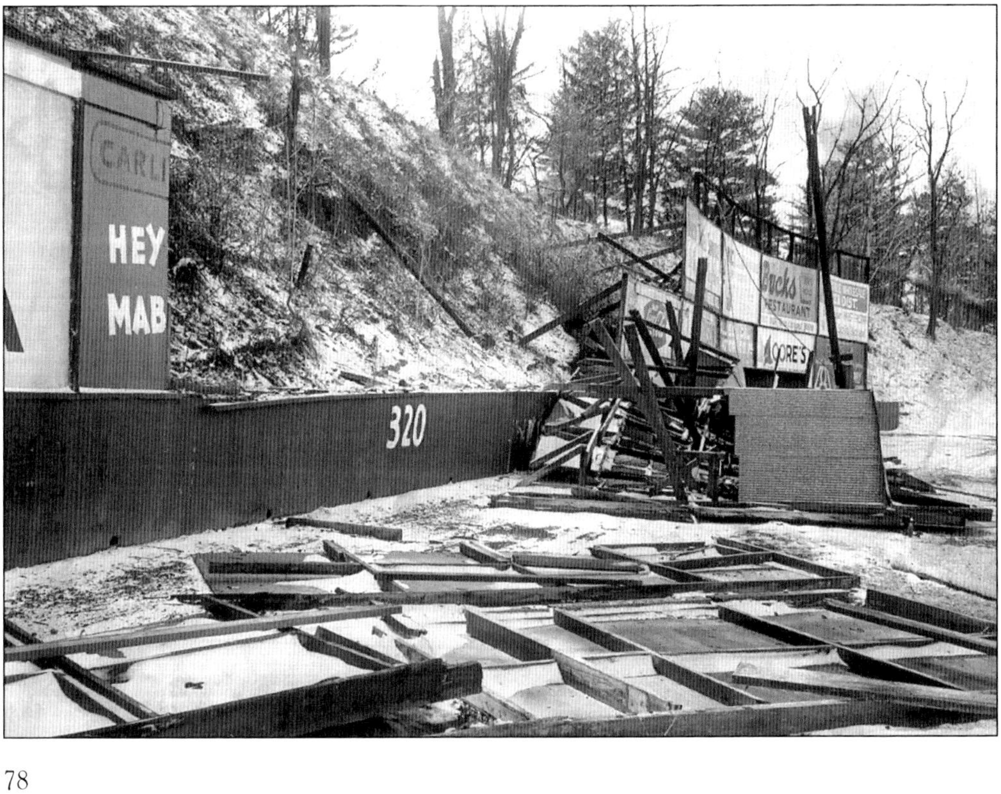

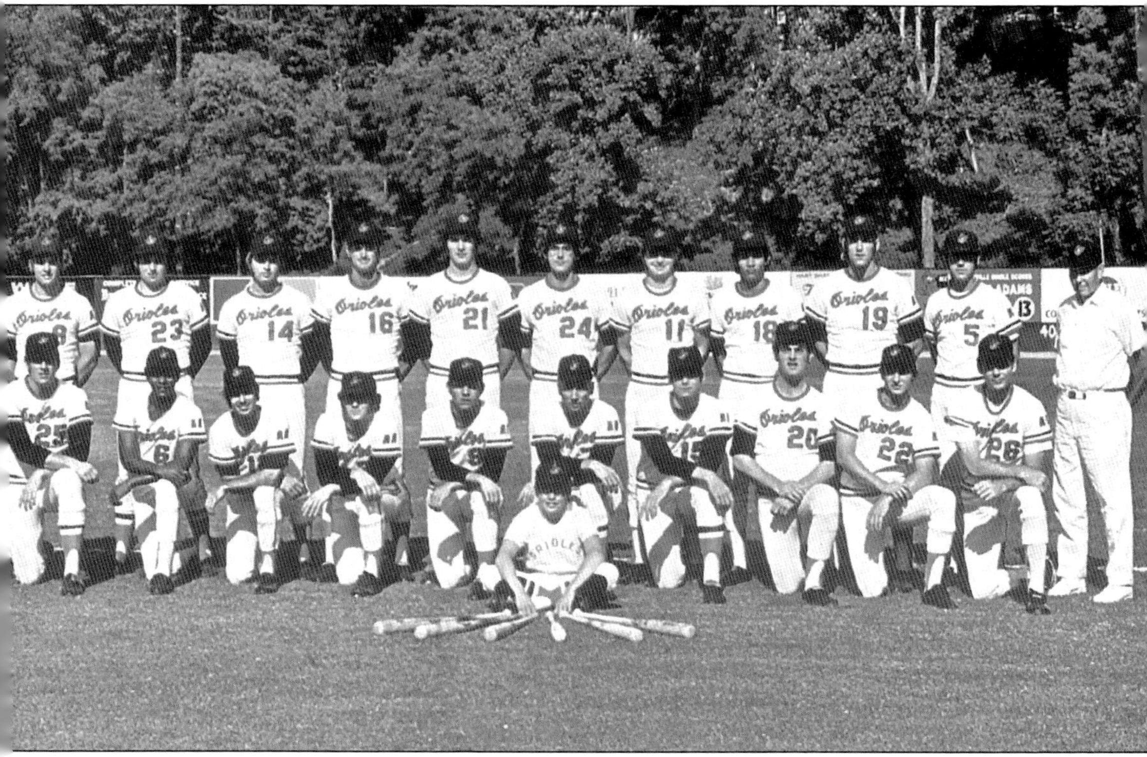

The Orioles came to town in 1972 and donned uniforms similar to those worn in the major leagues. Pictured from left to right are (front row) John Austin, Javier Andino, Rich Emard, Don Hickey, Rich Richardson, manager Cal Ripken, Paul Mitchell, Don Belluomini, Royle Stillman, and Donnie Collins; (back row) Bill Wood, Herb Hutson, Mark Weems, Doug DeCinces, Ed Blake, Dave Johnson, Mike Reinbach, Victor Agosto, Jim Fuller, Tim Nordbrook, and trainer Bill Cole. In front is batboy Larry McSwain. (Asheville Tourists photograph.)

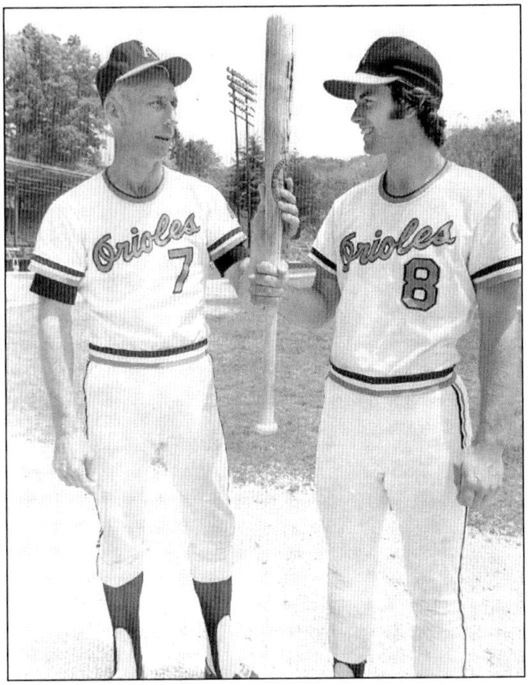

Cal Ripken Sr. managed the Asheville Orioles from 1972 to 1974, the first three of Baltimore's four-year working agreement with the city. Ripken guided Asheville to 222 victories, fifth on the franchise's managerial wins list. He served as a coach in Baltimore from 1976 to 1992 and managed the major league club for all of the 1987 campaign. Ripken is pictured with Bill Wood. (Asheville Tourists photograph.)

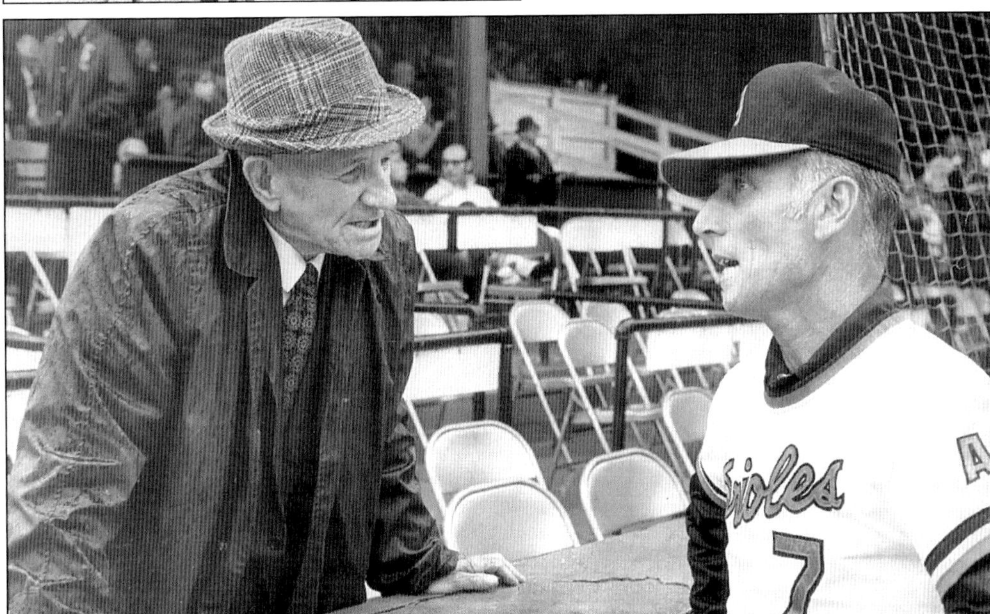

Charles "Struttin' Bud" Shaney chats with Cal Ripken prior to an Asheville game at McCormick Field. Known as one of the craftiest pitchers in history, Shaney twirled five of his 22 seasons in the minors with the Tourists, winning 85 games during that span and serving as the ace of the 1928 club. His biggest stunt occurred on September 5, 1954, 12 years after his final season as a player. A 53-year-old Shaney, who served as the McCormick Field groundskeeper at the time, threw five shutout innings before giving way to 38-year-old manager Ray Hathaway in a 4-0 win over the Smokies. That outing proved to be Shaney's final appearance in a professional game. (*Asheville Citizen-Times* photograph.)

Outfielder Al Bumbry was named the American League Rookie of the Year in 1973, one year after he played 26 games in Asheville. The Southern League provided little competition for the fleet-footed outfielder, who hit .347 with four home runs, 10 RBIs, and 10 stolen bases in 126 at-bats. (Asheville Tourists photograph.)

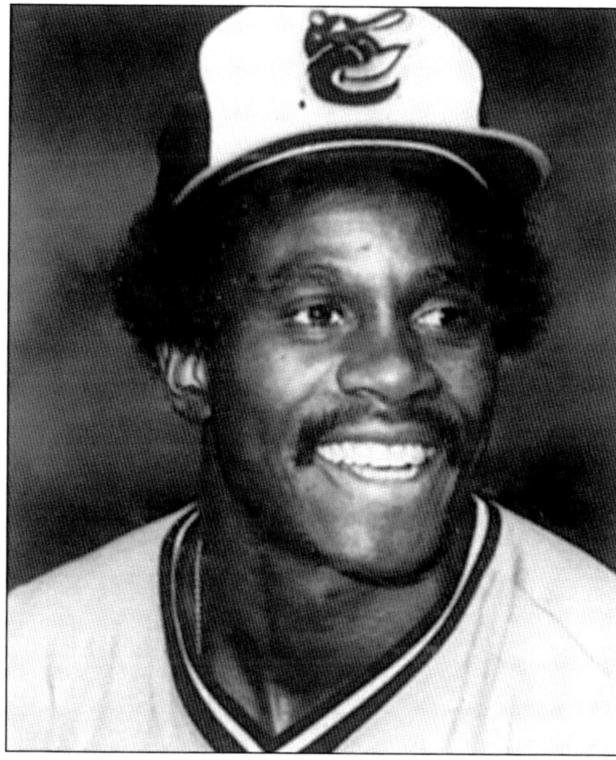

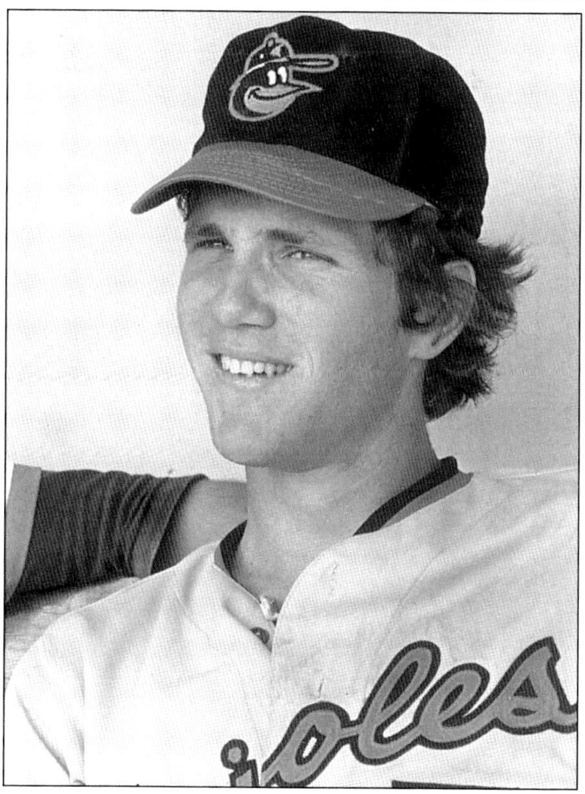

Second baseman Rob Andrews set the table for teammate Terry Clapp, who led the Southern League with 35 home runs and 98 RBIs during the 1973 season. Andrews paced the Double-A circuit with a .309 batting average, 167 hits, and 98 runs scored. Andrews played in the major leagues from 1975 to 1979 with the Astros and Giants. (Asheville Tourists photograph.)

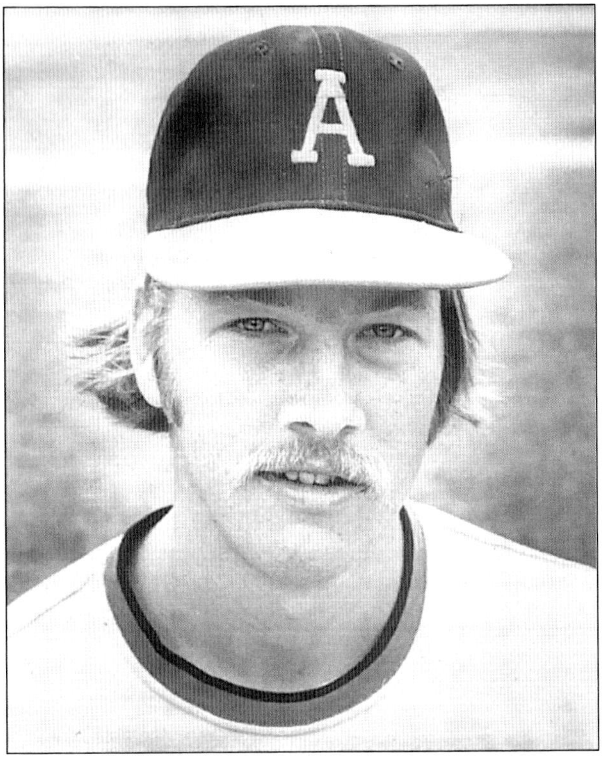

Dave Skaggs played all of the 1974 season and half of the 1975 campaign in Asheville. An excellent receiver, Skaggs led Southern League catchers in fielding and assists in 1974 while hitting .251 with five home runs and 38 RBIs. He batted .266 with 24 RBIs during his return trip to McCormick Field in 1975 before receiving a promotion to Class AAA Rochester. Skaggs played 205 games in the major leagues, mostly with Baltimore from 1977 to 1980. (Asheville Tourists photograph.)

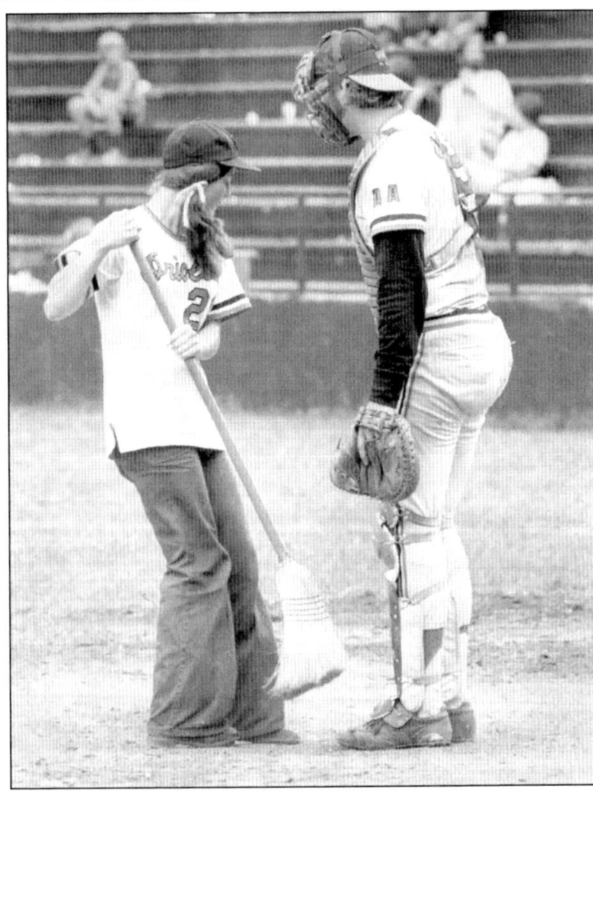

Ball girls were hired at McCormick Field during the 1970s. One Asheville employee sweeps home plate as well as the shoes of catcher Dave Skaggs in 1975. (Asheville Tourists photograph.)

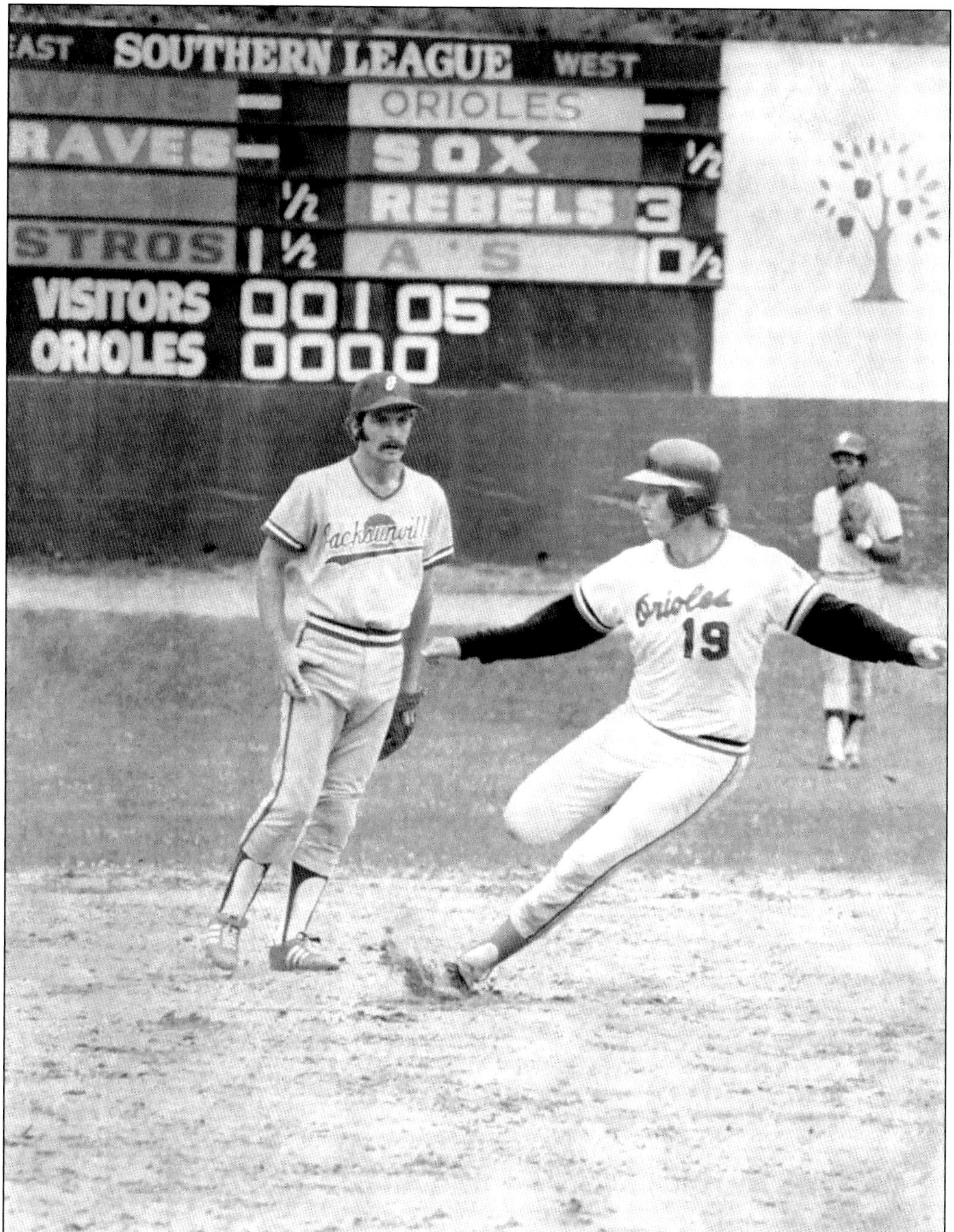

Dave Skaggs rounds second base during a game against Jacksonville in 1975. The background includes the old McCormick Field scoreboard, which featured the Southern League standings in both the East and West divisions. (Asheville Tourists photograph.)

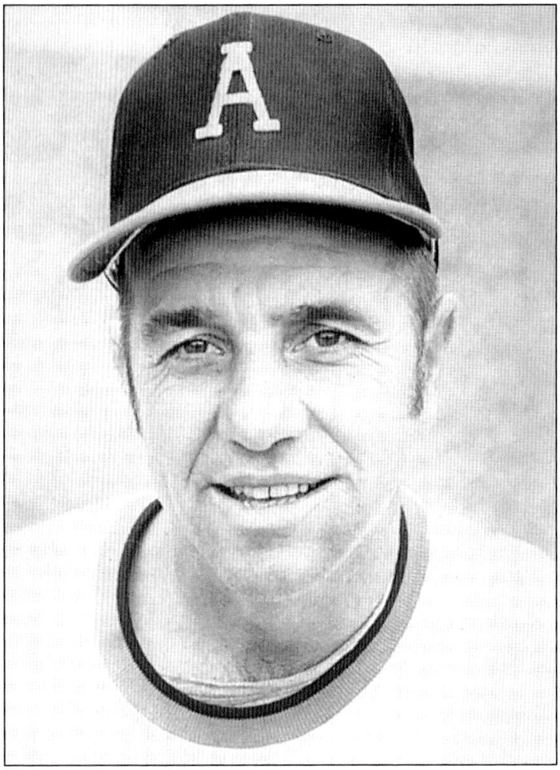

Jim Shaeffer's efforts in Asheville during the 1975 season benefited Baltimore for many years. Shaeffer helped teach Eddie Murray, a naturally right-handed batter, how to switch-hit during his days in Asheville. By the time Murray retired, the Hall of Famer earned the reputation as one of the most prolific switch-hitters in baseball history. (Asheville Tourists photograph.)

Jim Shaeffer is named manager of the Asheville Orioles for the 1975 campaign. Shaeffer's club featured modest talent, headlined by Southern League batting champ Chuck Heil and budding first baseman Eddie Murray. The Orioles finished in last place in the Southern Leagues's West Division with a 63-75 record in what proved to be Baltimore's final season in Asheville. (Asheville Tourists photograph.)

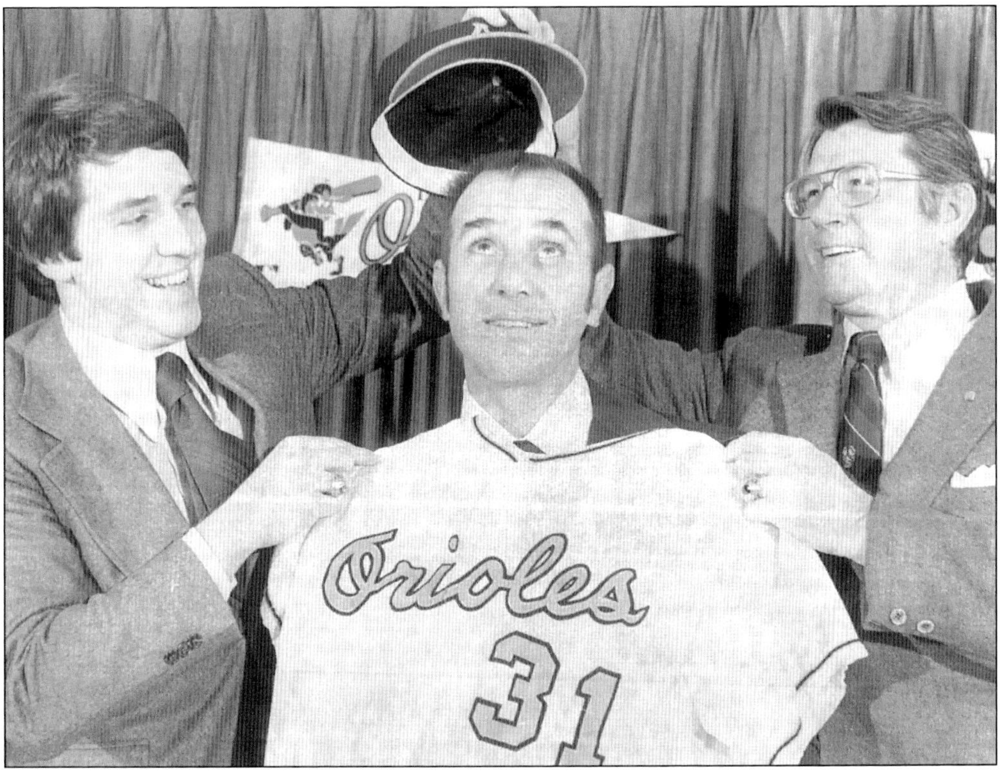

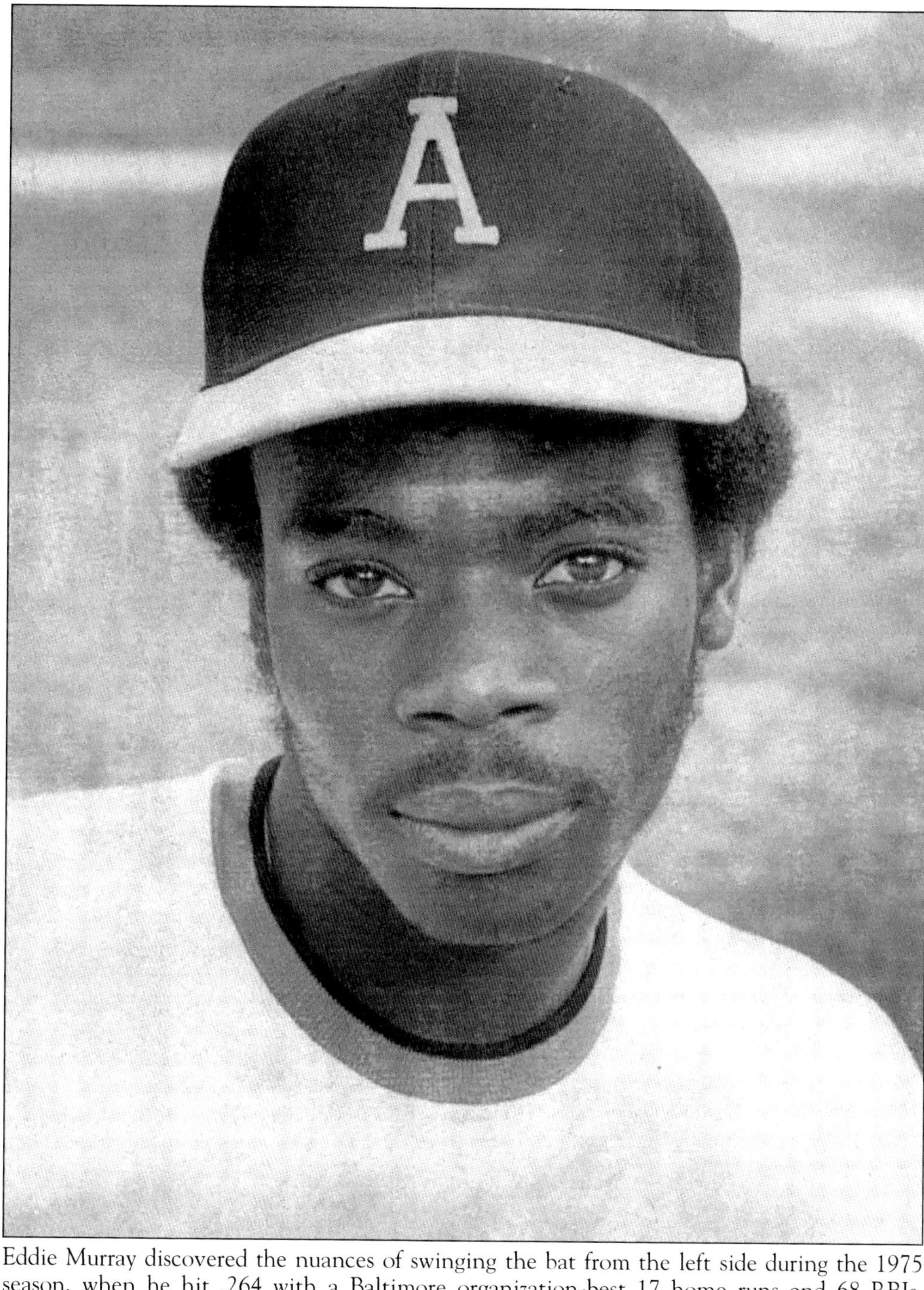

Eddie Murray discovered the nuances of swinging the bat from the left side during the 1975 season, when he hit .264 with a Baltimore organization-best 17 home runs and 68 RBIs. Murray was named the American League Rookie of the Year in 1977 and, in 2003, became the second former Asheville player to be inducted into the Baseball Hall of Fame. (*Asheville Citizen-Times* photograph.)

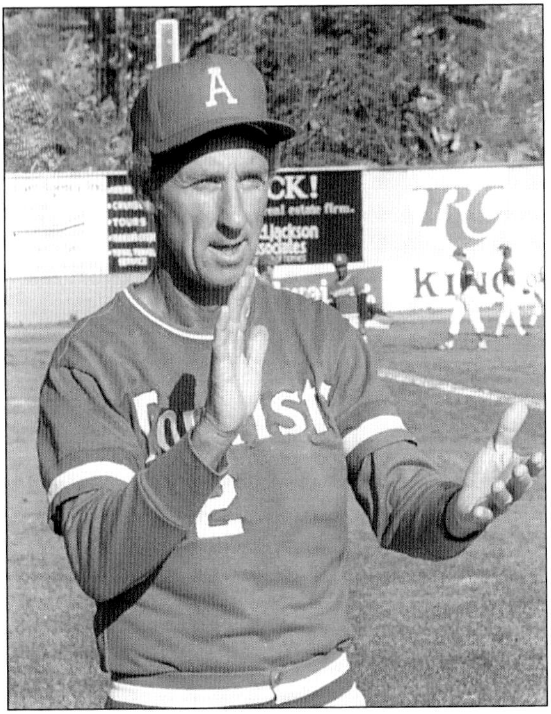

The Asheville team was known as the Tourists once again in 1976 when the franchise entered into a working agreement with the Texas Rangers. Wayne Terwilliger managed the Tourists for four straight seasons, from 1976 to 1979, and recorded 305 wins, the second-highest total in Asheville annals upon entering the 2004 season. (Asheville Tourists photograph.)

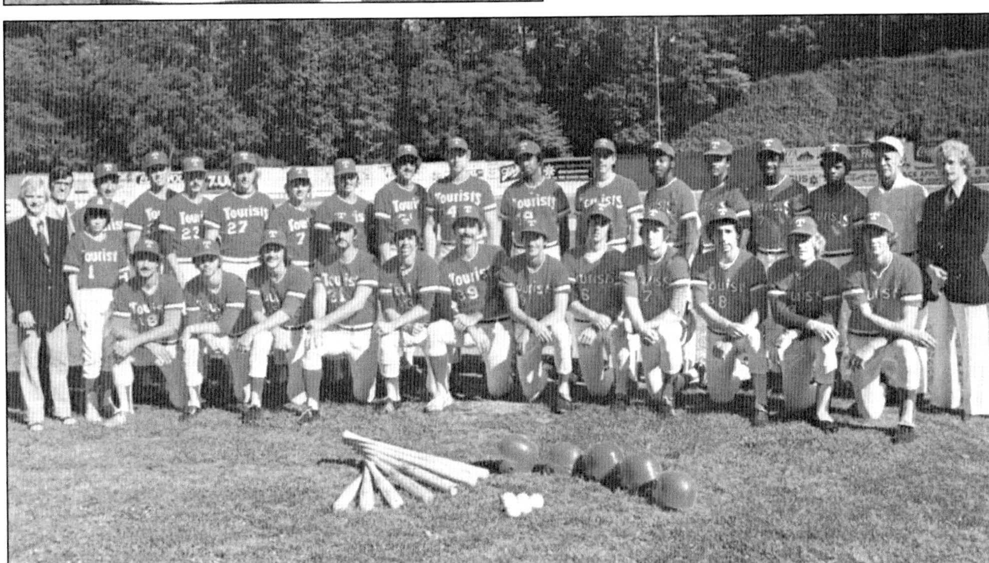

In the city's first year at the Class A level since 1967 as Houston's Carolina League affiliate, the 1976 Tourists placed first in the Western Carolinas League with a 76-62 record. From left to right are (front row) Randy Reynolds, Danny Tidwell, Dave McCarthy, Mike Arrington, Ward Smith, Mark Soroko, Wayne Pinkerton, Hal Kelly, Len Glowzenski, Paul Mirabella, Joe Russell, and Rick Lisi; (back row) operations director Jeff Johnson, general manager Merrill Eckstein, manager Wayne Terwilliger, coach Jeff Scott, Pat Moock, Bob Carroll, Bill Stone, Mark Miller, Glen Purvis, Pat Putnam, Larue Washington, Dave Rivera, Joe Stewart, Jerry Gaines, Eddie Miller, Richard Couch, trainer Paul Raibon, and public relations director Michael Lindner. (National Baseball Hall of Fame Library, Cooperstown, New York.)

Pat Putnam set the Tourists' franchise and South Atlantic League records with 194 hits, 142 RBIs, 305 total bases, and 15 intentional walks in 1976. That effort, along with 24 home runs, 100 runs scored, 33 doubles, and a South Atlantic League-leading .361 batting average, earned Putnam the *Sporting News*'s Minor League Player of the Year award, the lone Asheville player to receive a national honor. Said Putnam, who was elected to the South Atlantic League Hall of Fame in 1996, "I remember that in Asheville we had running spring water in the dugout and I mean it was good water. I also really enjoyed getting up early in the morning and going fishing at Bea Tree Lake, before going to the ballpark." (Author's collection.)

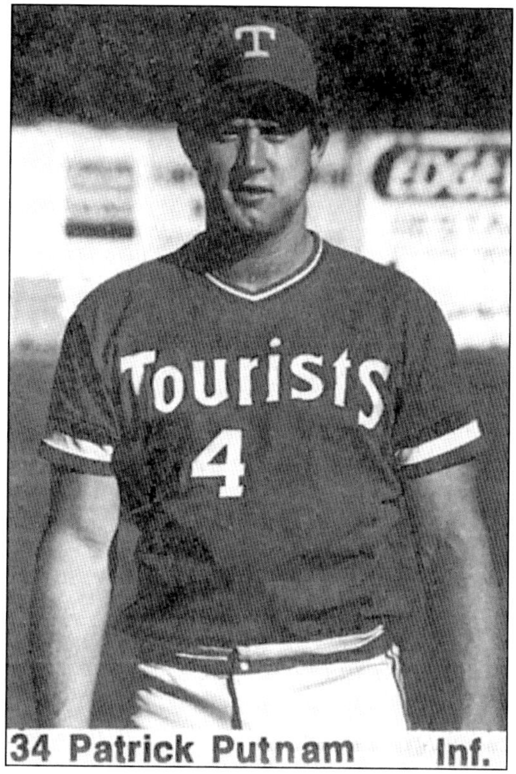

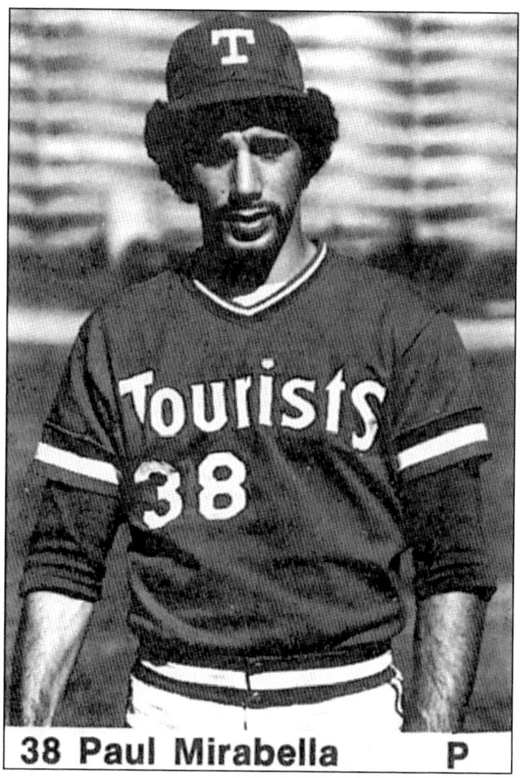

Pitcher Paul Mirabella tied for second as a member of the Tourists with 10 wins; he also posted a 3.99 ERA in 22 starts in 1976. Mirabella pitched 13 seasons in the major leagues, from 1978 to 1990. (Author's collection.)

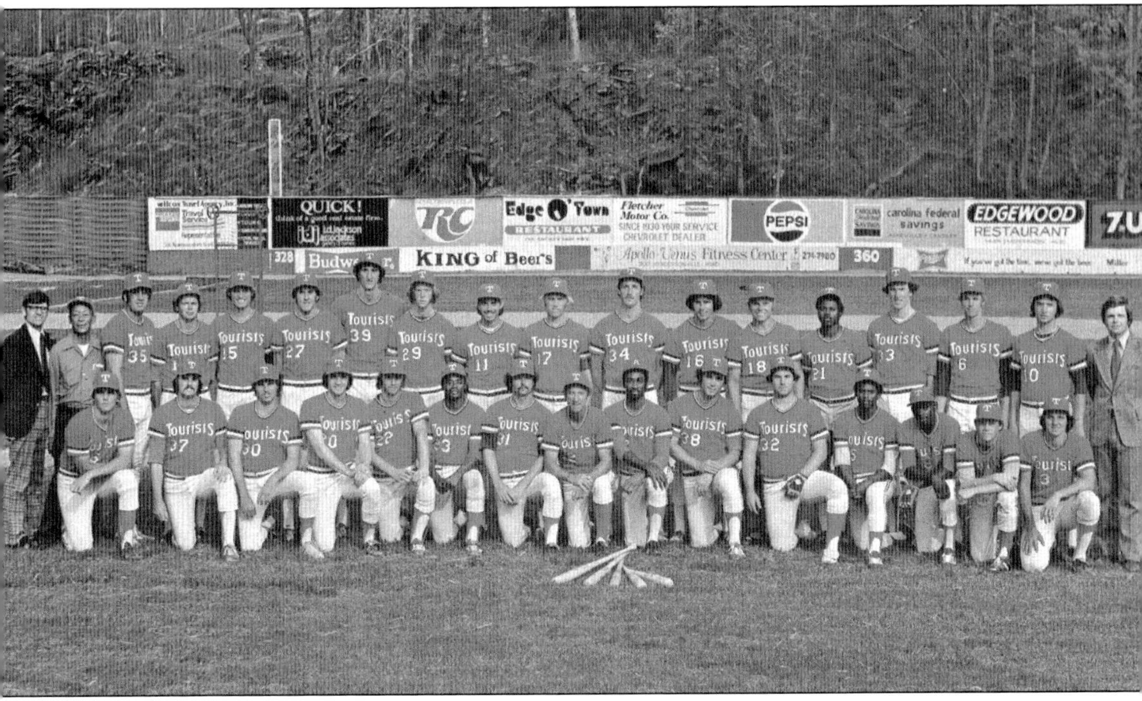

The 1977 Asheville Tourists finished in second place, one game behind the Gastonia Cardinals, by posting an 81-59 record during the 1977 Western Carolinas League campaign. Pictured in this giant postcard given out at McCormick Field are (front row) Coach Jeff Scott, Mike Hicks, Stan Jakubowski, Dave McCarthy, Vic Mabee, Jerry Gaines, Phil Watson, manager Wayne Terwilliger, Greg Jemison, Glenn Williams, Dennis Doyle, Richard Couch, Al Thompson, Len Whitehouse, and Jahn Takacs; (back row) General Manager Merrill Eckstein, trainer Paul Ralbon, Joe Zagarino, Mike Jaccar, Steve Bianchi, Phil Roddy, Kerry Keenan, Steve Finch, Dave Rivera, Wayne Wilkerson, Mike Williamson, Bill Simpson, Scott Peterson, Arnold McCrary, Mike Griffin, Bryan Allard, Ron Patrick, and public relations director Jerry Waselik. (National Baseball Hall of Fame Library, Cooperstown, New York.)

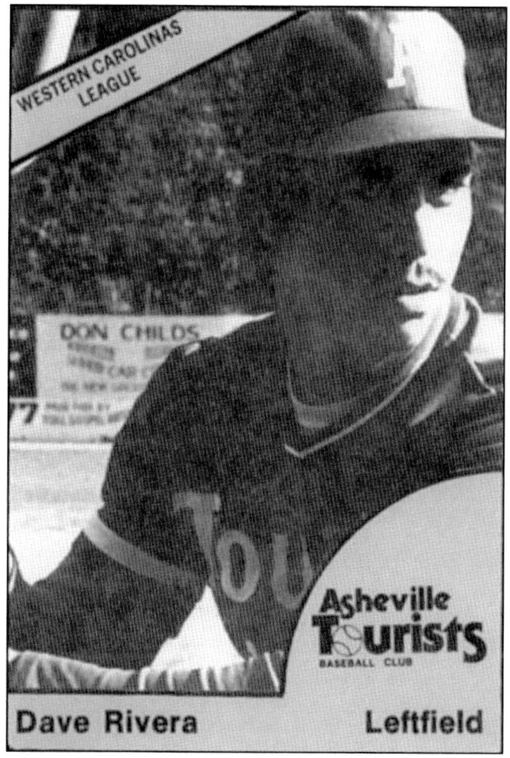

Left fielder David Rivera won the Triple Crown in the Western Carolinas League in 1977 by leading the loop with a .346 batting average, 26 home runs, and 118 RBIs. Rivera, who batted .199 with three homers and 19 RBIs during a short stint with Asheville in 1976, also topped the Class A circuit with 176 hits. (Author's collection.)

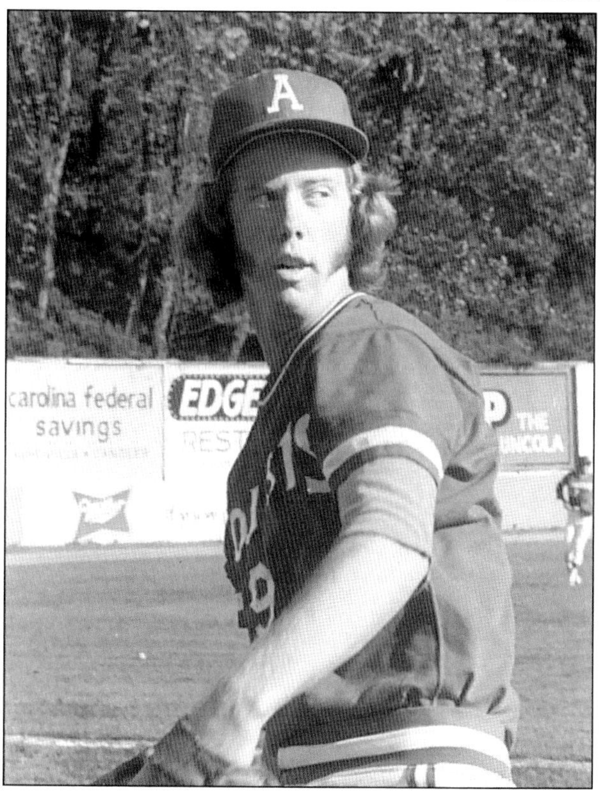

Right-hander Steve Finch ranked fourth in the Western Carolinas League with a 2.92 ERA during the 1977 season. Finch posted a 15-5 record with 13 complete games and 193 strikeouts in 191 innings. (Asheville Tourists photograph.)

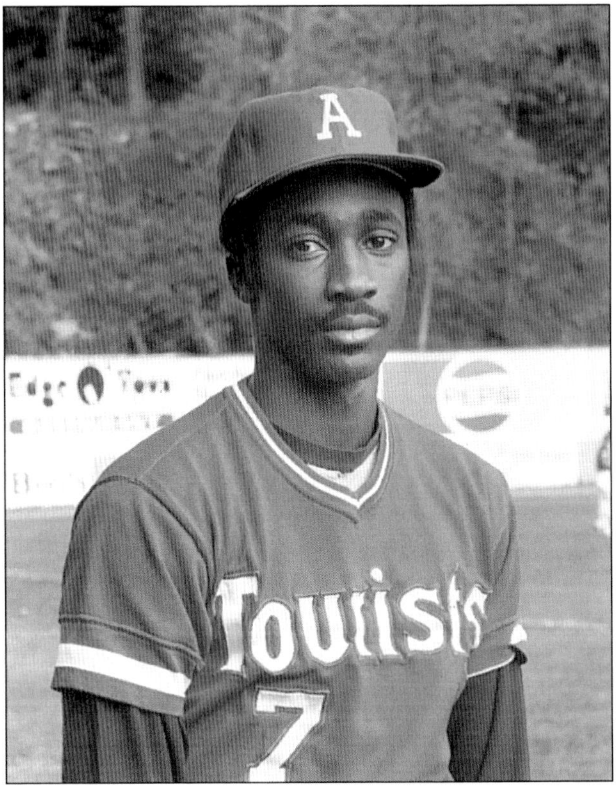

Outfielder Greg Jemison led the Western Carolinas League with 125 runs scored and an Asheville franchise-record 82 stolen bases during the 1977 season. Jemison also ranked third in the league with a .307 batting average and walked 118 times. (Asheville Tourists photograph.)

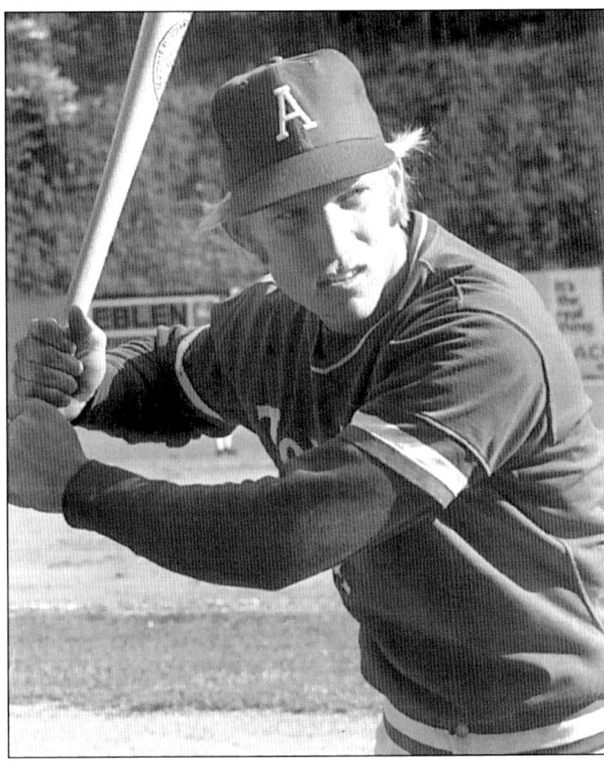

Third baseman Wayne Wilkerson placed fourth in the Western Carolinas League batting race in 1977 with a .304 average. Wilkerson also ranked second on the team with 105 RBIs while crushing 15 home runs. (Asheville Tourists photograph.)

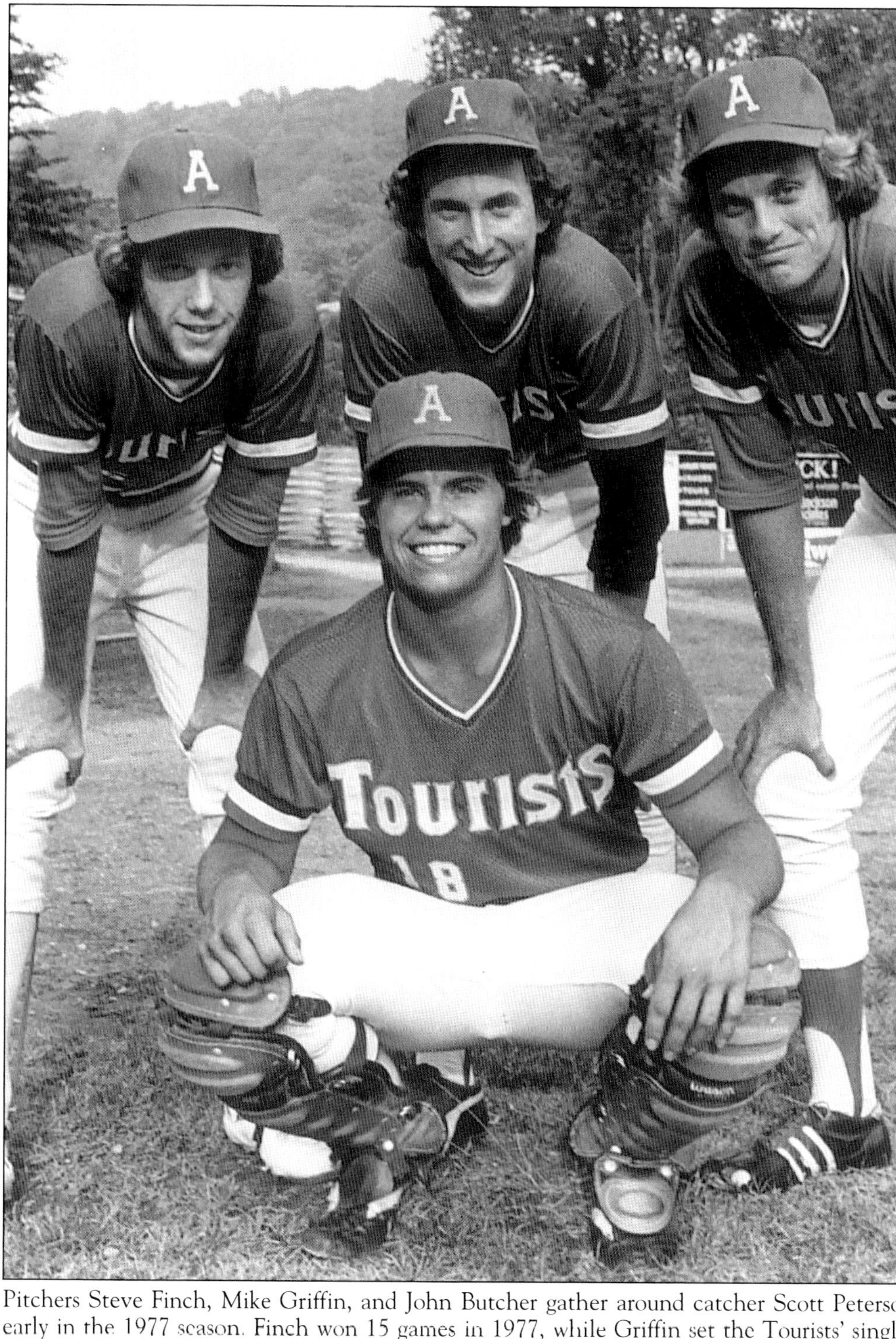

Pitchers Steve Finch, Mike Griffin, and John Butcher gather around catcher Scott Peterson early in the 1977 season. Finch won 15 games in 1977, while Griffin set the Tourists' single-season record with 201 strikeouts during his 17-win campaign. Butcher pitched in two games with Asheville in 1977 before going 10-9 with the Tourists a year later. Peterson contributed five home runs and 41 RBIs during the 1977 campaign. (*Asheville Citizen-Times* photograph.)

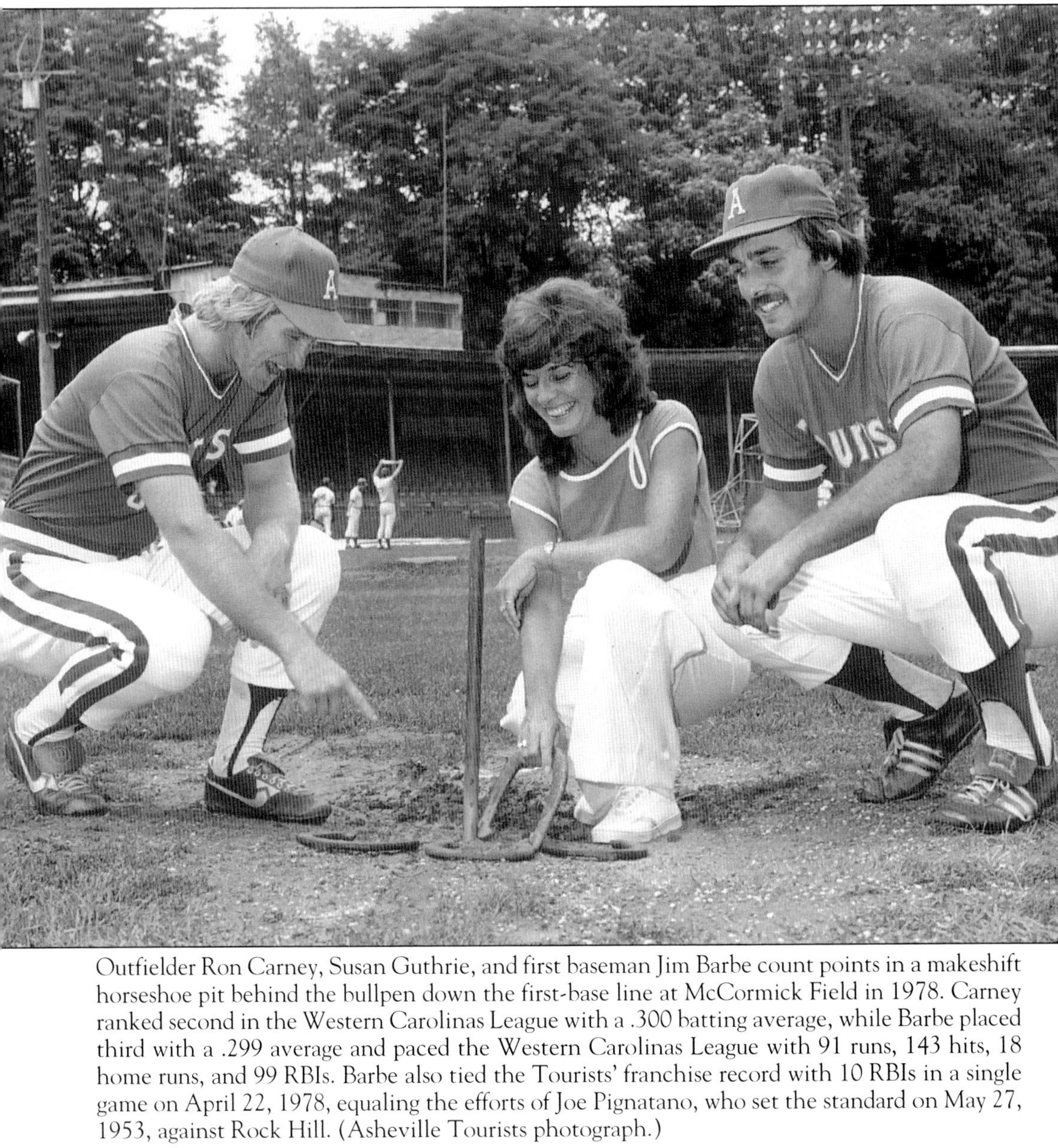

Outfielder Ron Carney, Susan Guthrie, and first baseman Jim Barbe count points in a makeshift horseshoe pit behind the bullpen down the first-base line at McCormick Field in 1978. Carney ranked second in the Western Carolinas League with a .300 batting average, while Barbe placed third with a .299 average and paced the Western Carolinas League with 91 runs, 143 hits, 18 home runs, and 99 RBIs. Barbe also tied the Tourists' franchise record with 10 RBIs in a single game on April 22, 1978, equaling the efforts of Joe Pignatano, who set the standard on May 27, 1953, against Rock Hill. (Asheville Tourists photograph.)

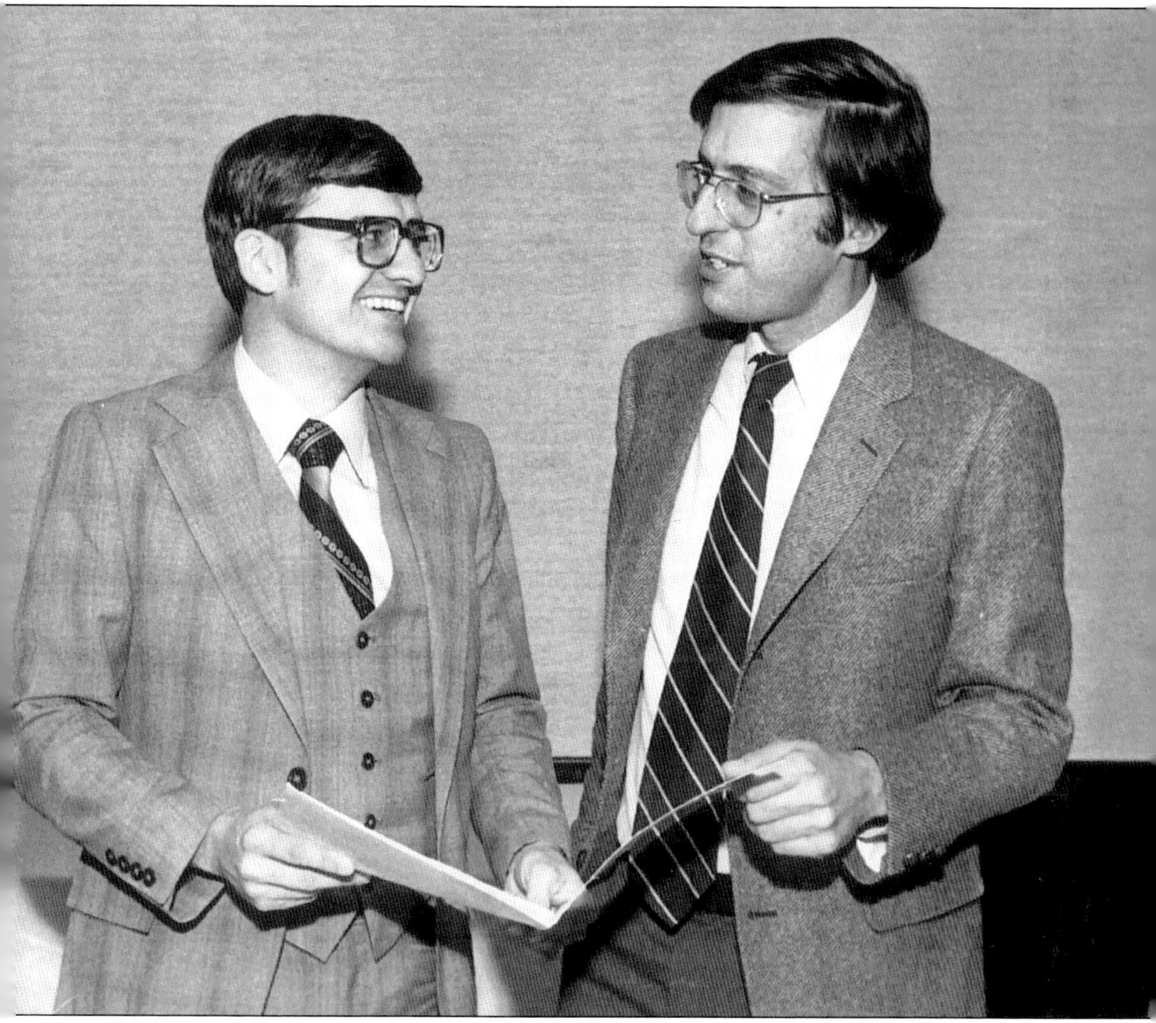

Merrill Eckstein (left) owned and operated the Tourists from 1975 to 1979. Eckstein hired Ron McKee as the team's general manager in 1980, and current owner Woody Kern purchased the club in 1981. Eckstein is pictured with partner Miles Wolff, who owned *Baseball America* magazine and the Durham Bulls in the 1980s and 1990s before becoming the founder and president of the independent Northern League in the mid-1990s. (*Asheville Citizen-Times* photograph.)

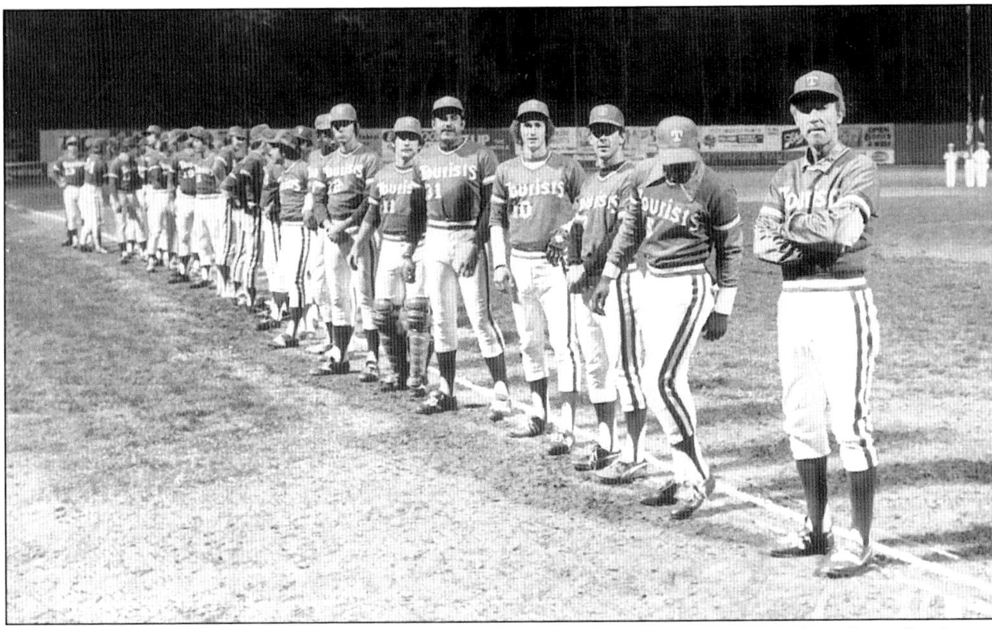

Headed by manager Wayne Terwilliger (far right), the Tourists are introduced at the home opener of the 1979 season at McCormick Field. Asheville finished the season in second place in the Western Carolinas League with a 75-63 record, three games behind the first-place Greenwood Braves. (*Asheville Citizen-Times* photograph.)

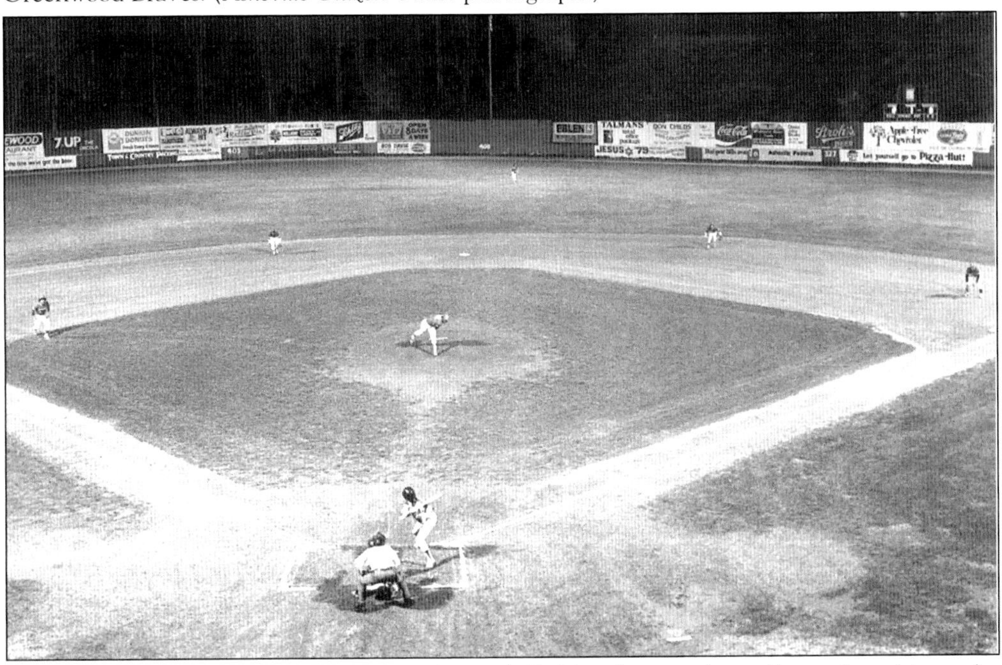

The first pitch of the 1979 season at McCormick Field is thrown. A small scoreboard is on the right-field wall, topped with a clock that had supposedly graced the scoreboard of Brooklyn's Ebbets Field in the 1940s. That story proved to be false, for several minor league towns throughout North Carolina had bought similar clocks from an uncouth traveling salesman. (*Asheville Citizen-Times* photograph.)

FOUR

A New Sheriff for the Tourists

Baseball in Asheville mirrored most of the minor leagues during the late 1970s. Franchises were struggling to survive, and attendance at games could be counted on fingers and toes. Located among the partial sellouts at McCormick Field were several rowdy fans that did little to increase the ambience among the paying customers.

That scenario changed in 1980 when Ron McKee became general manager of the Tourists. A former batboy for the club in the early 1960s, McKee disposed of the rowdies and instituted a more fan-friendly environment. With the help of his wife and team business manager Carolyn McKee, he also brought in special attractions, held giveaway nights, and created such innovative promotions as "Thirsty Thursday" and "Shirt Off Your Back Night." Attendance increased to 49,066 fans in McKee's first year; by 1986, the Tourists attracted more than 100,000 patrons for the first time since 1959, signaling the rebirth of the game throughout Western North Carolina.

"All I try to do is treat people the best that I can," said McKee shortly after taking the job in 1980. "When they enter the ballpark, they are entering my living room. I want only the best for the fans. It's like they are in my house."

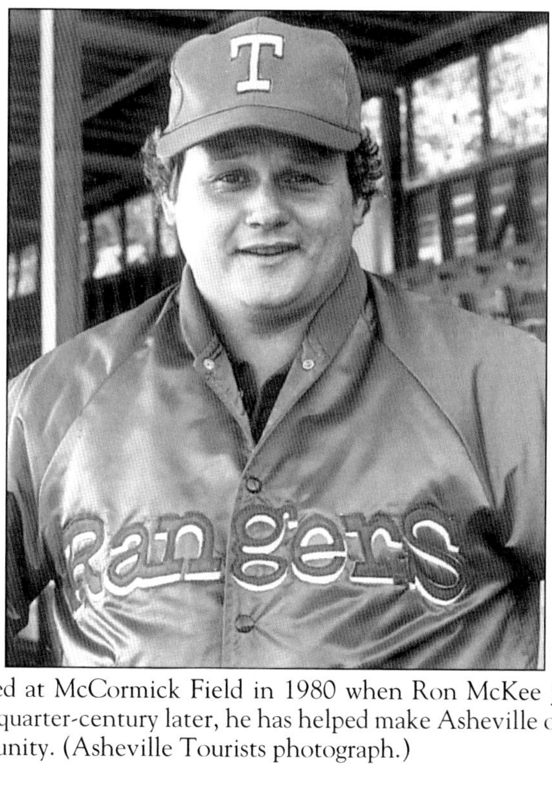

A new sheriff arrived at McCormick Field in 1980 when Ron McKee joined the Tourists as general manager. A quarter-century later, he has helped make Asheville one of the pillars of the minor league community. (Asheville Tourists photograph.)

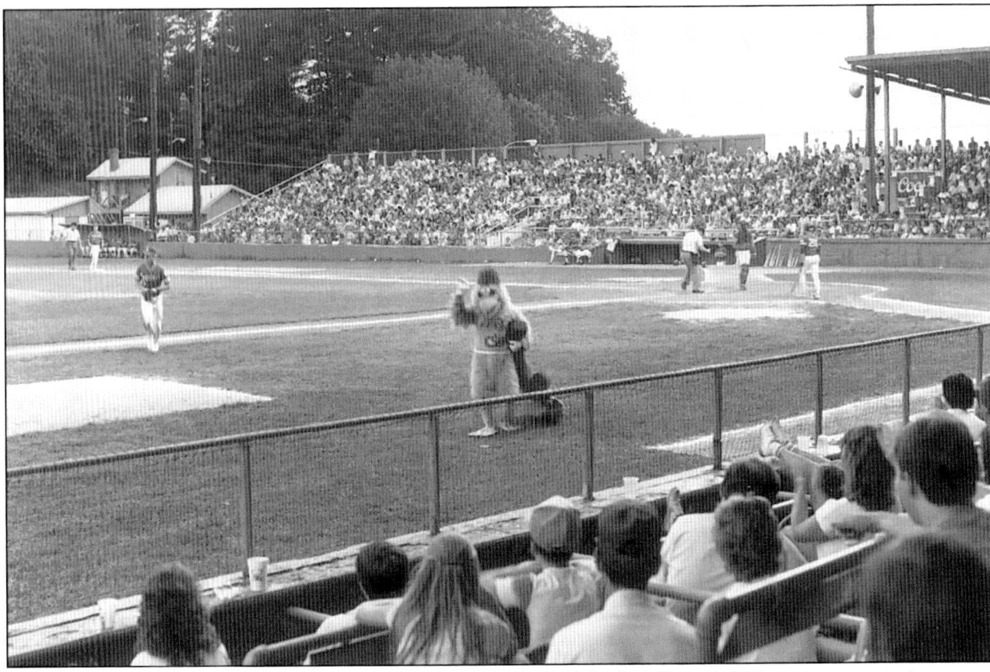

Promotions became commonplace at McCormick Field after Ron McKee was named general manager in 1980. One of the most popular attractions during the 1980s was The Famous Chicken, who performed at Tourists games in front of sellout crowds. (Bob Terrell collection.)

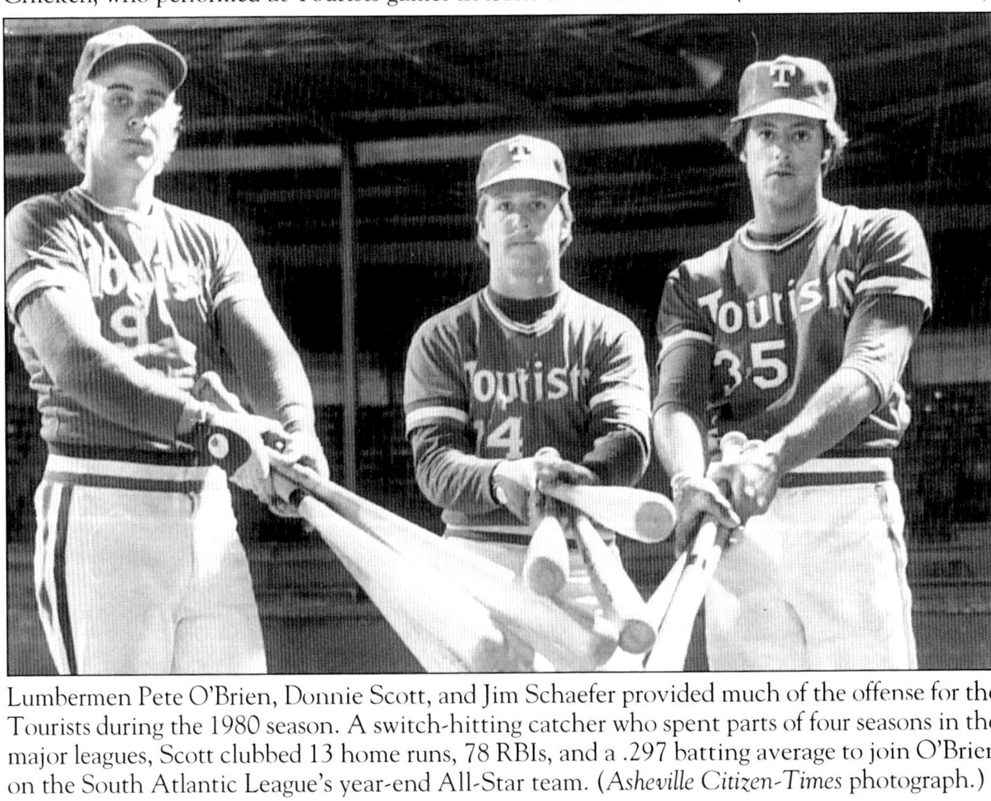

Lumbermen Pete O'Brien, Donnie Scott, and Jim Schaefer provided much of the offense for the Tourists during the 1980 season. A switch-hitting catcher who spent parts of four seasons in the major leagues, Scott clubbed 13 home runs, 78 RBIs, and a .297 batting average to join O'Brien on the South Atlantic League's year-end All-Star team. (*Asheville Citizen-Times* photograph.)

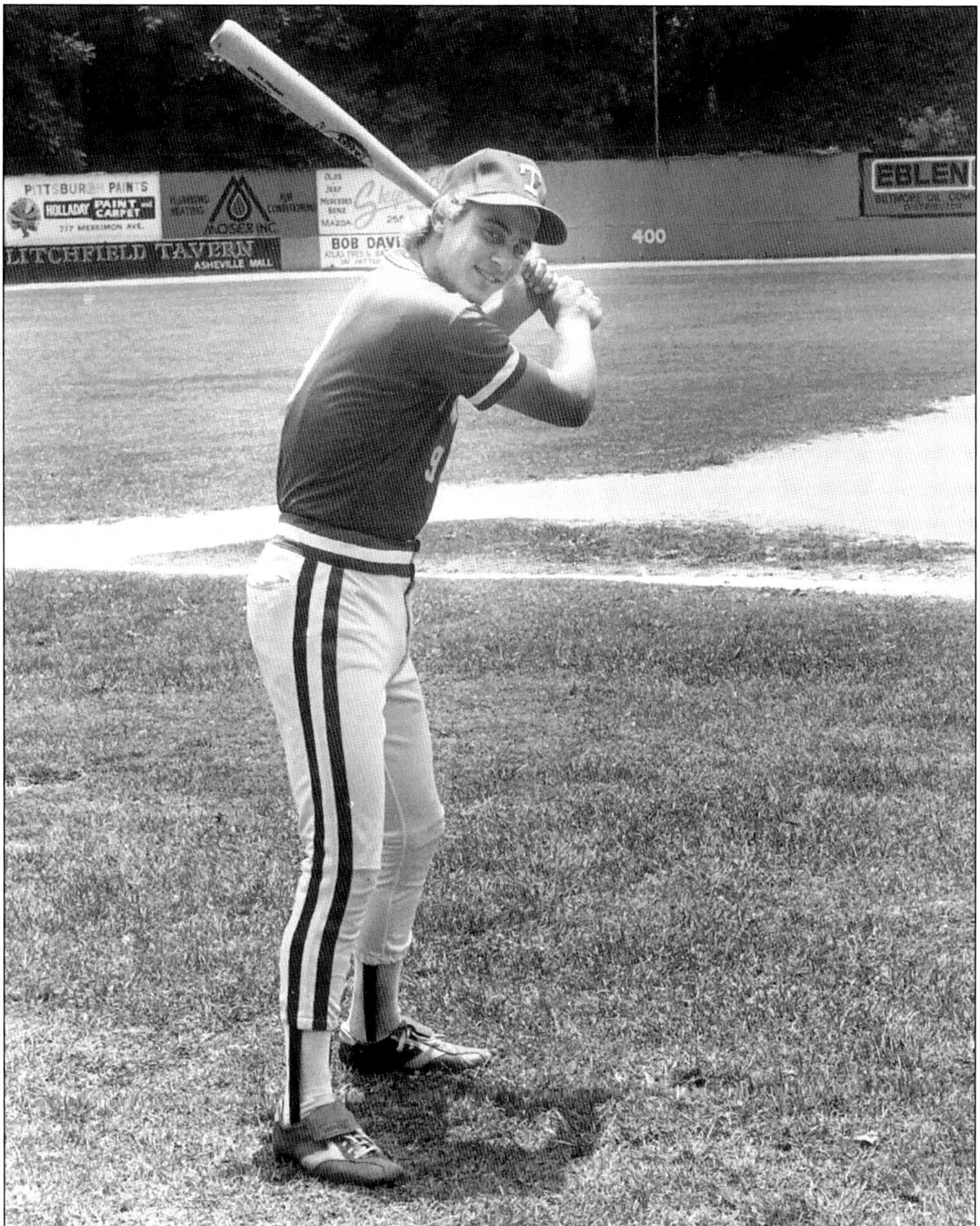

Pete O'Brien was named to the Topps Class A All-Star team in 1980 after he batted .295 with 34 doubles, 17 home runs, and 94 RBIs and led South Atlantic League first basemen in putouts and assists. O'Brien played 11 seasons in the major leagues with Texas, Cleveland, and Seattle. (Asheville Tourists photograph.)

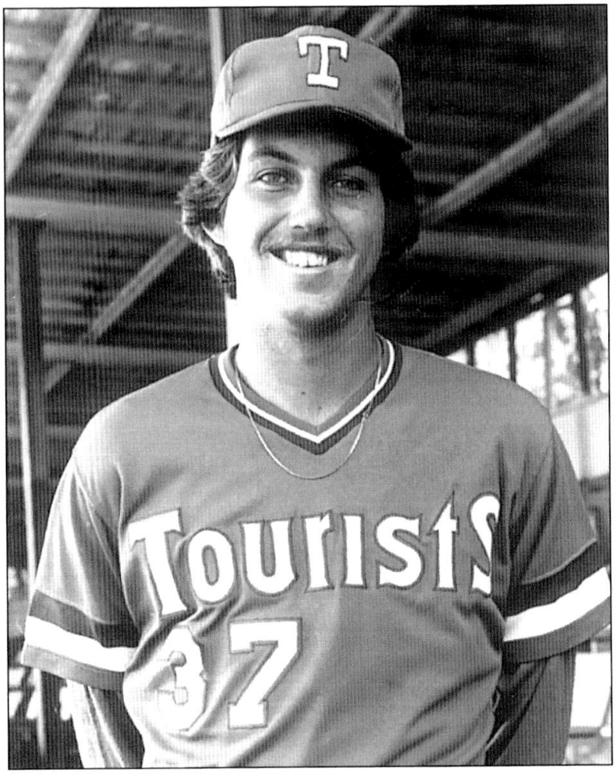

Six-foot-eight left-hander Billy Taylor spent parts of his first two professional seasons with Asheville, going 0-2 in six games with the Tourists in 1980 and 1-7 with a 4.64 ERA in 11 starts and one relief appearance in 1981. After 14 years in the minors, covering 11 cities, 467 games, and 1,314 innings, 32-year-old Taylor was the major leagues' oldest rookie when he reached the game's top level in 1994. (Asheville Tourists photograph.)

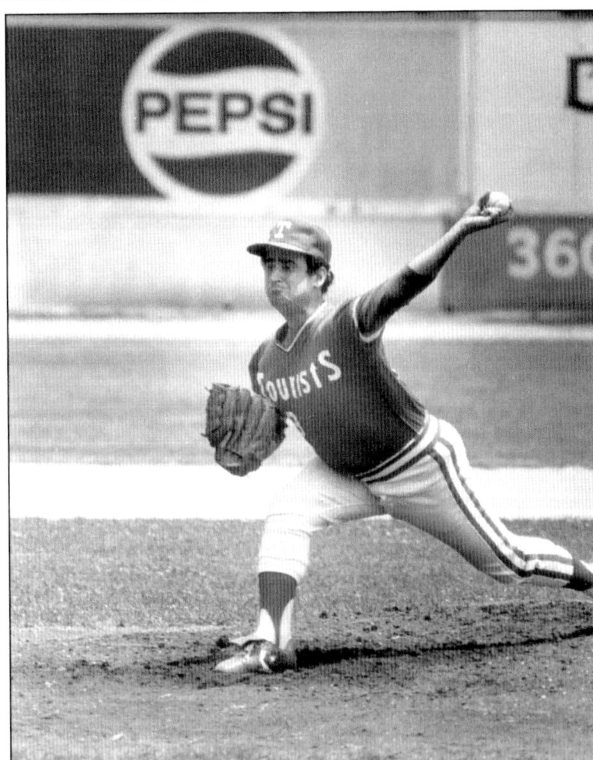

Cuban-born Tony Fossas went 12-8 with a 3.15 ERA and eight complete games for the Tourists in 1980. The left-hander led the South Atlantic League with 197 innings pitched and tied for the league lead with 27 starts. Fossas pitched five seasons in the major leagues, appearing in 212 games from 1988 to 1992. (Asheville Tourists photograph.)

Tom Robson managed the Tourists to 143 wins during the 1980 and 1981 seasons. Asheville finished in second place in the South Atlantic League's Northern Division with a 74-68 record in 1981. (Asheville Tourists photograph.)

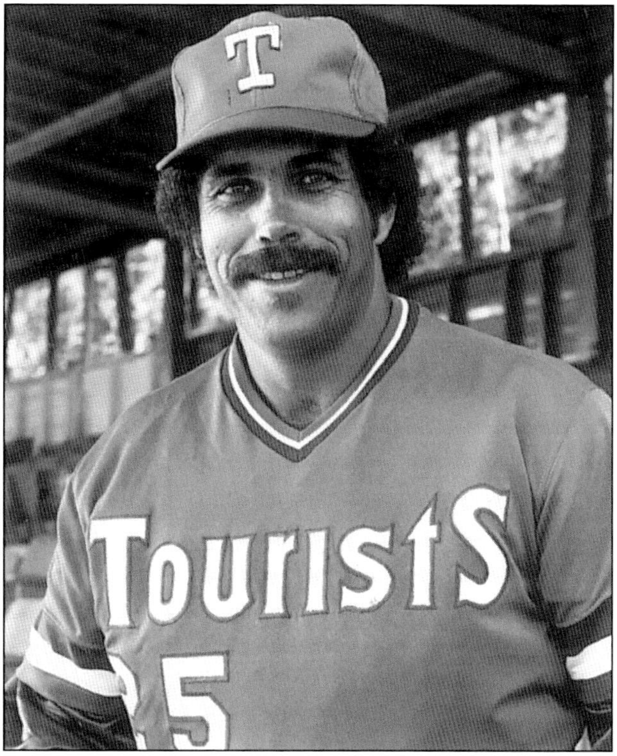

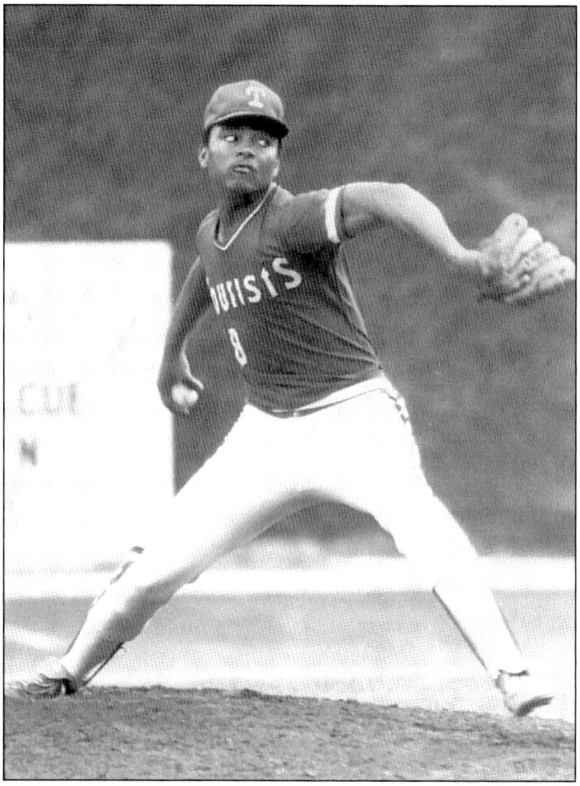

Dwayne Henry pitched parts of 11 seasons in the major leagues despite undergoing Tommy John surgery in 1982. The surgery was in its infancy in the early 1980s, involving the removal of a tendon from the pitcher's non-throwing wrist and forearm that is used to reconstruct a ruptured ligament in the throwing elbow. The right-hander's elbow started to hurt in 1981 at Asheville while posting an 8-7 record with a 4.43 ERA in 25 starts. (*Asheville Citizen-Times* photograph.)

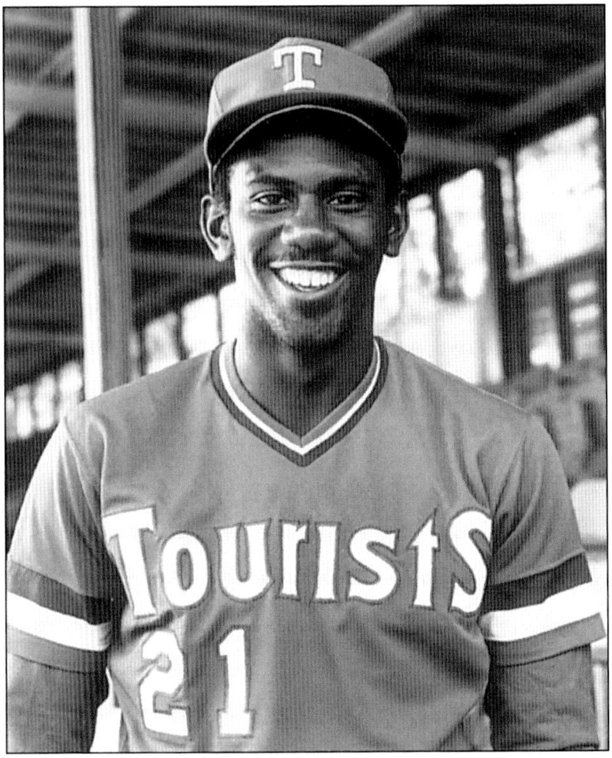

Right-hander Daryl Smith tied with Greensboro's Kelly Scott for the South Atlantic League lead with 16 wins during the 1981 season. Smith also posted a 2.76 ERA and a .762 winning percentage. (Asheville Tourists photograph.)

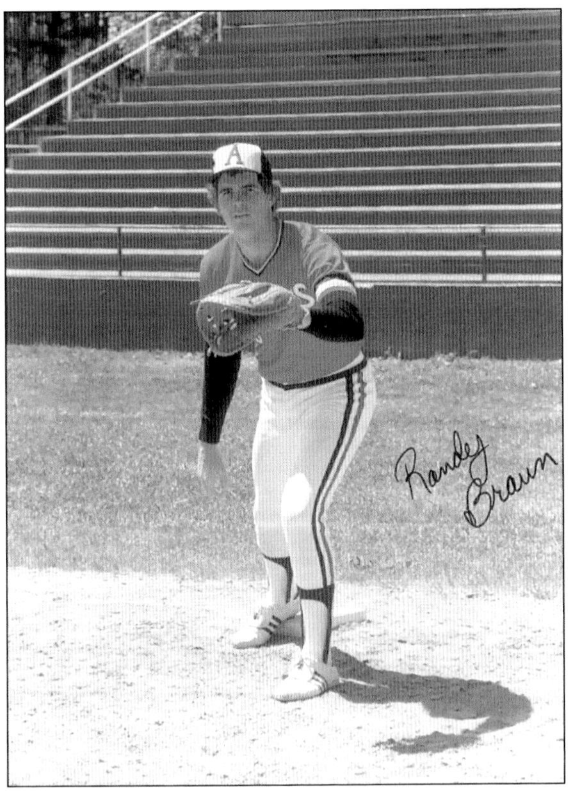

Asheville switched major league organizations prior to the 1982 season, changing from the South Atlantic League affiliate of the Texas Rangers to the Houston Astros. First baseman/designated hitter Randy Braun provided many of the thrills during the 1982 campaign by leading the South Atlantic League with 23 home runs. (Asheville Tourists photograph.)

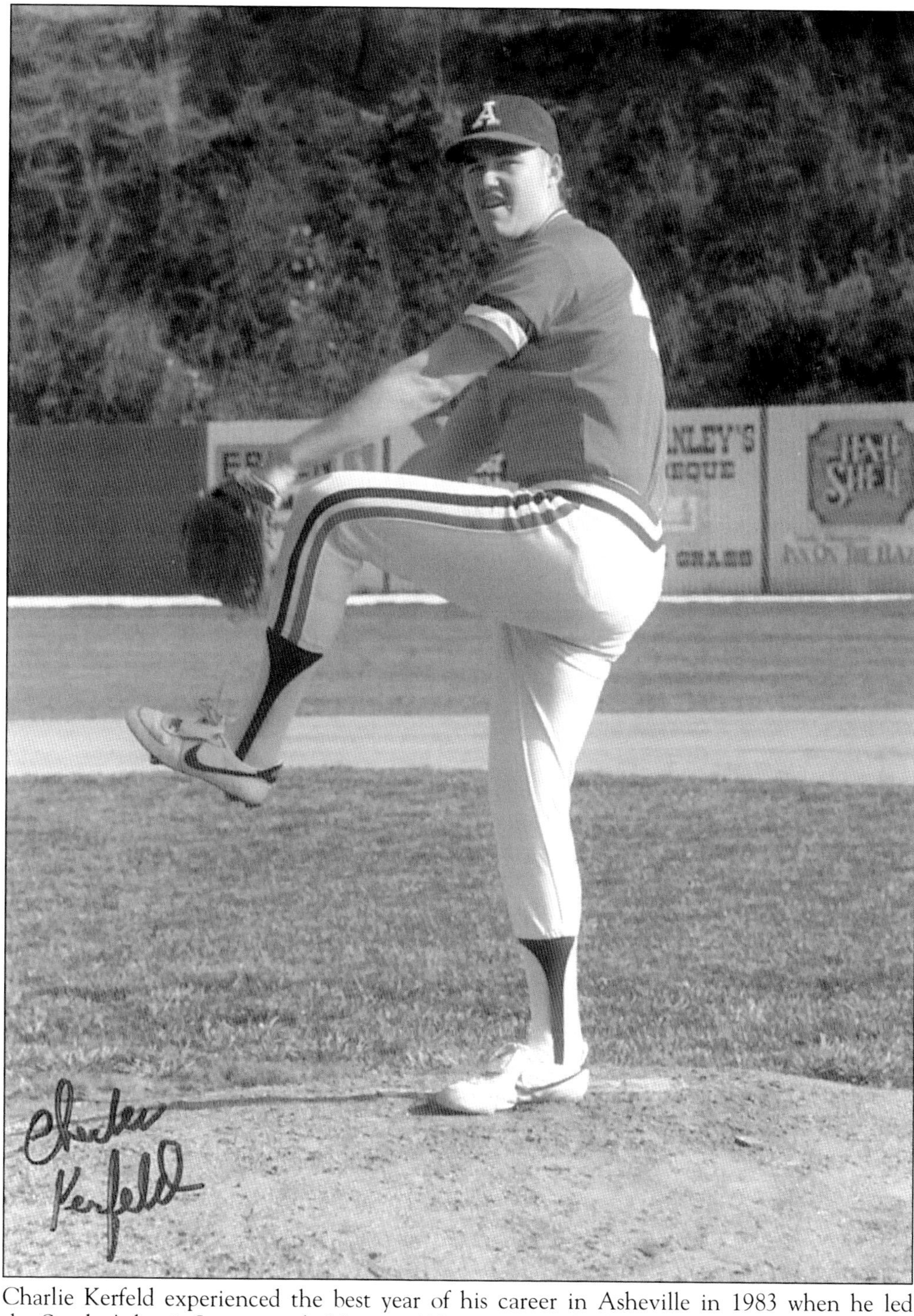

Charlie Kerfeld experienced the best year of his career in Asheville in 1983 when he led the South Atlantic League with 16 wins, 192 innings pitched, and 12 complete games while ranking second with 189 strikeouts. The right-hander, who earned South Atlantic League All-Star honors, reached the major leagues for his first of four years as a reliever in 1985. (Asheville Tourists photograph.)

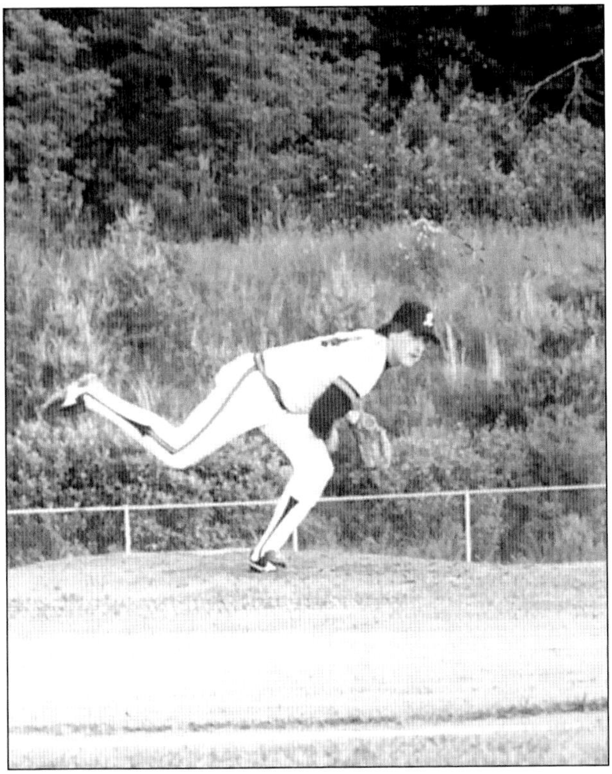

Right-hander Darren Holmes guided T.C. Roberson High School to the state title in 1983, a year before he was drafted in the 16th round by the Los Angeles Dodgers. Holmes spent 13 seasons in the major leagues through the 2003 slate, going 35-33 with a 4.25 ERA and 59 saves. The Fletcher, North Carolina, resident also pitched three games for the Tourists on a rehabilitation assignment in 1994 while with the Colorado Rockies. (Tom Smith collection.)

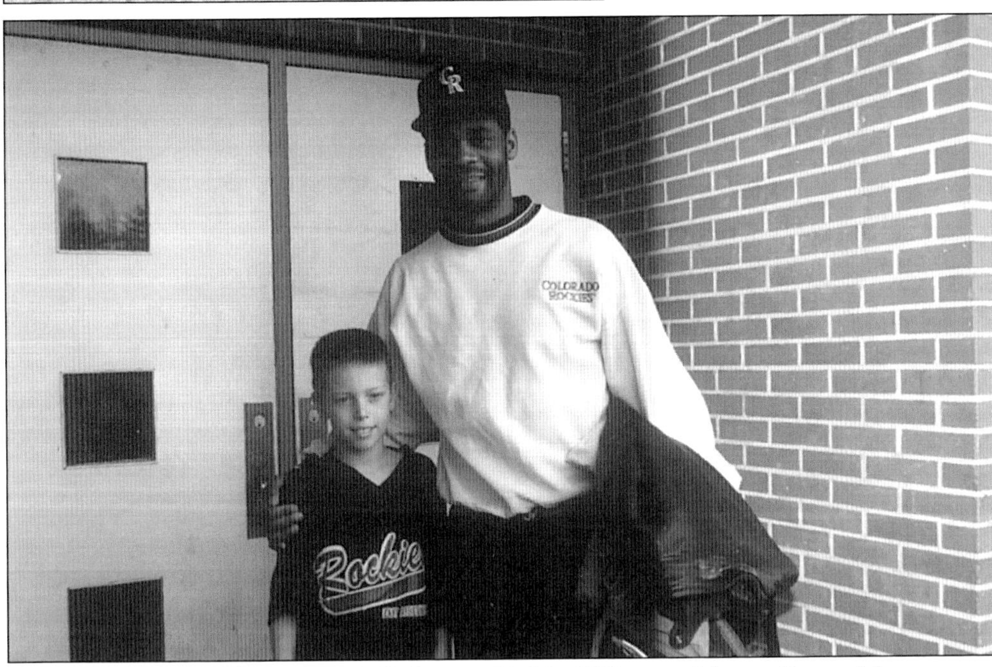

Another major contributor to T.C. Roberson High's 1983 state title was Danny Montgomery, who signed as a shortstop with the Los Angeles Dodgers' organization after graduating from high school. Montgomery is currently a national cross checker for the Colorado Rockies. (Tom Smith collection.)

The University of North Carolina-Asheville started its baseball program at the Division I level in the mid-1980s. The Bulldogs graduated their first player to the major leagues when third baseman Ty Wigginton earned a starting job with the New York Mets in 2002. (UNC-Asheville photograph.)

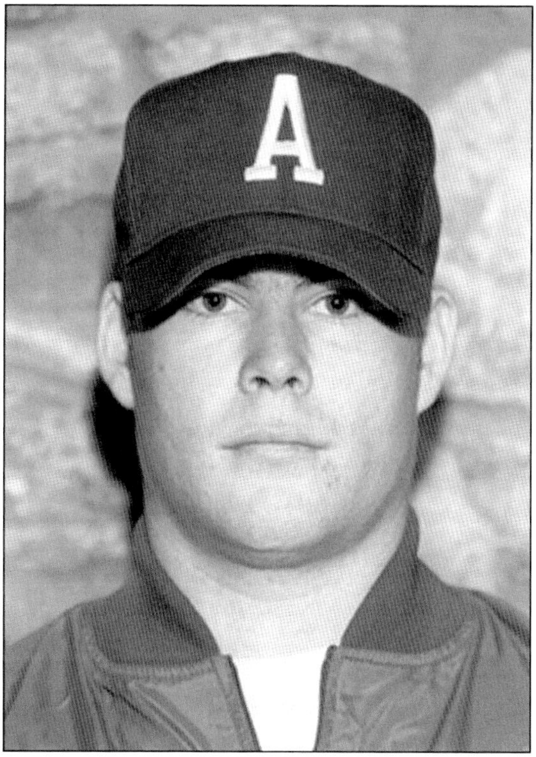

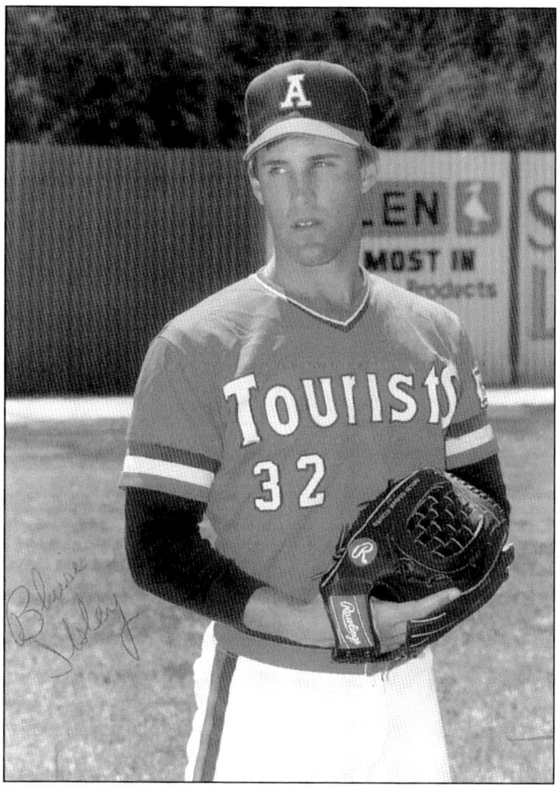

Blaise Ilsley was the only pitcher in the minors to win 20 games in 1986. The left-hander split the campaign between Asheville and Osceola, going 12-2 with a 1.95 ERA in 15 games with the Tourists. The South Atlantic League's pitcher of the year, Ilsley's nine complete games and three shutouts led the circuit even though he was promoted to the Florida State League at midseason. Ilsley pitched 68 games in relief for Chicago Cubs in 1994. (Asheville Tourists photograph.)

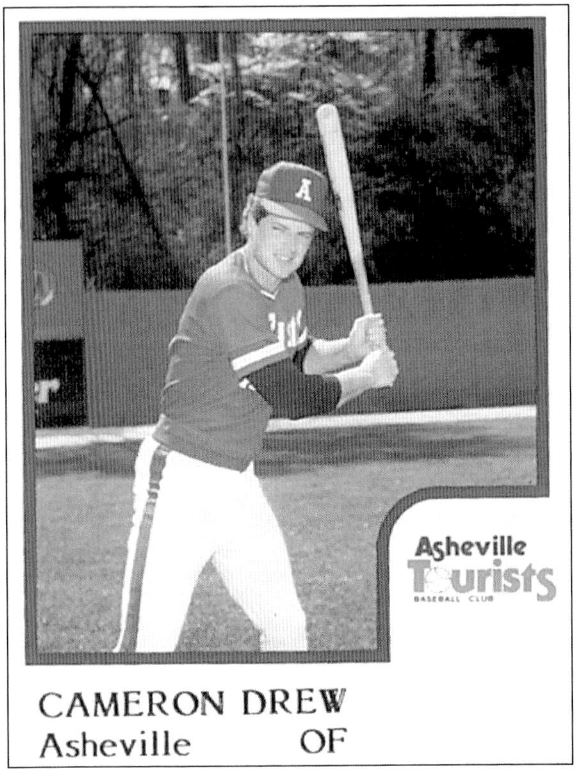

Employing a wide-open stance and a powerful stroke that rained baseballs beyond the right field wall, Cameron Drew was tabbed by the managers of the South Atlantic League as the loop's top major league prospect after narrowly missing the triple crown with Asheville in 1986. Drew led the league with 26 home runs and 117 RBIs and finished second with a .326 batting average. Named to the Topps Class A All-Star team, Drew played seven games with Houston in 1988. (Author's collection.)

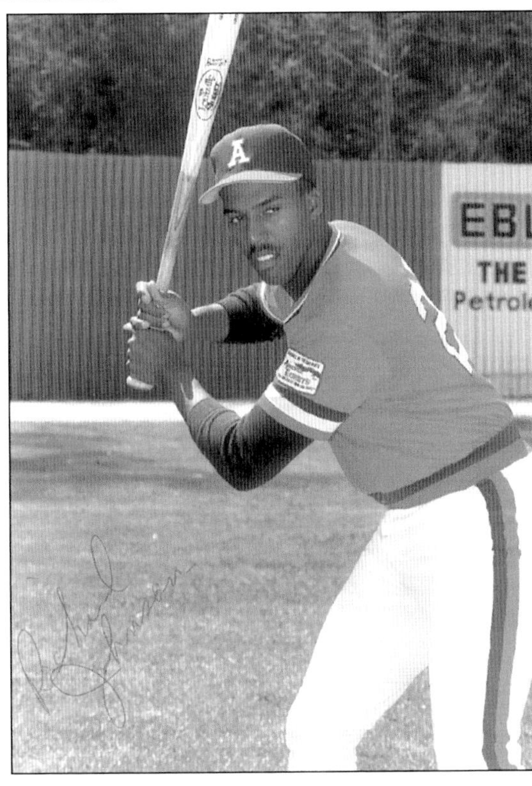

Richard Johnson made the most of McCormick Field's short porch in right field during the 1986 season. The right-handed hitter from Sam Houston State University clubbed 24 home runs with 78 RBIs and batted .395 in 68 games before hitting five more home runs after a promotion to Class A Osceola. Unfortunately for Johnson, his power never played consistently in leagues higher than the South Atlantic. (Asheville Tourists photograph.)

Mike Simms established the Asheville and South Atlantic League single-season home run records with 39 roundtrippers during the 1987 campaign. The first baseman clubbed three homers at Greensboro on June 8 before dominating the playoffs with nine hits in 18 at-bats, including three homers and 10 RBIs against Myrtle Beach. In Game 2 versus the Blue Jays, Simms went 5-for-5, including two home runs and six RBIs, then went 3-for-4 with four RBIs in Game 3. (Author's collection.)

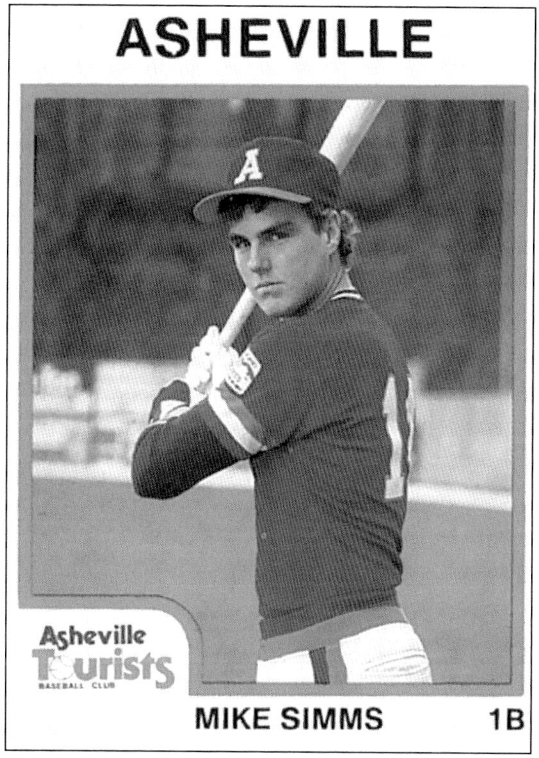

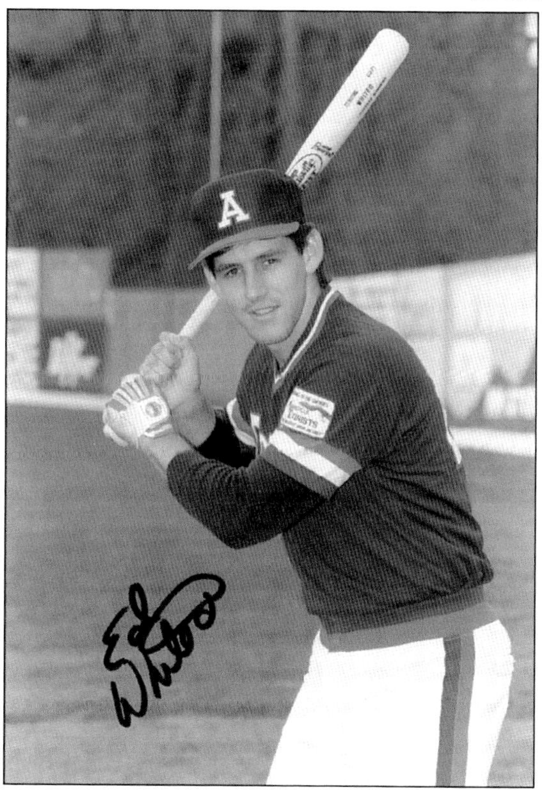

Third baseman Ed Whited earned South Atlantic League Most Valuable Player honors for his dominating performance in 1987. Whited led the South Atlantic League with a .327 batting average, 126 RBIs, 37 doubles, 18 game-winning RBIs, a .598 slugging percentage, and a .407 on-base percentage. He also set the South Atlantic League record with four grand slams while ranking second on the circuit with 28 home runs. Whited was traded to Atlanta in exchange for shortstop Rafael Ramirez after the 1987 season and played 36 games in the major leagues in 1989. (Asheville Tourists photograph.)

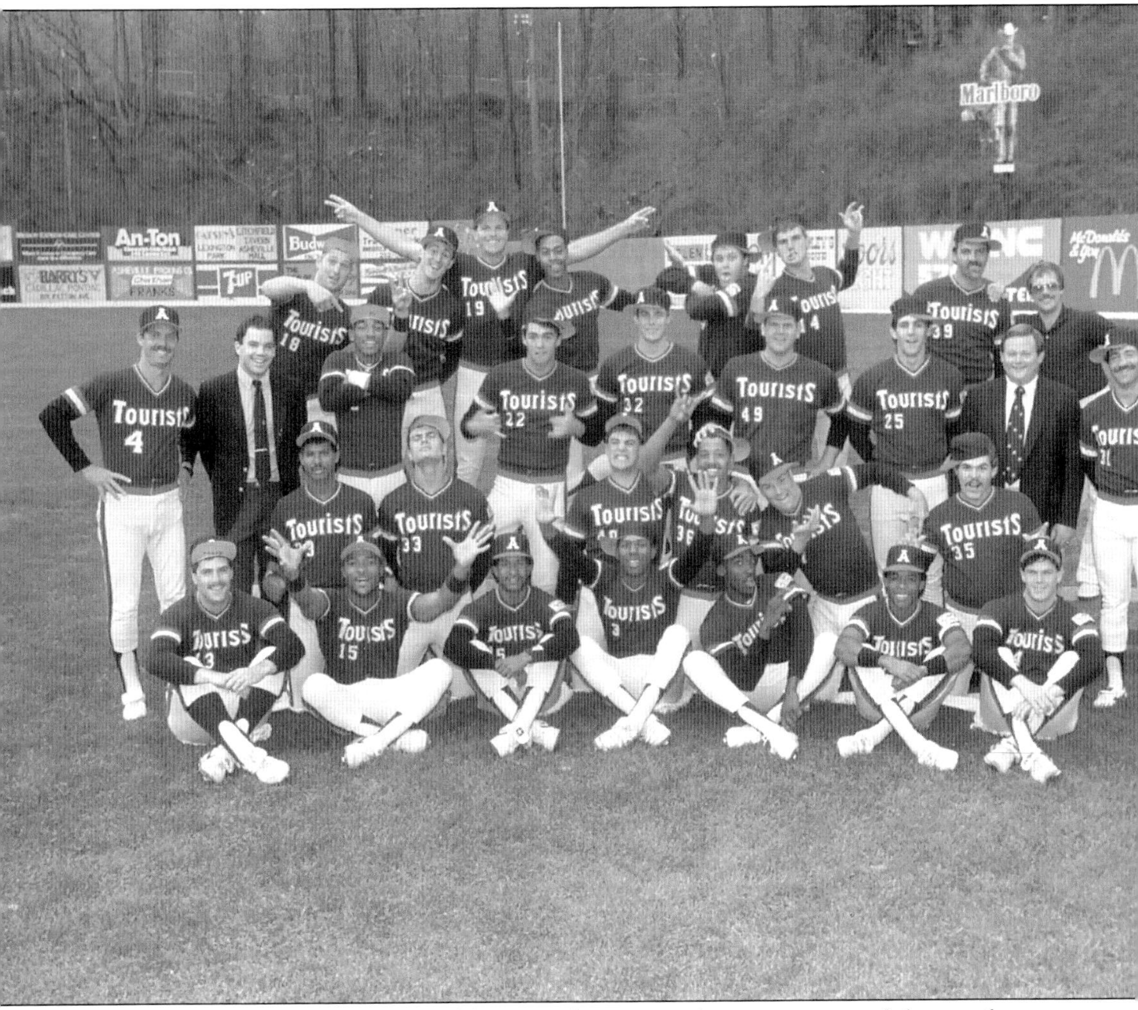

The 1987 Tourists are considered by many long-time observers as one of the top four teams in franchise history, challenged only by the 1928, 1948, and 1961 clubs. Asheville won 91 games that year, third-highest total ever. The team's 91-48 record produced a .655 winning percentage, good for second in team history, yet dropped the championship series to Myrtle Beach, three games to two. (Asheville Tourists photograph.)

Karl "Tuffy" Rhodes hit .252 with three home runs and 50 RBIs in 129 games with the Tourists in 1987. He made his biggest splash in the United States as a Chicago Cub by hitting three home runs off Dwight Gooden on Opening Day in 1995. In 2003, he became the first foreign player in Japanese baseball history to have four seasons of 40 or more home runs. (Asheville Tourists photograph.)

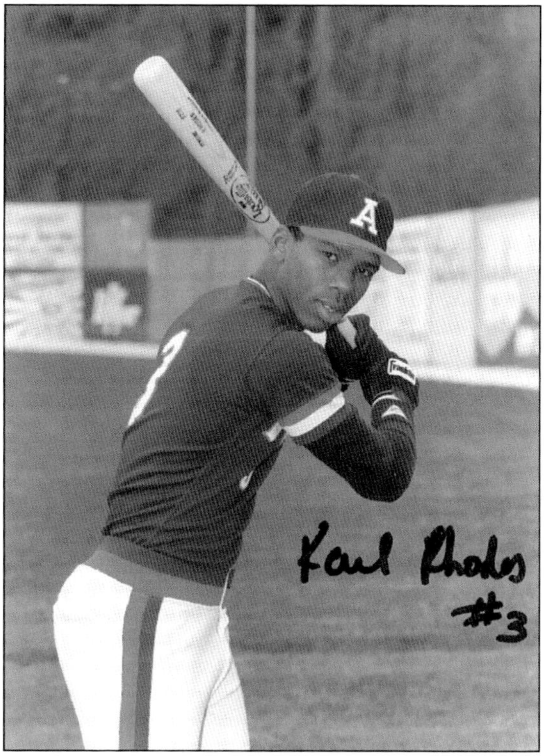

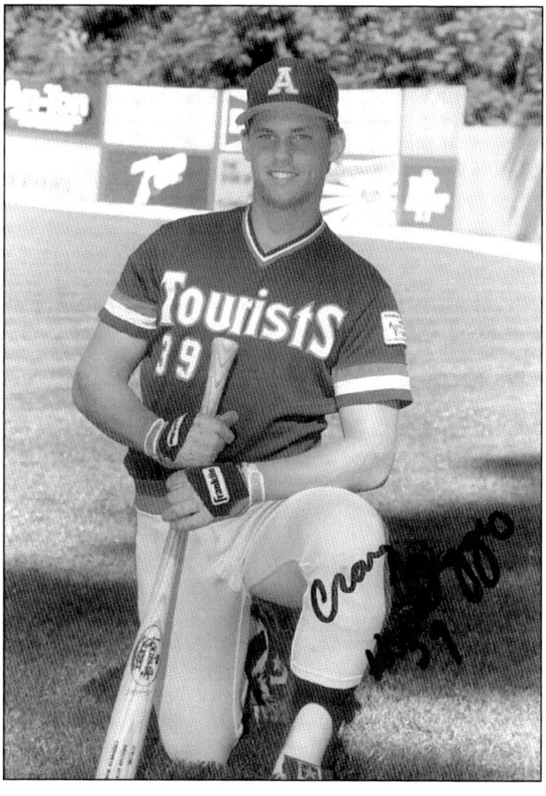

Asheville served as Craig Biggio's first stop in the minor leagues after being drafted by Houston in the first round in 1987 out of Seton Hall University. Biggio became a key component in the Tourists' Northern Division crown in the South Atlantic League by hitting .375 with nine home runs, 49 RBIs, and 31 stolen bases in 64 games. Since 1988, Biggio has been one of the most popular players in Houston Astros' history. (Asheville Tourists photograph.)

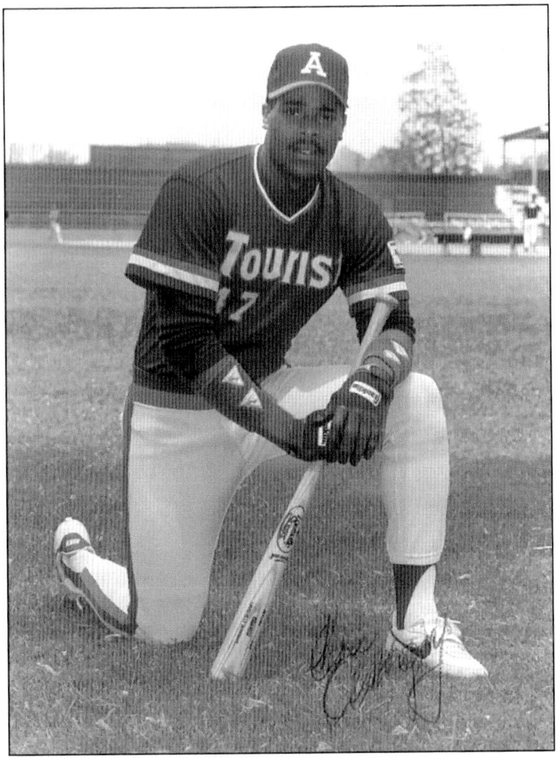

Outfielder Eric Anthony established the Tourists' franchise record as well as the South Atlantic League standard with 66 extra-base hits in 1988. Despite missing the first month of the season with a sprained right ankle, Anthony paced the minor leagues with 29 home runs, topped the South Atlantic League with 37 doubles, and led the Tourists with 73 runs and 120 hits. He hit 78 home runs in parts of nine seasons in the major leagues. (Asheville Tourists photograph.)

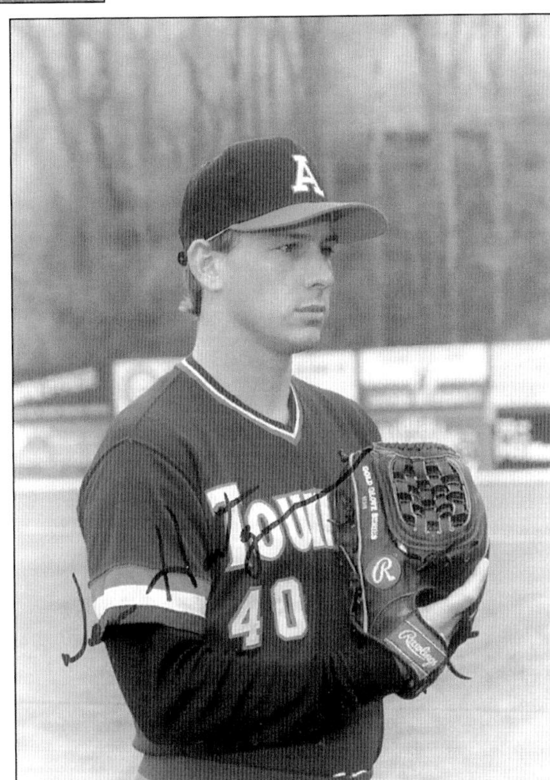

Dean Hartgraves celebrated his 22nd birthday on August 12, 1998, by tossing a no-hitter against Myrtle Beach during the nightcap of a doubleheader. The Tourists won the game 3-0. The left-hander went 5-9 with a 4.49 ERA in 39 games with Asheville in 1988. In 1989 he went 5-8 in 19 starts with the Tourists prior to a promotion to Class A Osceola. Hartgraves made 86 relief appearances in the major leagues from 1995 to 1998. (Asheville Tourists photograph.)

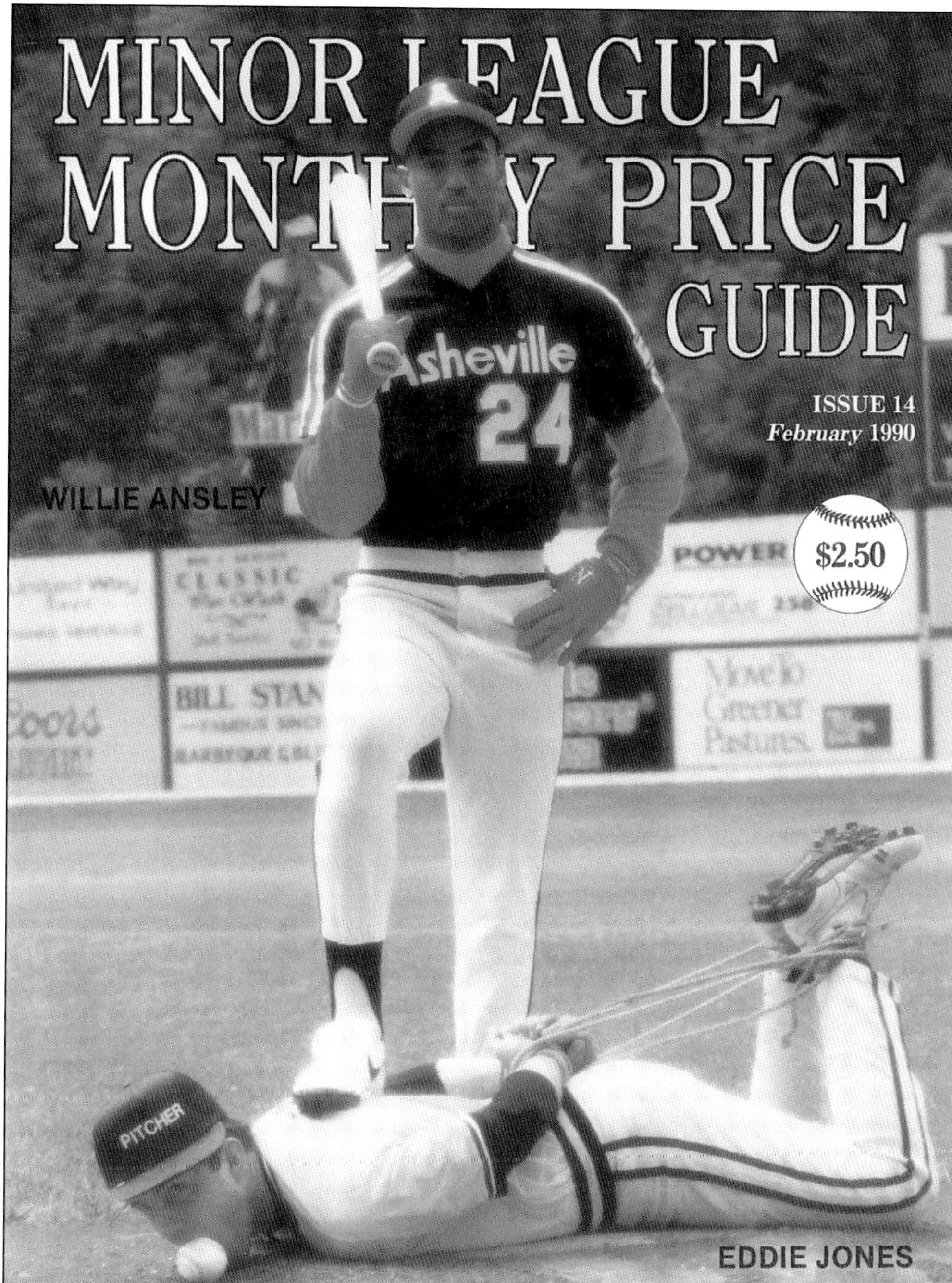

The future looked bright for outfielder Willie Ansley after he made his professional debut with the Tourists in 1989. Houston's top pick in the 1988 draft, Ansley placed second in the South Atlantic League with a .309 batting average and third with 53 stolen bases. In addition to being named a starter in the league's All-Star game, Ansley was tabbed by South Atlantic League managers as the circuit's top offensive and defensive prospect as well as the most exciting player. He appeared on the cover of the February 1990 issue of the short-lived *Minor League Monthly Price Guide*. (Author's collection.)

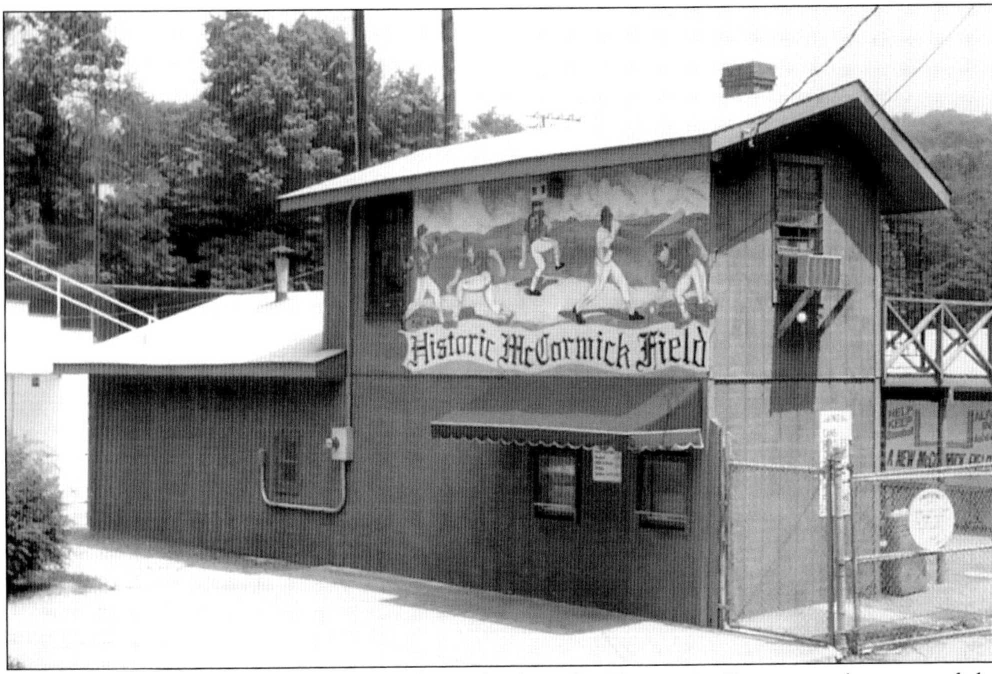

The mural above the ticket booth and attached to the Tourists' offices served as one of the distinctive landmarks during the latter years of old McCormick Field. This picture was taken in August 1989. (Author's collection.)

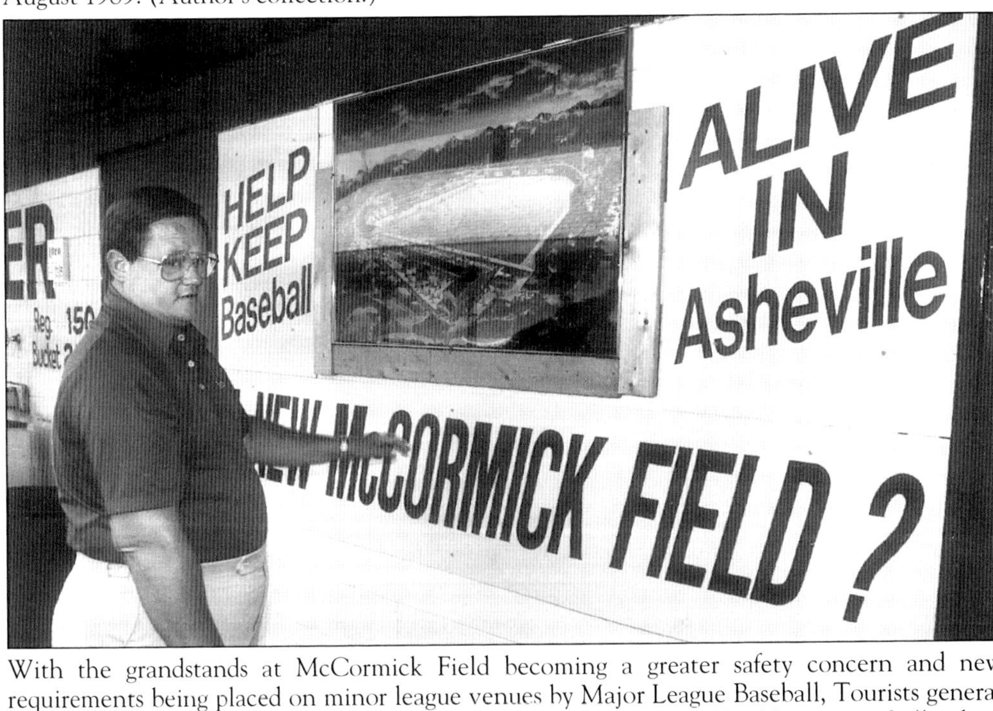

With the grandstands at McCormick Field becoming a greater safety concern and new requirements being placed on minor league venues by Major League Baseball, Tourists general manager Ron McKee undertook a project in 1989 with the hope of building a new ballpark in Asheville. McKee's hard initiative paid off when the new McCormick Field opened in 1992. (Bob Terrell collection.)

Shortstop Andujar Cedeno led the South Atlantic League with 146 hits, and ranked second with 223 total bases, third with 93 RBIs, and fourth with a .300 batting average during the 1989 season. Cedeno also earned South Atlantic League All-Star honors and paced the Tourists with six triples. He played a total of seven seasons in the major leagues with the Astros, Padres, and Tigers. (Author's collection.)

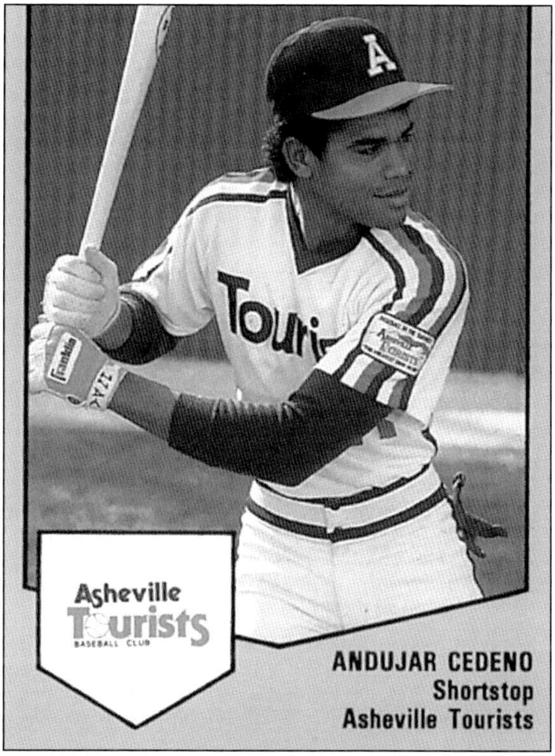

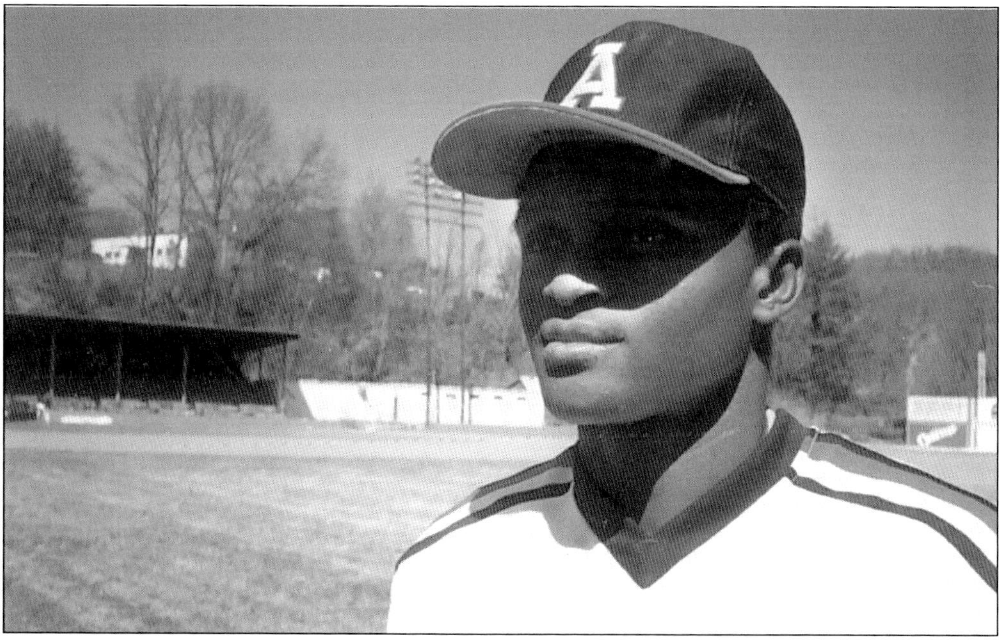

Orlando Miller was named to the South Atlantic League All-Star team in 1990 and was ranked by the circuit's managers as the loop's 10th-best prospect. A native of Panama, Miller tied for second in the South Atlantic League with 29 doubles and ranked fifth in batting with a .313 average. The slick-fielding shortstop played in the major leagues from 1994 to 1997, including the first three years with Houston. (Asheville Tourists photo.)

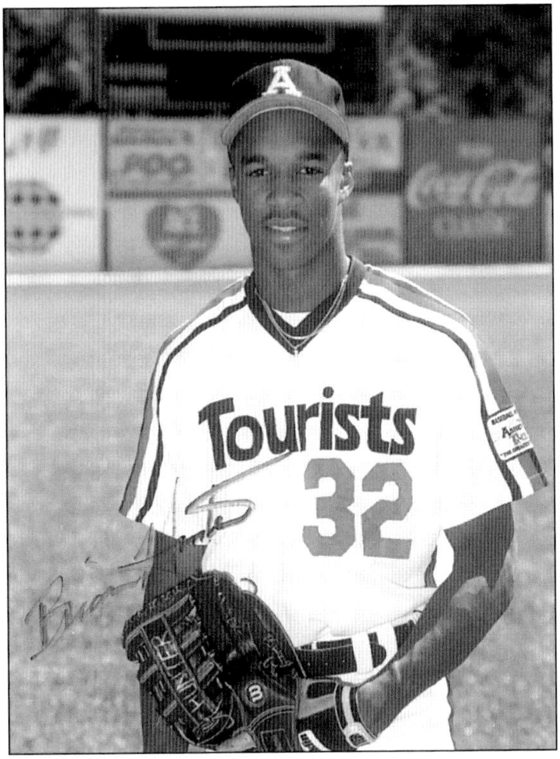

Brian Hunter's blazing speed was undeniable, but many fans at McCormick Field wondered if the outfielder would hit consistently enough to play in the major leagues. In 1990, Hunter batted .250 with only 16 RBIs in 127 games while leading the Tourists and ranking fifth in the South Atlantic League with 45 stolen bases. He wound up making enough contact to celebrate his 10th season in the major leagues during the 2003 campaign. (Asheville Tourists photograph.)

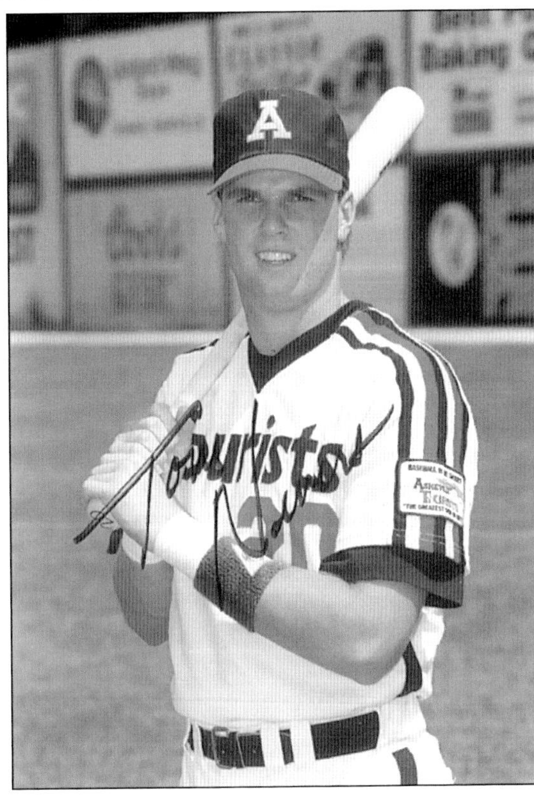

Tom Nevers, the Astros' first-round draft pick in 1990, said prior to the final game at McCormick Field that he wanted to hit the last home run in the historic ballpark. He accomplished the feat on September 1, 1991, with a three-run shot in the third inning over the right-field wall. Nevers led the Tourists with 16 home runs while hitting .251 with 71 RBIs. He remained active in the minor leagues through the 2003 campaign. (Asheville Tourists photo.)

FIVE

The New McCormick

Nary had a day passed after the final pitch of the 1991 season before McCormick Field's wooden grandstand, built in 1923, was little more than a memory. The building of a new ballpark with a seating capacity of approximately 4,000 was erected by Leader Construction and designed by architects Bowers, Ellis, and Watson. Some observers wondered if the facility would be ready for the 1992 season, but exhaustive hours through February and March and into April made the campaign at the corner of Biltmore Avenue and Charlotte Street a reality.

The new McCormick Field maintained the layout of the original ballpark and kept the playing field intact. For fans, the improvements centered on expanded restrooms, modern concession stands, more comfortable seats, and a large plaza area for group outings. New clubhouses and lights served as the major benefits for the players, although one new twist altered the thought process of pitchers as well as hitters from both sides of the plate. Only 301 feet from home plate, right field had always been a target of left-handed power hitters. The feat became tougher prior to the 1993 season when the wall's height more than tripled to its current 36 feet.

The new facility led to a new major league affiliate. The Tourists had been the Houston Astros' Class A South Atlantic League club since 1982 until general manager Ron McKee collaborated with the expansion Colorado Rockies, beginning in 1994. Colorado general manager Dan O'Dowd said, "The first-class situation is one that makes us very comfortable to put our young players in. We are as proud to be a part of the Asheville Tourists as any major league organization can be."

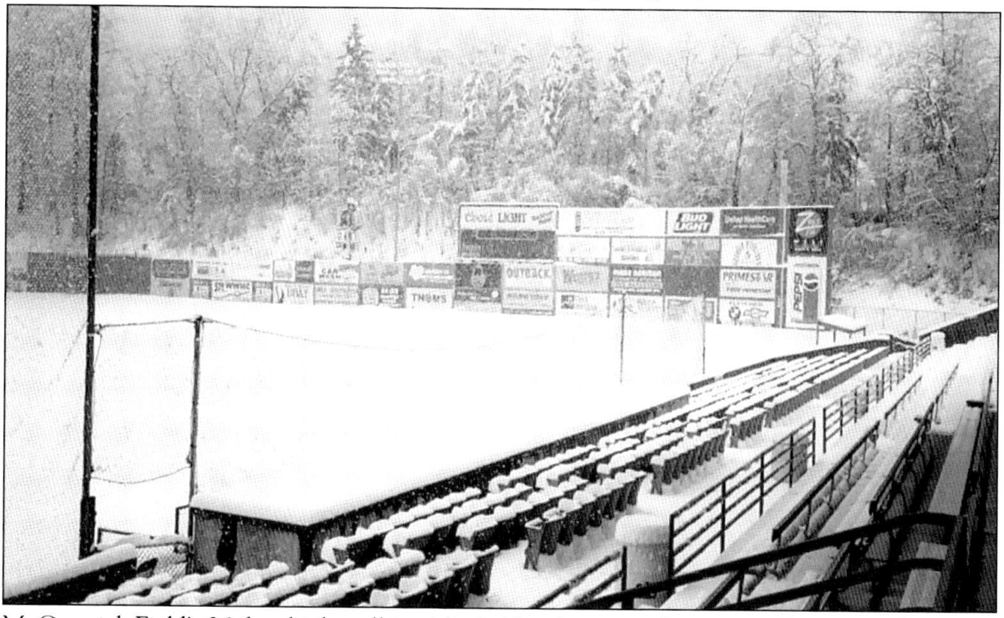

McCormick Field's 36-foot high wall in right field is the minors' answer to Fenway Park's Green Monster in the major leagues. (Asheville Tourists photograph.)

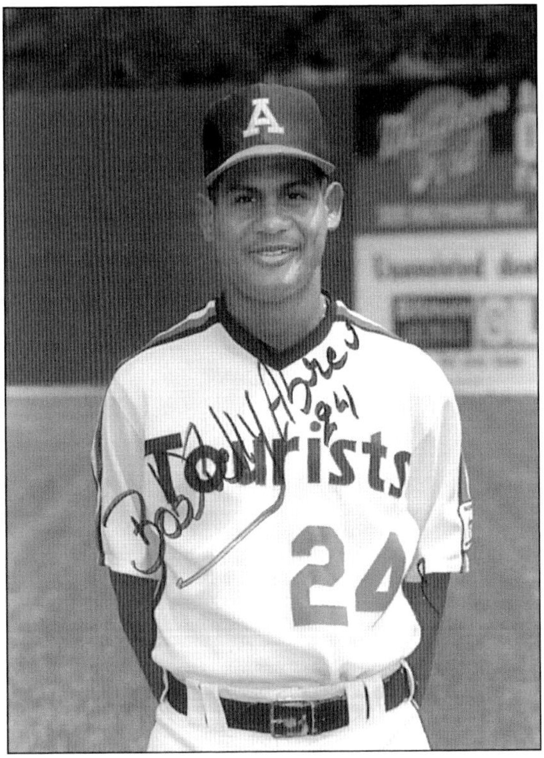

Bobby Abreu displayed one of the strongest throwing arms ever seen in right field with the Tourists, as evidenced by his 15 assists during the 1992 season. As an 18-year-old with Asheville, Abreu ranked among the Houston organizational leaders with 81 runs scored, 8 home runs, 140 hits, 48 RBIs, and 63 walks. He reached the major leagues with the Astros in 1996 and spent his sixth season with Philadelphia in 2003. (Asheville Tourists photograph.)

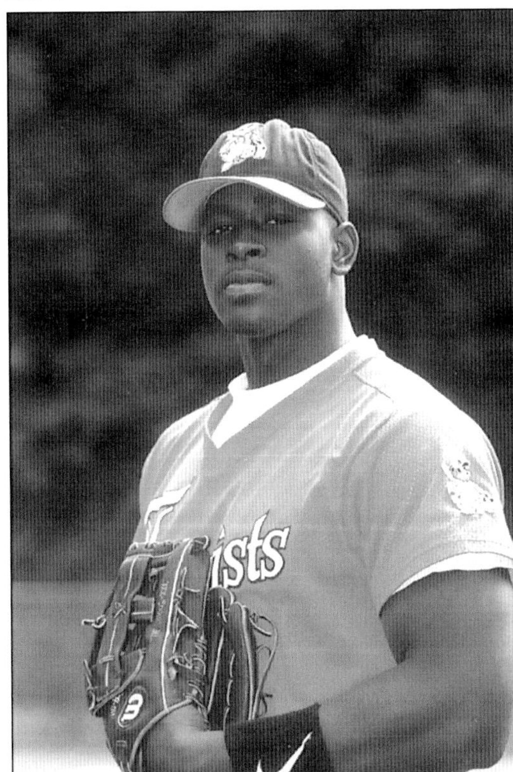

Derrick Gibson was the only player in the minor leagues to make the 30-30 Club during the 1995 season. Toiling for the Tourists, the outfielder crushed a South Atlantic League-best 32 home runs and swiped 31 bases. He also paced the South Atlantic League with 115 RBIs and hit at a .292 clip. He reached the major leagues briefly in 1998 and 1999 before his diamond pursuits stalled, leading Gibson to give professional football a brief try with the Cleveland Browns. (Asheville Tourists photograph.)

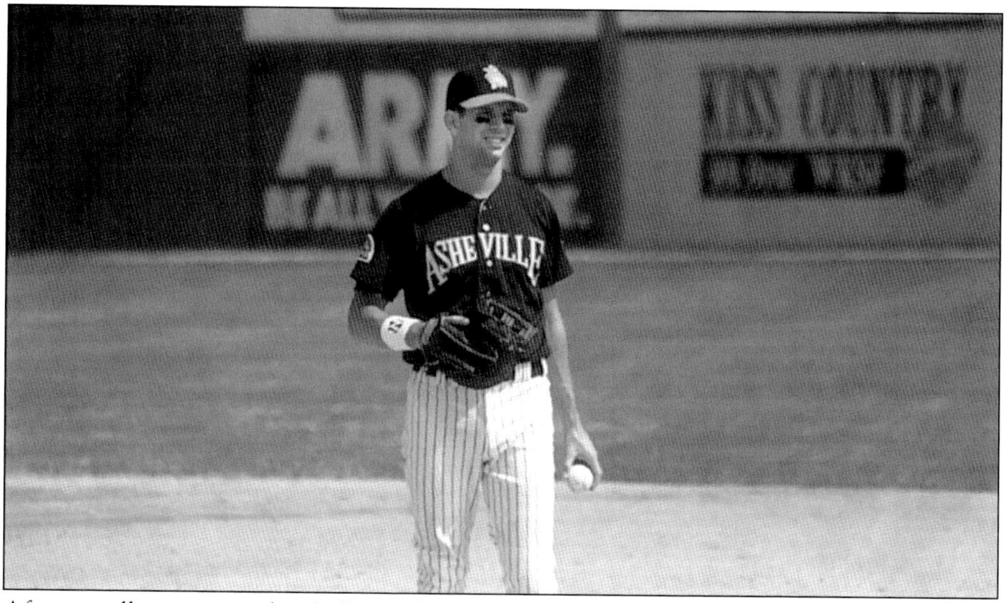

After a stellar career in baseball and football at the University of Tennessee, Todd Helton traveled two hours east to Asheville to make his professional debut after being drafted by Colorado in the eighth overall pick in 1995. The first baseman looked nothing like a future batting champ and Gold Glove winner while with the Tourists. Exhausted after playing in the College World Series with the Volunteers, Helton hit just .254 with a home run and 15 RBIs in 54 games with Asheville. He made up for lost time shortly thereafter and placed second in National League Rookie of the Year balloting in 1998. (Tony Farlow photograph.)

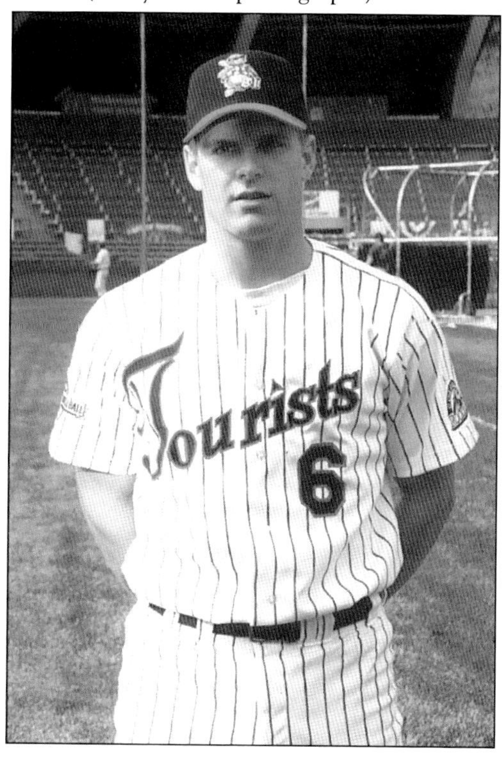

Catcher Ben Petrick spent his first professional season in Asheville as an 18-year-old after being drafted in the first round by Colorado in 1995. His best day with the Tourists occurred on July 7, 1996, when he hit two home runs and drove in six runs in a 10-6 win over Hickory. For the season, Petrick batted .235 with 14 home runs and 52 RBIs. He debuted in the major leagues with Colorado in 1999. (Tony Farlow photo.)

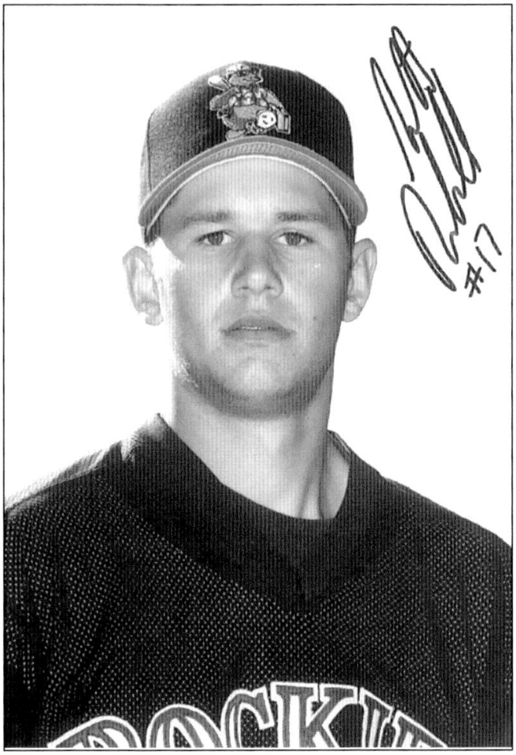

With the aid of one of the best curveballs in the minor leagues, Scott Randall started the 1996 season with a 6-0 record and earned team Most Valuable Player honors after posting a 14-4 record and a 2.74 ERA. Randall fired a no-hitter at Fayetteville on July 17 during a 4-0 victory. A month later, he tossed 11 no-hit innings with 11 strikeouts, yet received a no-decision in what proved to a 2-1, 19-inning victory for the Tourists. The right-hander reached the major leagues seven years later, in 2003, when he appeared in 15 games with Cincinnati. (Asheville Tourists photo.)

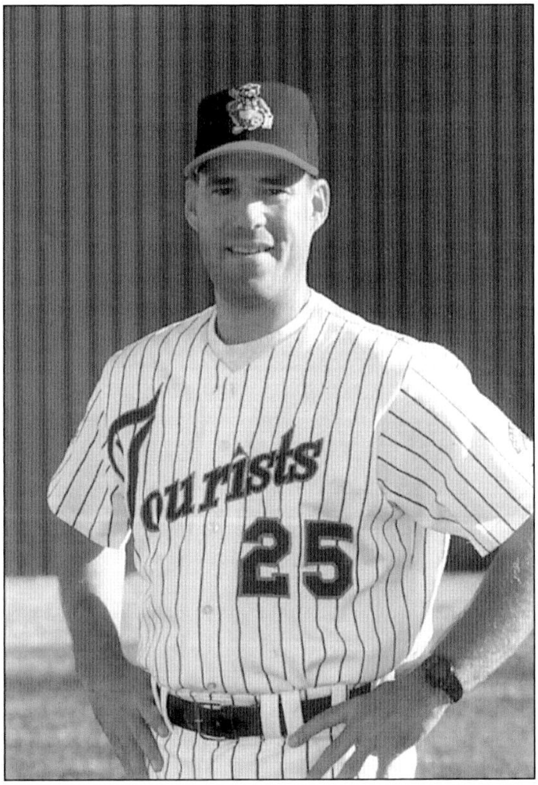

Ron Gideon managed the Tourists to 133 wins during the 1997 and 1998 seasons. Gideon used his no-nonsense approach and knowledge as a former catcher to help numerous prospects, particularly pitchers, make the necessary adjustments in their professional careers. (Asheville Tourists photo.)

David Lee arrived in Asheville in 1997 as an unheralded relief pitcher and departed as a solid prospect after saving a team-best 22 contests and leading the South Atlantic League with 49 games finished. The hard-throwing right-hander reached the big leagues in 1999, and has appeared in 92 games through the 2003 season during stints with the Rockies, Padres, and Indians. (Asheville Tourists photo.)

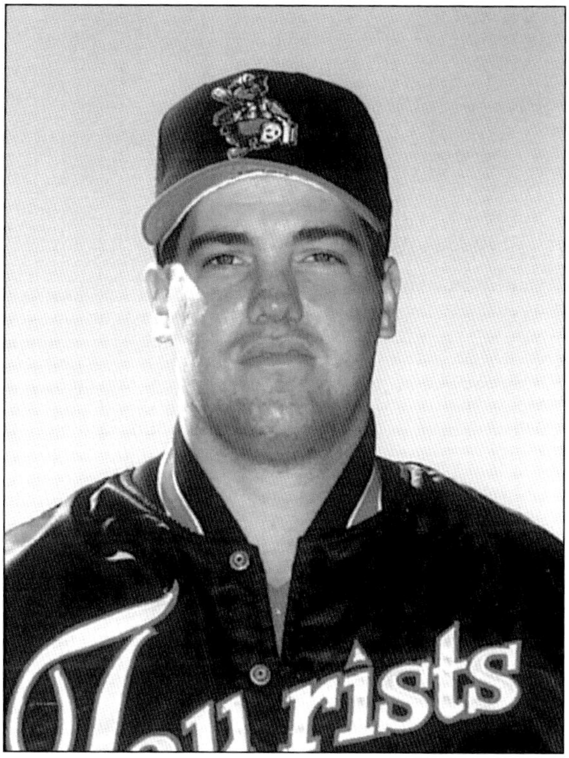

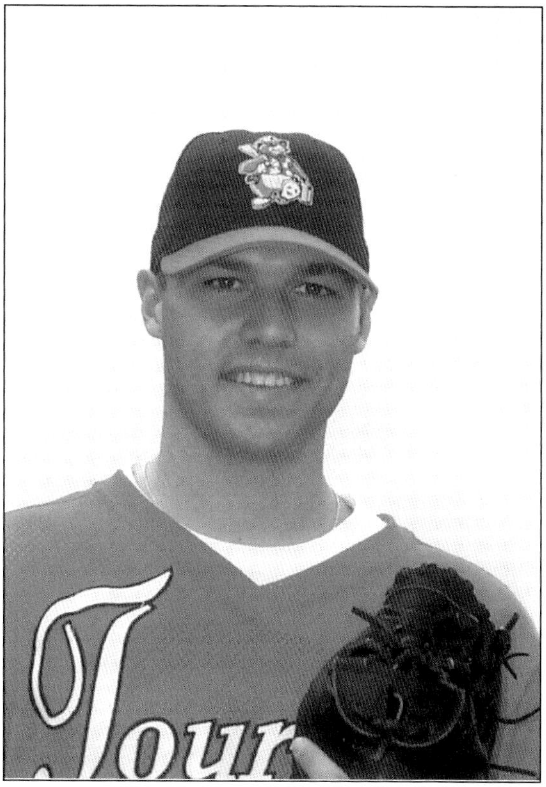

Colorado's first-round draft pick in 1996, right-hander Jake Westbrook headlined Asheville's prospect-laden rotation in 1997 and led the Tourists in wins with a 14-11 record and three complete games. Traded to Montreal a year later, Westbrook debuted in the major leagues with the Yankees in 2000 before spending parts of three seasons, from 2001 to 2003, with the Cleveland Indians. (Asheville Tourists photo.)

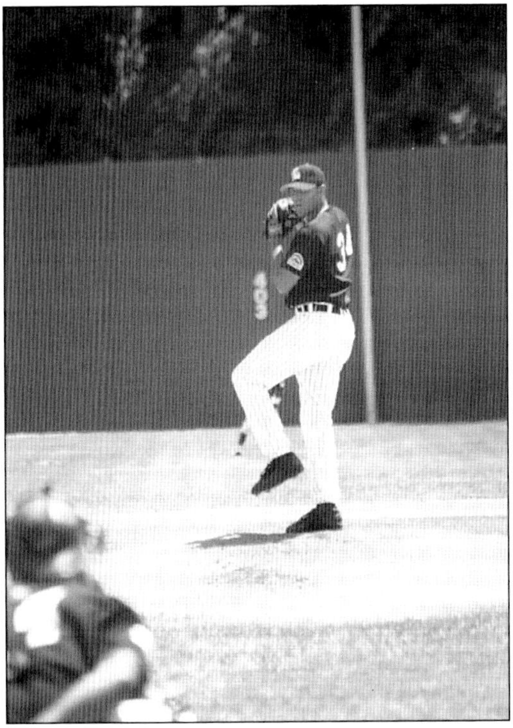

Shawn Chacon became the first player drafted by the Rockies directly out of a Colorado high school when the team selected the Greeley product in the third round in 1996. The right-hander won 11 games as a Tourist in 1997 and led the team with 149 strikeouts and paced the rotation with a 3.89 ERA. Chacon was named the Rockies' Rookie of the Year in 2001 after making 27 starts for Colorado. (Tony Farlow photograph.)

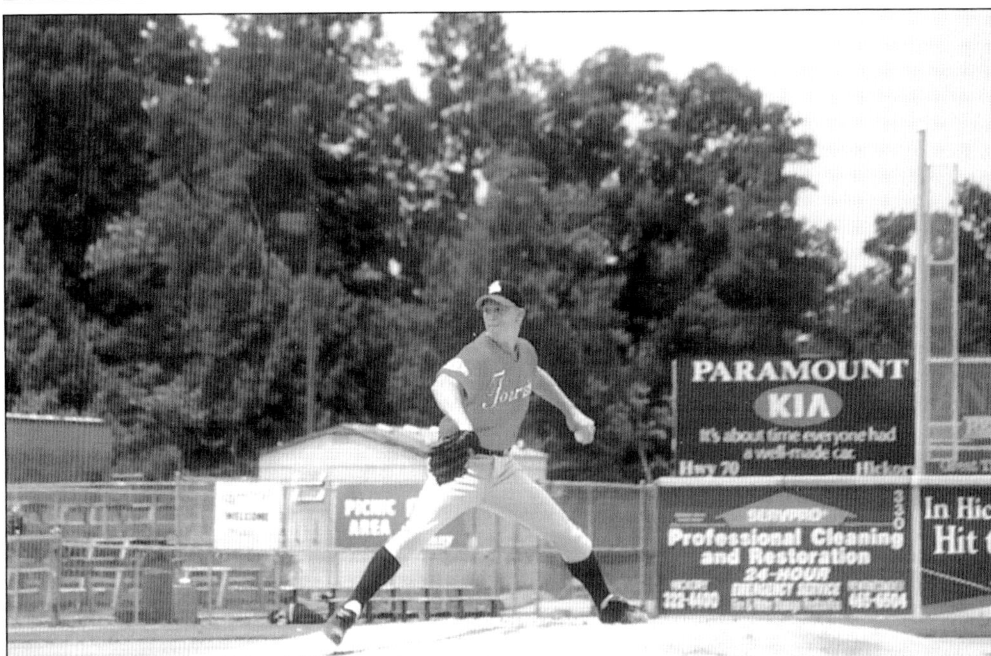

Josh Kalinowski is shown during his 17-strikeout performance at Hickory's L.P. Frans Stadium on June 28, 1998. The Asheville left-hander also tossed a complete-game no-hitter against the Charleston RiverDogs on August 26. Kalinowski finished the season with a 12-10 record and a franchise-record 215 strikeouts, the second-highest total in the minor leagues during the 1998 campaign. (Asheville Tourists photo.)

Choo Freeman was considered to be Colorado's top minor league prospect upon his arrival to Asheville at the start of the 1999 season. Drafted by the Rockies in the first round in 1998, Freeman displayed an impressive combination of power and speed. He glided to the ball while patrolling center field, and hit a solid .274 with 14 home runs, 66 RBIs, and 16 stolen bases. He concluded his tenure in Asheville with home runs in his last two games, including a grand slam versus Hickory in the season finale on September 6. (Asheville Tourists photo.)

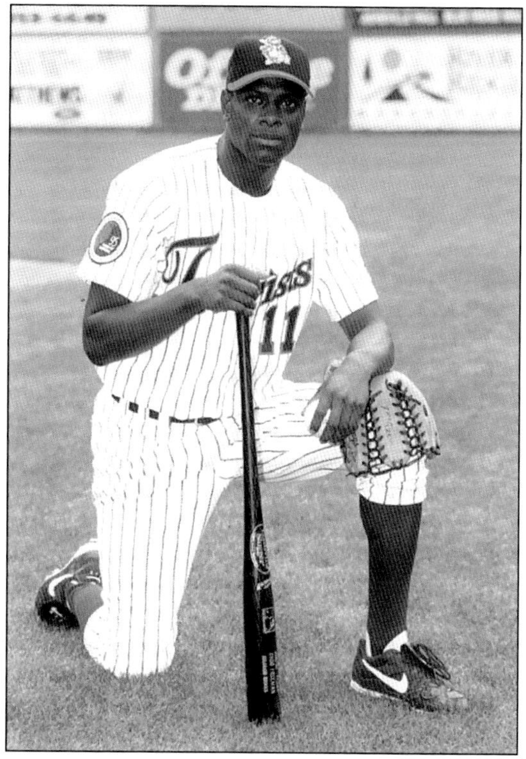

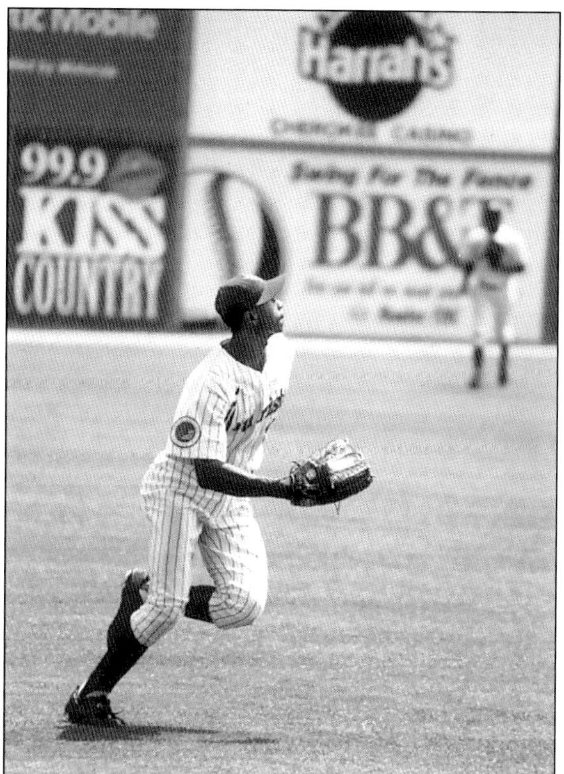

Outfielder Juan Pierre continued to prove the critics wrong, yet he received little attention for his accomplishments. A 13th-round draft pick out of the University of South Alabama in 1998, Pierre led professional baseball with 101 hits in June, but was not selected to play in the 1999 South Atlantic League All-Star game. He used that snub as motivation for the remainder of the season and wound up leading the South Atlantic League with 187 hits. He also ranked second with 66 stolen bases and fourth with a .320 batting average. Pierre debuted in the major leagues with Colorado in 2000 before helping guide the Florida Marlins to the World Series crown in 2003. (Tony Farlow photograph.)

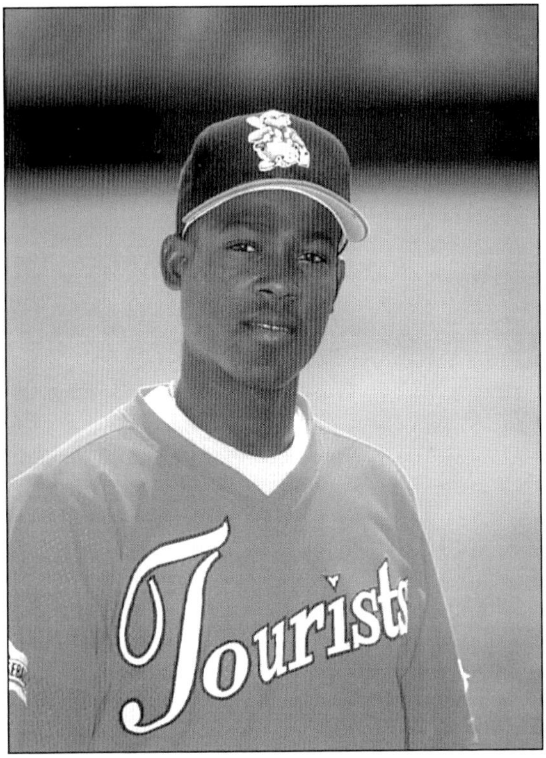

Dominican dandy Juan Uribe dazzled the McCormick Field faithful with his defense and displayed one of the quickest releases of any shortstop in Asheville history during the 1999 season. After hitting .267 with nine home runs and 46 RBIs, Uribe made the jump to the major leagues in 2001 and remained the Rockies' starting shortstop through the 2003 campaign. (Asheville Tourists photo.)

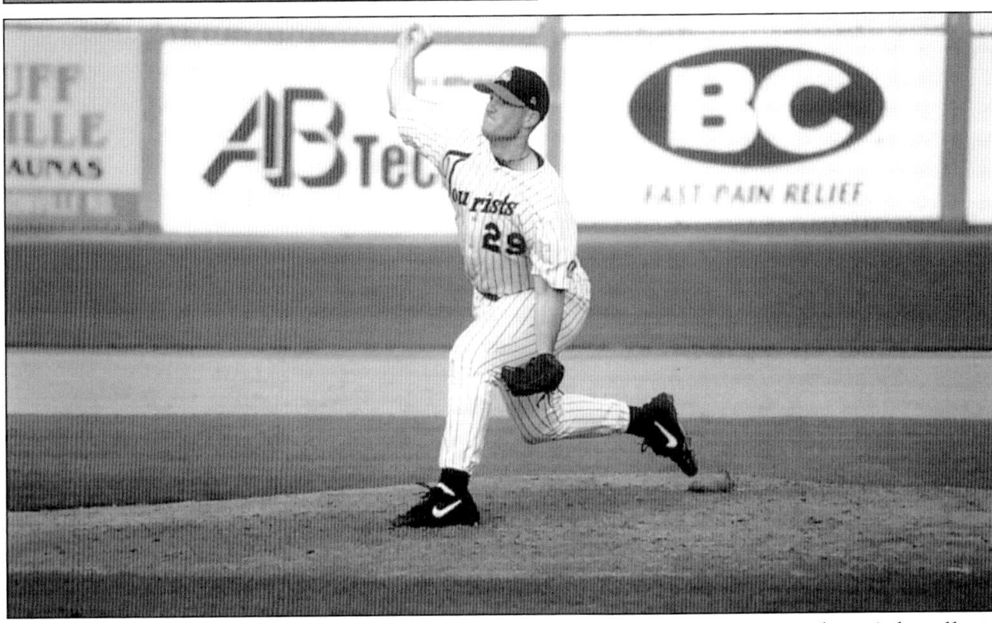

Colorado's first-round draft choice in 1999, pitcher Jason Jennings reported to Asheville in July and paid immediate dividends. A two-way player who led Baylor University to the College World Series and was named the College Player of the Year by *Baseball America* in 1999, Jennings struck out 69 batters in 58.1 innings while splitting his four decisions with the Tourists. The thick-legged right-hander was named the National League Rookie of the Year in 2002. (Tony Farlow photograph.)

Fifteen years after starring on the diamond at McCormick Field, Joe Mikulik returned to the Tourists as the team's manager, beginning with the 2000 season. A resident of nearby Candler, Mikulik entered the 2004 campaign as Asheville's skipper, his fifth straight at the dugout helm, representing the longest consecutive year run for a Tourist manager in franchise history. He won 272 games in his first four seasons, the third highest total in Asheville annals, and was named South Atlantic League Manager of the Year in 2001. (Tony Farlow photo.)

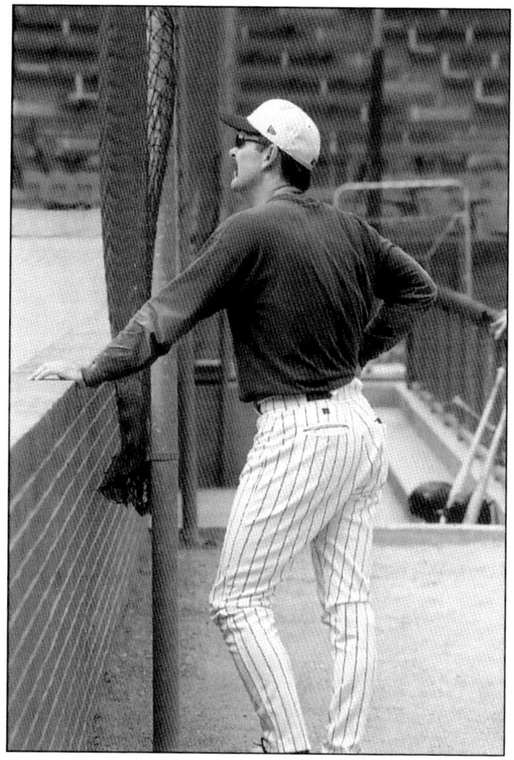

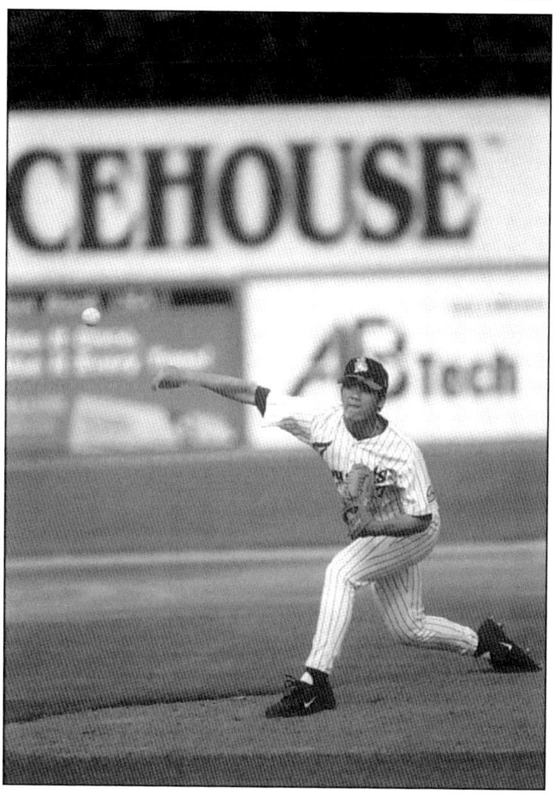

Tsao Chin-hui joined the Tourists with considerable fanfare in 2000 and lived up to the lofty expectations. Using an explosive fastball in the mid-to-upper 90s and a wicked slider, the native of Taiwan proved he was worth every penny of his $2.2 million signing bonus by tying for second in the South Atlantic League with 187 strikeouts and ranking third with a 2.73 ERA. He finished the year with an 11-8 record before suffering a major elbow injury in March 2001. Tsao bounced back to make his major league debut with the Rockies in 2003. (Tony Farlow photograph.)

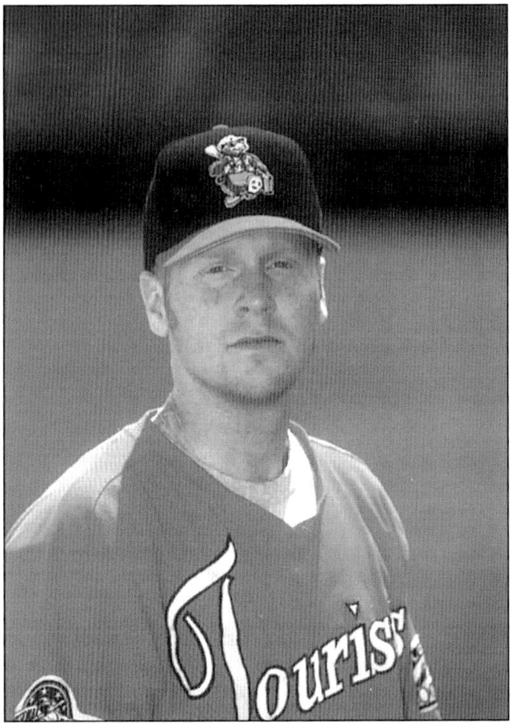

While Tsao Chin-hui and Julio DePaula received most of the headlines, right-hander Aaron Cook was Asheville's steadiest starter during the 2000 campaign. Cook fired a two-hitter and a pair of three-hitters on his way to a 10-7 record and a 2.96 ERA with the Tourists prior to his promotion to Class A Salem on July 25. Cook, who also pitched in Asheville in 1999 with a 4-12 record, debuted in the big leagues with Colorado in 2002. (Asheville Tourists photograph.)

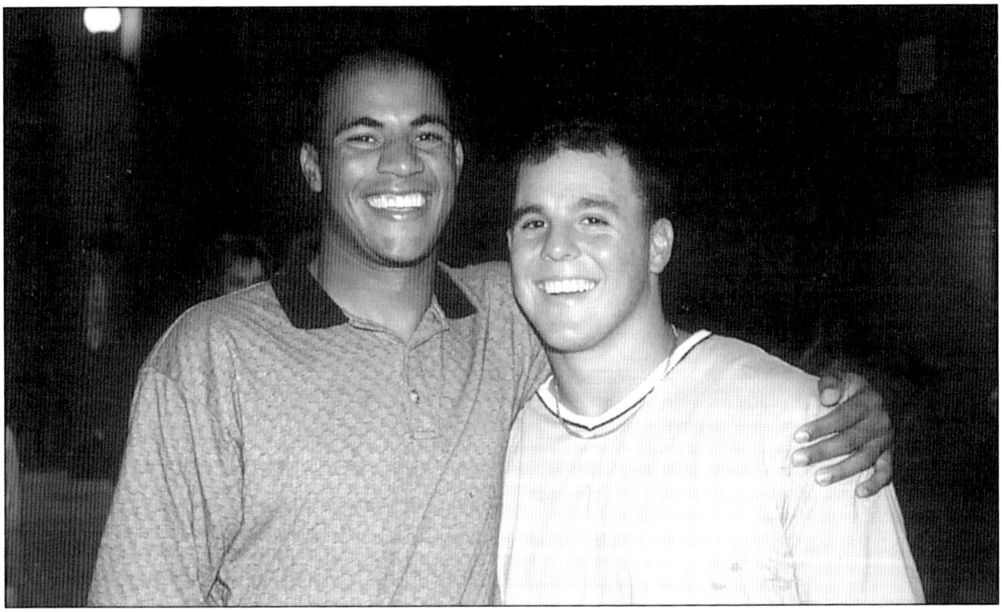

Julio DePaula and catcher Jeff Winchester are all smiles after DePaula threw the most dominating no-hitter in Asheville history, on June 26, 2000. DePaula allowed only a hit batsman in the first inning and a walk to open the second frame to silence the Cape Fear Crocs, 1-0. The right-hander, who went 8-13 with a 4.70 ERA for the Tourists in 2000, fanned 12 batters in the nine-inning gem and retired the last 24 batters he faced. He was traded to the New York Yankees a year later and made his major league debut in 2003. (Tony Farlow photograph.)

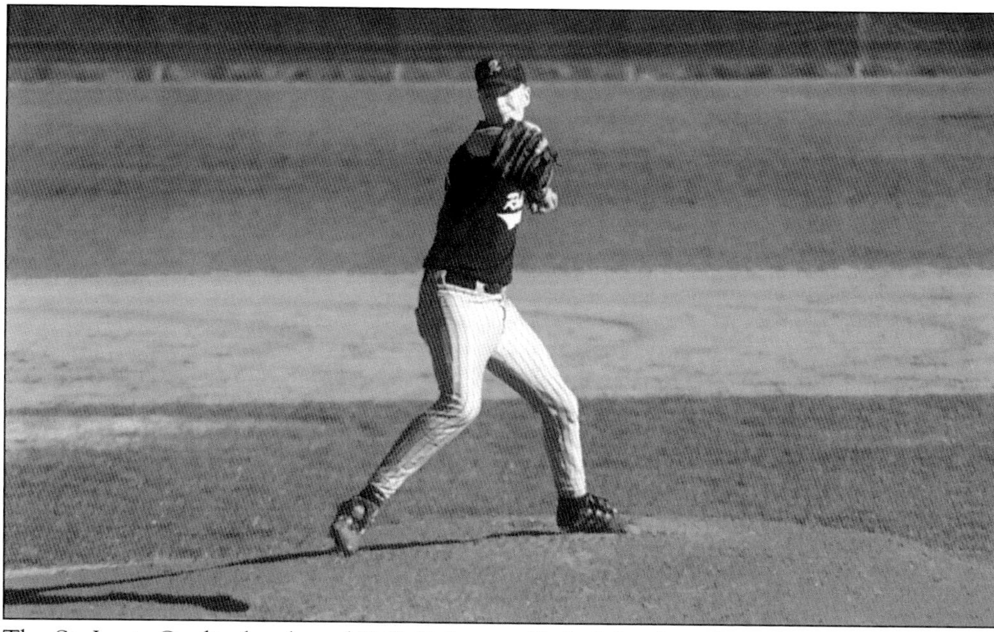

The St. Louis Cardinals selected T.C. Roberson High School pitcher Chris Narveson in the second round in the 2000 draft after the left-hander won all 13 of his decisions and posted a 0.67 ERA for the state's top-ranked team. Narveson attracted scouts with his low-90s fastball and excellent command, enabling him to strike out 133 batters while walking only 19 in 69 innings as a senior. (Tom Smith collection.)

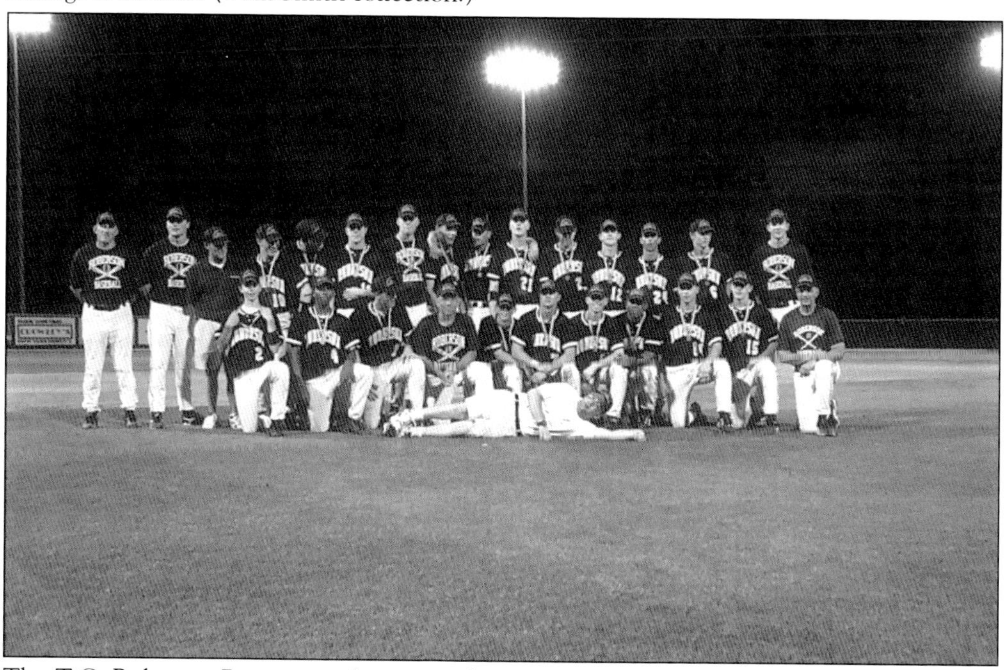

The T.C. Roberson Rams won their second state title under head coach Tom Smith during the 2000 campaign. The Rams also won the state championship in 1983 and 2002, giving Smith three state titles during his quarter-century at the Roberson High dugout helm. (Tom Smith collection.)

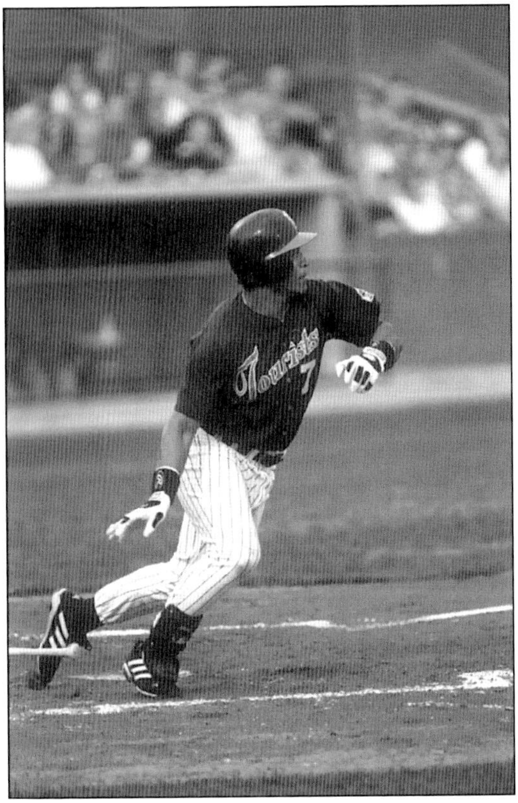

Rene Reyes won the South Atlantic League batting crown with a .322 average to accompany his 11 home runs and 61 RBIs while stealing 53 bases during the 2001 season. The Venezuelan product also ranked second on the circuit with 156 hits and was named the South Atlantic League Most Valuable Player at the end of the campaign. Reyes made his major league debut with Colorado in 2003. (Tony Farlow photograph.)

The 2001 Tourists enjoyed one of the most exciting seasons in franchise history when they went from a last-place finish in the campaign's first half with a 27-43 record to a Southern Division title with a 41-28 mark in the second half. Asheville swept Augusta in two games in the first round of the playoffs. The Tourists then trailed Lexington 2-0 in the championship series before the finals were cancelled due to the events of September 11. (Asheville Tourists photo.)

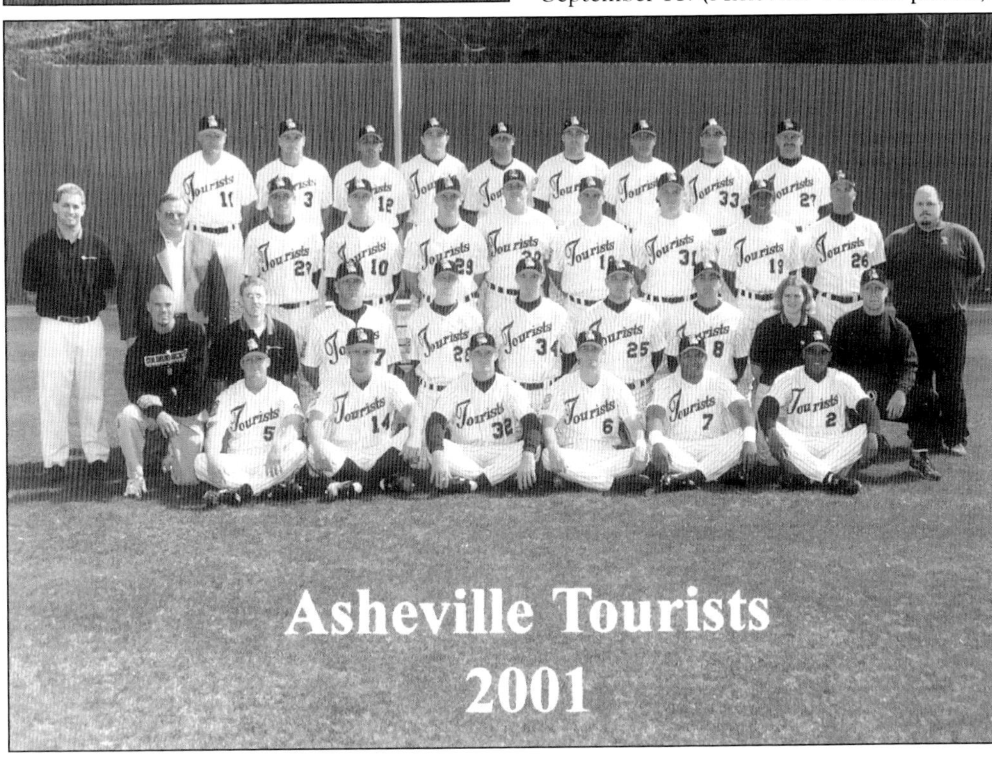

Jayson Nix showed Asheville fans why he was picked in the 44th overall selection in the 2001 draft. The second baseman made impressive strides with his ability to turn the double play while hitting .246 with 14 home runs and a team-best 79 RBIs. (Asheville Tourists photograph.)

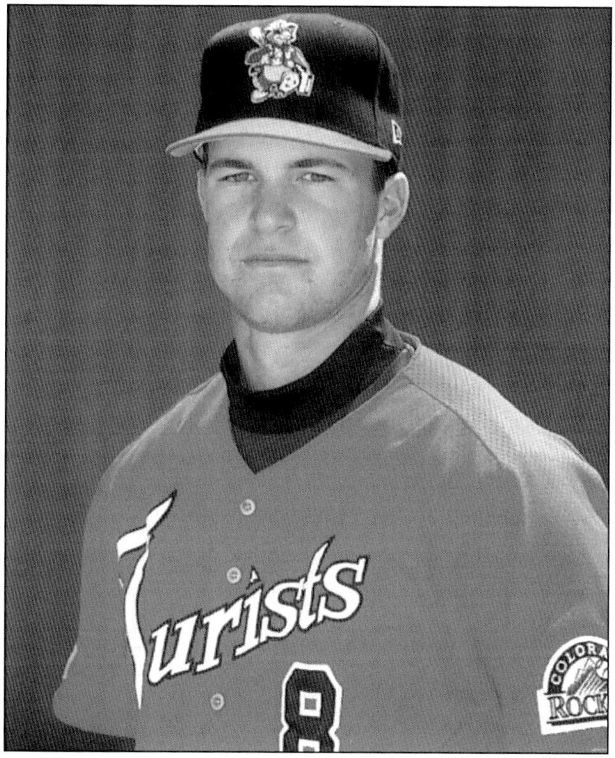

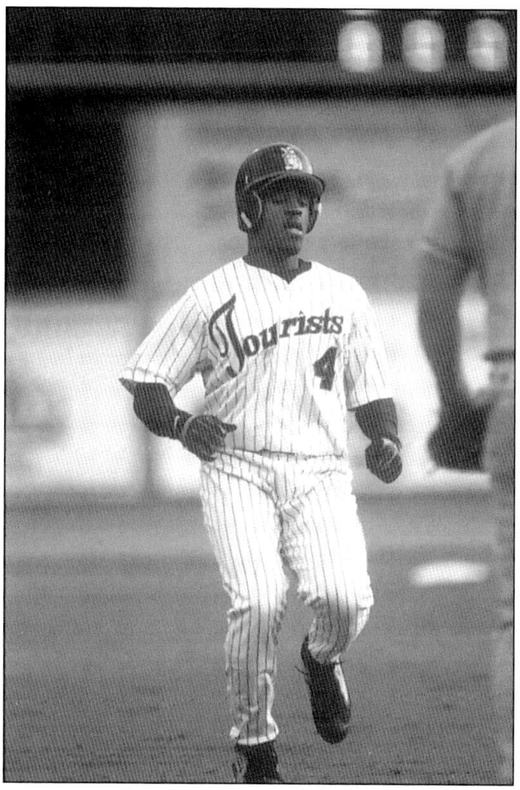

A former football player at the University of Toledo, outfielder Tony Miller overcame his lack of experience on the diamond to earn team Most Valuable Player honors with Asheville in 2002. Miller led the South Atlantic League with 109 runs and 88 walks; his 50 stolen bases and 142 hits ranked fifth on the circuit. The center fielder and leadoff hitter also led the team with 17 home runs and posted a .283 batting average. (Tony Farlow photograph.)

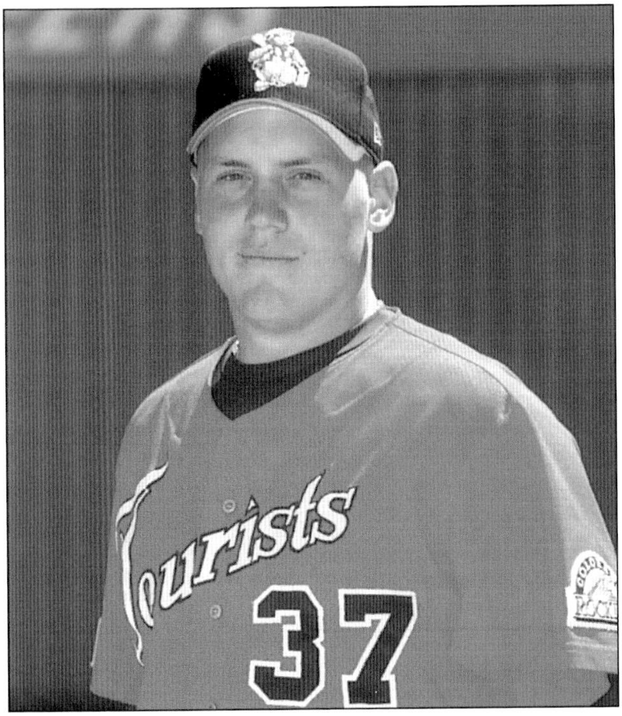

After struggling with injuries and inconsistency during his first four professional campaigns, hard-throwing Matt Roney found his groove with the Tourists in 2002, his second season in Asheville. Roney, who went 8-10 in 2001, registered a 4-6 record with 88 strikeouts in 83 innings before he received a mid-June promotion to Class AA Carolina. Acquired by Detroit prior to the 2003 season, he appeared in 45 games with the hapless Tigers in his first major league campaign, posting a 1-9 record. (Asheville Tourists photograph.)

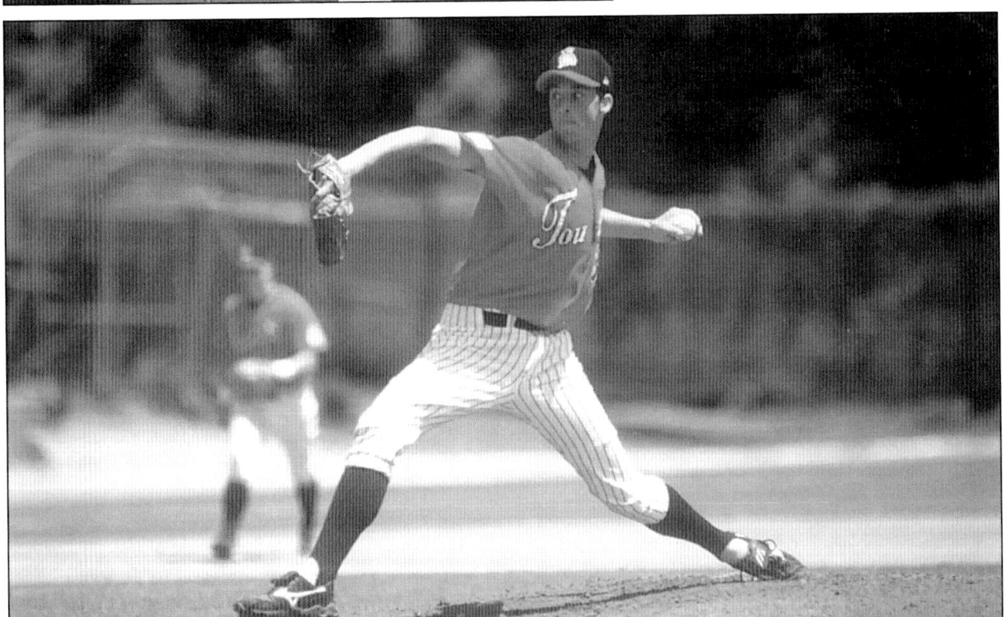

Asheville became a focal point for Canadian baseball fans in the summer of 2002 when pitcher Jeff Francis joined the Tourists in late July. Drafted by the Colorado Rockies with the ninth overall pick in 2002 out of the University of British Columbia, Francis received a bonus of $1.85 million upon signing his first professional contract. The left-hander had a 1.80 ERA in four starts before being struck in the side of the head with a foul ball while standing in the McCormick Field home dugout. The injury caused him to miss the remainder of the campaign before returning to the mound at Class A Visalia in 2003. (Tony Farlow photograph.)

After earning All-America recognition for three straight seasons at Clemson University, Jeff Baker made his professional debut with the Asheville Tourists in 2003. Baker struggled with a hand injury for most of the campaign, yet still managed to post a .289 batting average with 11 home runs and 44 RBIs. An outstanding defensive third baseman, Baker proved that his reputation as one of the game's premier prospects is deserved. (Tony Farlow photograph.)

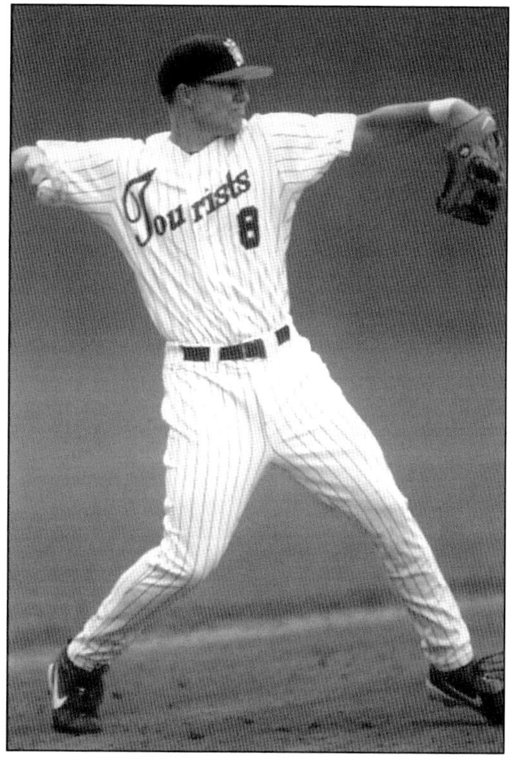

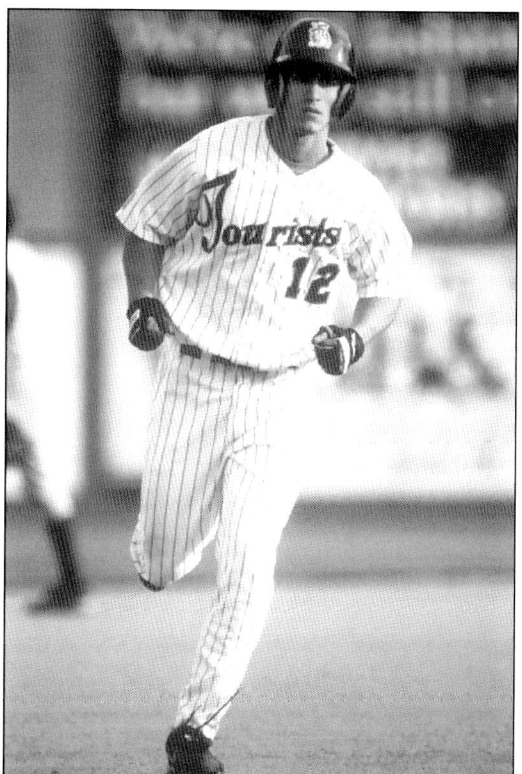

Outfielder Jeff Salazar put together the best all-around season of any player in the South Atlantic League in 2003. A product of Oklahoma State University, Salazar was considered the circuit's best defensive outfielder and topped the South Atlantic League with 29 home runs, 98 RBIs, and 109 runs scored while ranking second with 56 extra-base hits. (Tony Farlow photograph.)

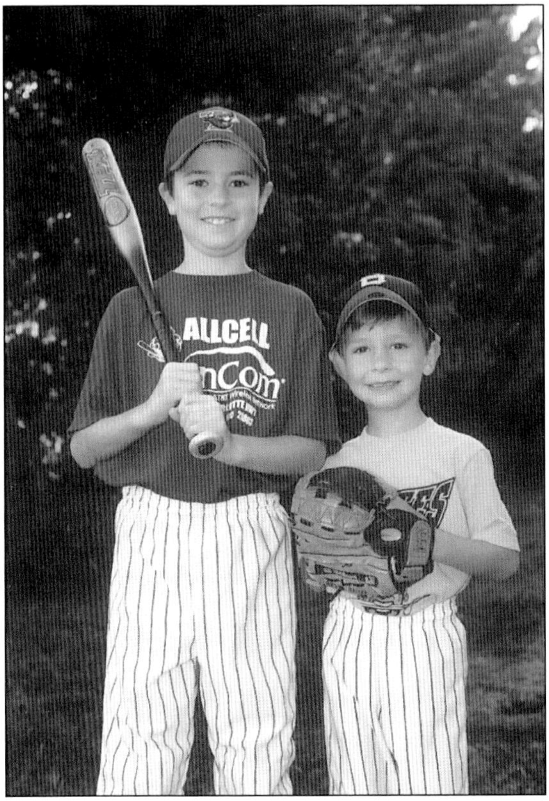

Thanks to Western North Carolina Fall Baseball, under the direction of Bill Stewart, youngsters are able to play the diamond game in the Asheville area from August through October, in addition to the spring and summer. Eight-year-old Brad Ballew (left) and five-year-old Bryce Ballew participated in the 2-A and T-ball fall circuits, respectively, in 2003. (Author's collection.)

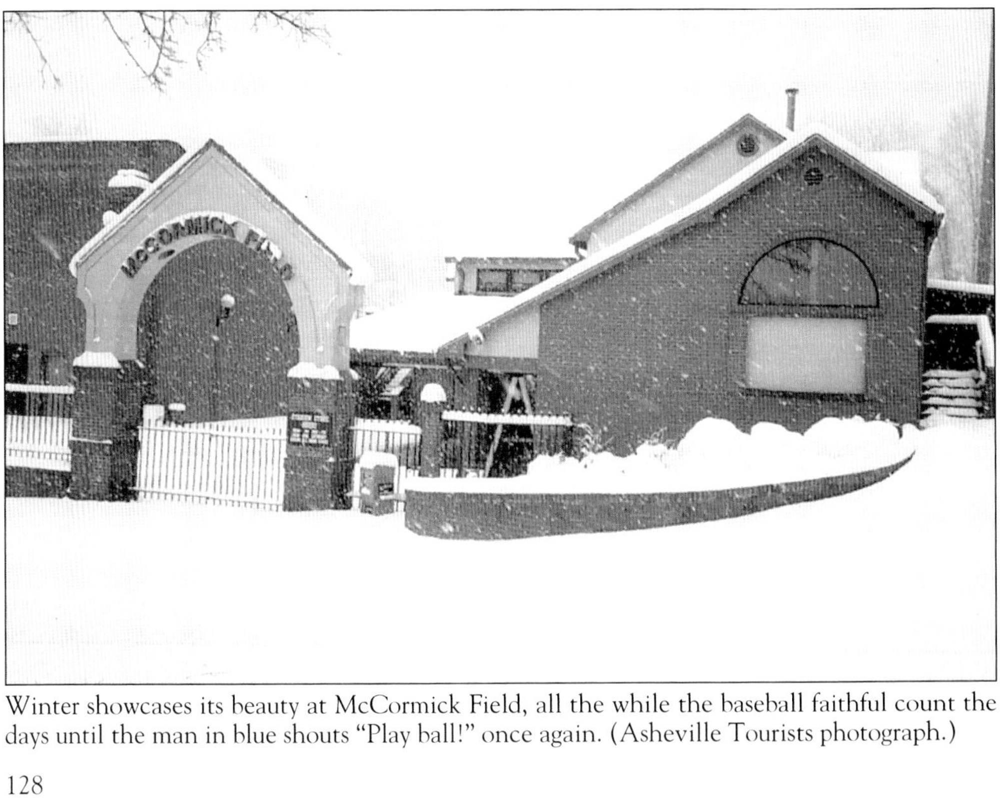

Winter showcases its beauty at McCormick Field, all the while the baseball faithful count the days until the man in blue shouts "Play ball!" once again. (Asheville Tourists photograph.)